LAST SCENE OF ALL
REPRESENTING DEATH ON THE WESTERN STAGE

LEGENDA

LEGENDA is the Modern Humanities Research Association's book imprint for new research in the Humanities. Founded in 1995 by Malcolm Bowie and others within the University of Oxford, Legenda has always been a collaborative publishing enterprise, directly governed by scholars. The Modern Humanities Research Association (MHRA) joined this collaboration in 1998, became half-owner in 2004, in partnership with Maney Publishing and then Routledge, and has since 2016 been sole owner. Titles range from medieval texts to contemporary cinema and form a widely comparative view of the modern humanities, including works on Arabic, Catalan, English, French, German, Greek, Italian, Portuguese, Russian, Spanish, and Yiddish literature. Editorial boards and committees of more than 60 leading academic specialists work in collaboration with bodies such as the Society for French Studies, the British Comparative Literature Association and the Association of Hispanists of Great Britain & Ireland.

The MHRA encourages and promotes advanced study and research in the field of the modern humanities, especially modern European languages and literature, including English, and also cinema. It aims to break down the barriers between scholars working in different disciplines and to maintain the unity of humanistic scholarship. The Association fulfils this purpose through the publication of journals, bibliographies, monographs, critical editions, and the MHRA Style Guide, and by making grants in support of research. Membership is open to all who work in the Humanities, whether independent or in a University post, and the participation of younger colleagues entering the field is especially welcomed.

Last Scene of All

Representing Death on the Western Stage

❖

Edited by Jessica Goodman

l

LEGENDA

Modern Humanities Research Association

2022

Published by Legenda
an imprint of the Modern Humanities Research Association
Salisbury House, Station Road, Cambridge CB1 2LA

ISBN 978-1-78188-686-1 (HB)
ISBN 978-1-78188-690-8 (PB)

First published 2022

Copy-Editor: Richard Correll

CONTENTS

❖

ACKNOWLEDGEMENTS

❖

The conference at which this volume originated was generously funded by the Modern Humanities Research Association (MHRA), the Oxford Research Centre for the Humanities (TORCH) and the Oxford University Modern Languages Faculty; thanks are due to all of them, as well as to St Catherine's College, for hosting the event, and providing funding for indexing. Many thanks, too, to all at Legenda: Jonathan Long and our anonymous reviewers for their invaluable suggestions on the contents and direction of the volume, Richard Correll for copy editing, and Graham Nelson for all manner of support and guidance throughout the project. Amanda Wrigley has provided an excellent and helpful index.

From conference to publication, this project has been bookended by my two maternity leaves, and punctuated by a global pandemic. It has thus taken even longer than might be usual in a Humanities research context, and I thank the contributors for their patience. And as for the 'mewling infants' that are the other two products of this four-year period: as the theatrical world comes back to life post Covid, I look forward to sharing with them my love for this captivating and endlessly fascinating medium.

J.G., Oxford, January 2022

NOTES ON THE CONTRIBUTORS

❖

María Bastianes is a Marie Curie Fellow at the University of Leeds, working on the documentation and promotion of the presence of Spanish theatre in the UK. She is an expert on twentieth-century European history of theatre and Spanish classical drama in performance. She is the author of *Vida Escénica de 'La Celestina' en España* (Peter Lang, 2020), a book on the performance and reception of *La Celestina* in Spain. She is currently working on her second monograph, *Performing 'Celestina' on the Italian Stage: From Mussolini to the Piccolo Teatro di Milano*, under contract with Routledge.

Sarah Burdett is Lecturer and Programme Lead in English at St Mary's University, Twickenham. She holds a PhD from the University of York, completed within the Centre for Eighteenth Century Studies. Her research focuses on representations and receptions of arms-bearing women on the British stage during the French revolutionary and Napoleonic periods. Her debut monograph, titled *The Arms-Bearing Woman and British Theatre in the Age of Revolution*, is under contract with Palgrave Macmillan. Sarah has published research pertaining to Romantic theatre practices, eighteenth-century gender politics and practice-led theatre research in journals including *Comparative Drama*, *Restoration and Eighteenth-Century Theatre Research*, and *Sound Stage Screen*.

Cecilia Feilla is Associate Professor of English and World Literatures at Marymount Manhattan College. Her research focus is French theatre and performance of the eighteenth century with special emphasis on the period of the French Revolution. Her publications include *The Sentimental Theater of the French Revolution* (Ashgate, 2013), a critical edition of *La Tribu indienne; ou Édouard et Stellina* by Lucien Bonaparte (MHRA, 2006), as well as numerous articles and chapters on eighteenth-century drama and the literature of revolution.

Stefano Giannini is Associate Professor of Italian at Syracuse University (NY). His research focuses on modern and contemporary Italian theatre, the notion of exile, and visions of Italy outside of Italy. He has authored *La musa sotto i portici: caffè e provincia nella narrativa di Piero Chiara e Lucio Mastronardi* (M. Pagliai, 2008); *Vittorio Sereni Niccolò Gallo: l'amicizia, il capirsi, la poesia. Lettere 1953–1971* (Loffredo, 2013); and co-edited *Tradition and the Individual Text: Essays in Memory of Pier Massimo Forni* (*MLN* Special Issue, 2019). His current research analyses the relationships among the cultures of the Mediterranean basin, in particular between Italy and Egypt. His project "Maps of Absence: Modern Italian Writers in Alexandria, Egypt" investigates the encounters of modern Italian artists with Northern Africa between the end of the nineteenth century and the twentieth century.

Dominic Glynn is Associate Professor in English at the University of Evry (Paris-Saclay). He is currently leading research projects on transnational theatre practices. Previously, he was the principal investigator of an AHRC Research Network Grant titled 'Literature under Constraint'. His publications include *(Re)Telling Old Stories* (Peter Lang, 2015) and *Lignes de fuite* (L'Harmattan, 2015), as well as the co-edited volumes *Littéraire: pour Alain Viala*, vols I & II (Artois Presses Université, 2018).

Jessica Goodman is Associate Professor of French at St Catherine's College, Oxford. She works in the field of eighteenth-century literature and thought, with a particular interest in the ways in which authors create a public image of themselves, both in their lifetime and after their death. She is the author of *Goldoni in Paris: La Gloire et le Malentendu* (Oxford University Press, 2017), and the editor of a critical edition of plays created around the death of Mirabeau, *Commemorating Mirabeau: 'Mirabeau aux Champs-Elysées' and other texts* (MHRA, 2017), and a collaborative open access translation of Palissot's *Les Philosophes* (Open Book, 2021). Her current project, *Imagined Afterlives*, examines the use of posterity as an imaginative tool in eighteenth-century France.

Joseph Harris is Professor of Early Modern French and Comparative Literature at Royal Holloway, University of London. An expert on early modern French literature, especially drama, he is author of *Hidden Agendas: Cross-Dressing in Seventeenth-Century France* (Narr, 2005) and *Inventing the Spectator: Subjectivity and the Theatrical Experience in Early Modern France* (Oxford University Press, 2014). He also wrote the Introduction to *Four French Plays* (Penguin Classics, 2013), and is currently co-editor of the journal *French Studies*. He has published widely on seventeenth- and eighteenth-century French literature, and is currently finishing a comparative project on misanthropy in European literature and thought from the late Renaissance to the early nineteenth century.

Fiona Macintosh is Professor of Classical Reception, Director of the Archive of Performances of Greek and Roman Drama (APGRD) and Fellow of St Hilda's College, University of Oxford. She is the author of *Dying Acts* (Cork University Press, 1994), *Greek Tragedy and the British Theatre, 1660–1914* (Oxford University Press, 2005; with Edith Hall), *Sophocles' Oedipus Tyrannus* (Cambridge University Press, 2009), and *Performing Epic or Telling Tales* (Oxford University Press, 2020; with Justine McConnell). She has edited eight APGRD volumes: *Medea in Performance* (Legenda, 2000), *Dionysus Since 69* (Oxford University Press, 2004), *Agamemnon in Performance, 458 BC to AD 2004* (Oxford University Press, 2005), *The Ancient Dancer in the Modern World* (Oxford University Press, 2010), *Choruses, Ancient and Modern* (Oxford University Press, 2012), *The Oxford Handbook of Greek Drama in the Americas* (Oxford University Press, 2015), *Epic Performances from the Middle Ages into the Twenty-first Century* (Oxford University Press, 2018) and *Seamus Heaney and the Classics* (Oxford University Press, 2019).

Barry Murnane is Associate Professor in German at the University of Oxford, and Fellow and Tutor at St John's College. He has published widely on modernism, theatre, and Anglo-German cultural relations from the eighteenth century to the present day, including *'Verkehr mit Gespenster': Gothic und Moderne bei Franz Kafka* (Ergon, 2008), *Popular Revenants: The German Schauerroman and its International Reception* (Cambridge University Press, 2012; ed. with Andrew Cusack), and *Zwischen Popularisierung und Ästhetisierung: Hanns Heinz Ewers und die Moderne* (Bielefeld Aisthesis Verlag, 2014; ed. with Rainer Godel). He has become increasingly interested in praxeological approaches to understanding the history of German Studies in the period, including most recently *Essen, töten, heilen: Praktiken literaturkritischen Schreibens nach 1700* (Wallstein Verlag, 2019; ed. with Ritchie Robertson, Christoph Schmitt-Maaß and Stefanie Stockhorst) and *Literature in the World: Material Networks of Books to and from Goethe's Weimar* (forthcoming 2021; ed. with Stefan Höppner).

Jonathan Patterson is Lecturer at St Edmund Hall and in the Sub-faculty of French at the University of Oxford. His research explores how literature interacts with broader cultural forces of early modern French society. His publications include *Villainy in France (1463–1610): A Transcultural Study of Law and Literature* (Oxford University Press, 2021), *Representing Avarice in Late Renaissance France* (Oxford University Press, 2015), and 'Variations of Vileness' (*Early Modern French Studies*, 39.2, 2017, co-edited with Emilia Wilton-Godberfforde).

Julie Vatain-Corfdir is associate professor of English at Sorbonne Université, where she teaches literature, translation and acting. She is the author of *Traduire la lettre vive* (Peter Lang, 2012; recipient of the SAES/AFEA book of the year award), and has edited several collections of essays and conversations with artists, among which are *American Dramaturgies for the 21st Century* (Sorbonne University Press, 2021), *American Musicals: Stage and Screen* (Sorbonne University Press, 2019; with Anne Martina), and *La Scène en version originale* (Sorbonne University Press, 2015). She has written many articles on anglophone playwrights, and translated several plays into French, including plays by Thornton Wilder and Sarah Ruhl.

INTRODUCTION

❖

Death on Stage:
A Never-Ending Ending

Jessica Goodman

St Catherine's College, Oxford

A glooming peace this morning with it brings,
The sun, for sorrow, will not show his head.
Go hence to have more talk of these sad things;
Some shall be pardon'd, and some punished:
For never was a story of more woe
Than this of Juliet and her Romeo.
— William Shakespeare, *Romeo and Juliet*, v. 3. 305–10[1]

When, in the final lines of *Romeo and Juliet*, the Prince commands the onstage onlookers — Montagues and Capulets alike — to 'have more talk of these sad things', he enjoins the audience, beyond the footlights, to do the same. Reflect on what you have seen here, this exemplary spectacle of woe, whose heaven-shifting crisis has resolved into a gloomy, peaceful morning. This is the time to look back on what has happened, and learn to manage passions and resulting actions better in the future.

The spectators, unlike the family members present onstage, are not directly implicated in the tragedy. Nonetheless, they are part of the crowd that is addressed here, drawn into the emotion of what they have witnessed despite their privileged knowledge that the 'star-crossed lovers' were doomed from the prologue, their fate written in their family situation and their impetuous actions, just as much as in Shakespeare's lines. This combination of pity and fear — identification with (or a perceived link to) the onstage subject, accompanied by the intuition of impending but undeserved tragedy — is the recipe traditionally required for tragic catharsis to take place: the peaceful morning is a figure for the calm after the emotional storm, when the audience has (according to the definition you follow) either become inured to misfortune in the world by learning to tolerate it, or refined its passions into a more balanced state, or discharged them completely. The deaths of the young lovers and their transformation into this model for contemplation resolve the tension set up by the prologue, conclude the play, and provide — in modern parlance — a sense of closure.[2]

But this is theatre. And so the actors get up, dust themselves off, and prepare to die again at the next performance — and the next, and the next. Moreover, these individual actors, repeatedly embodying Romeo and Juliet at this particular period in time, in this particular theatre space, are themselves part of a longer chain of repetition and re-presentation. These same deaths have occurred thousands of times since they were first written: on stage or screen; in quiet or melodramatic fashion; in any number of languages; in modern or contemporary dress; as verse or ballet or opera; read according to multiple cultural traditions: the variation is endless, even as the fact of that inevitable ending remains constant. Any stage death, then, is also a non-ending, a fact of which any individual audience member — whether witnessing it for the first or the fifty-first time — must be aware. What looks like resolution and closure, especially in the context of classically influenced tragedy, leaves something unresolved. There is an uneasy sense that the ending is false: quite literally only theatre.

The conflict between the very real emotions roused by theatre, and the know-ledge that what has been witnessed is — to borrow another Shakespearean closing speech — 'no more yielding but a dream',[3] is far from confined to the field of death and catharsis, and real spectator emotion in the face of theatrical artifice is a topic that has been explored at length elsewhere.[4] However, the tension is particularly strongly felt at these moments of death, especially climactic death, whose impact is ostensibly drawn from their status as ending, even as their practical existence as theatre resists such a status.

Spanning six centuries and seven countries, and moving broadly chronologically, this book considers how different dramatic authors have engaged with this tension, examining the representation of death as theme and practice, culturally inflected symbol and never-ending ending. We cannot, of course, capture all of theatre's shifting, ephemeral presence (let alone different productions, performances and audience reactions) through ten brief examples drawn solely from Western theatrical tradition, nor can we draw a single grand narrative about death or the stage or death on stage from these snapshots. However, as long as the fact that they are mere snapshots is kept in mind, we can nonetheless both draw productive conclusions about the individual cases, and make tentative suggestions about the patterns into which the kaleidoscope seems to fall, tracing how representations of death (as symbol and repetition) respond to the sign of catharsis under which they are inevitably born.

Theatre and Death

In his 2019 monograph, *Death in Modern Theatre*, Adrian Curtin identifies 'a nexus between theatre and death'.[5] This nexus, for Curtin, draws together (among other things) the notions of absence and presence entailed in representing the deceased people of the past[6] or fantastical figures such as Death itself through the flesh and blood of the actor, the language theatre shares with death (the actor 'corpses' when he laughs on stage), the theoretical notion of 'ghosting' created by Marvin Carlson, whereby the ghosts of past performances and past performers are always already present for actors and audience alike,[7] and the very mortal experience of sharing a live performance, created by breathing, ageing human bodies, with our fellow spectators.[8] He notes, too, the difficulties surrounding the presentation of death on stage: the danger of drifting into the comic register, the problems of realism, and whether it is better to describe or depict. This awkward practicality of theatrical death is another manifestation of the ending/repeating dichotomy already set out above. It exists somewhere between Stoppard's flippant '[death is] just a man failing to reappear, that's all — now you see him, now you don't',[9] and Maggie Vintner's observation that 'in theatre, death is not something you suffer, but something you do':[10] the former noting the ease with which an individual can visually, physically be removed from life and — by extension — the stage; the latter putting the emphasis on the continued work that the all-too-living actor has to do if the state of 'being dead' is to be portrayed.

Curtin's volume examines how Western dramatists from the nineteenth century onwards have exploited this deathly presence in their writing to address cultural attitudes to and practices surrounding death at specific historical moments: from wars, to nuclear destructions, to contemporary anxieties surrounding assisted suicide. Writing in the same year, Vinter, too, in her *Last Acts: The Art of Dying on the Early Modern Stage*, thinks about the political, social and economic implications of portraying death on stage, exploring how dramatists appropriate concepts from the *ars moriendi* to understand what it is to die 'well' under changing historical circumstances. Hutcheon and Hutcheon's *Opera: The Art of Dying* (2004) posits that death in opera in particular emulates this medieval tradition by allowing the audience to 'experience their own mortality by proxy',[11] an idea that Curtin echoes when he discusses theatre's communal nature 'potentially helping audiences to cope a little better with ontological insecurities'.[12] Michael Neill's *Issues of Death* (1997), meanwhile, suggests that English tragedy of the Renaissance allowed contemporary audience safely to rehearse their own encounter with death.[13] All of these scholars, therefore, write onstage death into an audience experience that might be described as cathartic, not just because it incites and purges general emotions of pity and fear, but because it alters and perhaps discharges a spectator's emotions on the specific subject of mortality.

This book does not claim to tackle all aspects of such a broad theme. Though eschatology is clearly a significant undercurrent in any discussion of death, the theological and the philosophical remain very much on the edges of our study. In concentrating on theatrical representation, we are largely concerned with the relationship of the dead and dying to the world they have left and in which these deaths are performed, as opposed to the world into which they may or may not be going, although some of the plays examined do touch on this crossover; our examples, after all, begin from the sixteenth century, when, Philippe Ariès argues, cultural imaginings of death were becoming increasingly secular.[14] Moreover, although our methodology echoes Curtin's in drawing together close reading, historical situation and performance analysis across a series of 'micro-narratives', unlike his examples, the texts and performances analysed here do not necessarily all take death as a theme, or present the allegorical figure itself on stage. Rather than linking external attitudes to death with its manifestation on stage at different moments, this volume instead uses its series of case studies of tragedies, comedies, onstage and offstage deaths, ghosts, funerals and ritual to examine very specifically how dramatists write death on stage — as theme and practice, culturally inflected symbol, and never-ending ending — into or against both theatrical practice and classical tradition, most specifically with respect to the desire for cathartic closure that seems more unproblematically present in the other critical works described above.

Catharsis and Death

For all that my account thus far, in common with many of the cited works, refers to a 'traditional' notion of catharsis, the term is notoriously far from stable. This is not the place for a full discussion of the different approaches taken to elucidating what, after all, receives only the briefest of mentions in Aristotle's *Poetics*: Stephen Halliwell, among others, has traced the multiple interpretations to which it has been subject in detail, and even calls for a moratorium on redefining it.[15] It is worth, however, taking a moment to consider various approaches in general terms, in order better to situate the authors and works to be discussed here.

A primary understanding, perhaps most prevalent in Neoclassical tragedy, is what Halliwell denotes the 'didactic' approach to catharsis: the spectator is provided with an example of the passions to avoid, experiencing them vicariously in the theatre to avoid experiencing them in life. This form of catharsis shares many features with the second category identified by Halliwell, in which catharsis creates emotional fortitude in the spectator through the exposure to trials onstage that they will learn to tolerate in reality.[16] Both forms (whose efficacy is decried by Rousseau as merely fleeting)[17] are linked to what Halliwell calls catharsis as 'outlet'; in other accounts called 'purgation'. This is often opposed to 'purification': a mode of catharsis by which passions are not removed but rather refined, in order that they be experienced in moderation and managed in the 'right' way.[18] This modified understanding is especially prevalent in the eighteenth century, for example in Lessing, for whom theatre allowed passions to be redirected towards civic virtue.[19] Between the two extremes — the catharsis centred on fear (what to avoid) and that centred on pity (a sympathetic understand of how to behave in that same situation of crisis) — is one born from admiration, in which love for the good inspires the rejection of vice.[20]

Crucially, catharsis in all of these senses is founded upon the idea of identification: the spectator feels some form of emotional link with those presented onstage, and is able to envisage him- or herself in their situation or a very similar one. It is this empathy that makes pity and fear nearly indistinguishable, with the spectator pitying in the character the experience that they fear for themselves. Yet this is not total identification: the distance between stage and auditorium, often combined with critical reflection on the part of the spectator, is what prevents total subsumption into the character portrayed, and allows catharsis to take place. This distance is related, too, to the aesthetic pleasure produced, even as tragic passions and situations are conveyed — a pleasure that might itself contribute to cathartic satisfaction. We stray once again, here, into the territory of non-endings, for, paradoxically, it might be admiration for the work done by the real body of a 'dead' actor — in other words, the knowledge that this is feigned death, feigned ending — that brings this aesthetically satisfying form of closure.

Death is not necessary for catharsis; however, given the need to arouse the heights of fear in the audience, it is its frequent companion. Writing in 1601, Battista Guarini described 'the purging Terror of Tragedy' with reference to both physical and moral death:

> The terror of the interior [moral] death, which, having been roused in the soul of the listener by means of the image of the things represented, attracts like a magnet — due to the similarity that one fear has with the other — the bad sinful death [the terror of physical death]: thus reason, which is nature, and the beginning of the life of the soul, abhorring it [the sinful affect] as its capital enemy, and being opposed to it, pushes it out, leaving only the good fear of infamy and of interior death, which is the foundation of virtue.[21]

The mere possibility of a terrible fate can suffice to create catharsis, even if it is overturned at the last moment: the dénouement of a play does not make its whole meaning. It is true too, of course, that a terrible fate does not always entail death, as the deathless ending of Racine's *Bérénice* serves to demonstrate. When death is present on stage, however, it is often a moment of high emotion, and/or climax, and might thus be considered a primary candidate for creating catharsis, in any one of its forms.

Even more prosaically, death frequently satisfies the criterion for Goethe's more structural understanding of catharsis: simply the conclusion of the plot that reconciles contradictory passions, a formal dénouement 'which is required by any drama and even any poetic work'.[22] This is the understanding that might be seen as feeding into Brechtian and Hollywood Golden Age conceptions of spectatorial satisfaction and closure (negative for Brecht, positive in Hollywood).[23] Significantly for our purposes, (actual) death and Goethe's version of catharsis find an even closer relationship in the intuition of their advent: the play, like life, must end, and thus all that precedes this ending is to some extent coloured by its anticipation.[24] The end of a play, though, is more clearly defined in its temporality than an individual's death: the spectator, aware of roughly how long they expect a performance to last, may second guess the outcome as the clock counts down; they may attempt, too, to interpret 'signs' in advance, based on their prior knowledge of a play, in a way that is only possible in retrospect in real life. And just as in the paradoxical example of aesthetic pleasure drawn from the knowledge of artifice set out above, it is the repetitious aspect of theatre, the non-finality of its ending, that allows such foreknowledge to colour experience in the moment, and — crucially — heightens a cathartic ending through the expectation of its arrival (or conversely, the frustration of its non-arrival).

Representing Death

Catharsis is therefore very clearly a property of the relationship of the audience to what appears before them: a property of the process of representation. Death is one of the few onstage actions that (a very few unfortunate examples aside![25]) is unmistakably 'mere' representation: in the eighteenth-century theoretical debates surrounding the veracity of emotion on stage, for all that some theorists claimed that 'only those born to love should play lovers',[26] it could not be argued that death could only be performed by the truly dying or deceased. Dominic Glynn's chapter in this volume considers in detail just how 'performable' death ever is, from either a moral or a literal standpoint. The grammar of dying brings sharply into focus the fact that *talking* about death in particular is necessarily always at one remove: we can discuss or describe the death of another, but 'I'm dying' refers to the process rather than the state or completed action, whilst 'I die' sounds at best overly stagey, the dramatic precursor to a melodramatic collapsing to the ground. Our lived experience of death, then, is always as a spectator, and Joseph Harris's essay examines plays in which Corneille exploits death-as-spectacle through 'aggressive suicides', which give neither the onstage nor the offstage spectator moral satisfaction.

Theatrical deaths are necessarily symbolic to a greater or lesser extent. For any form of catharsis or closure to result, these symbols must be 'read' by the audience, who might therefore be supposed to have some form of shared reference point or code for interpretation. Expectations of cultural and theatrical conventions and responses to them are of course conditioned by both genre and historical moment.[27] Death is presented differently and means something different in French classical tragedy and in contemporary American drama, and in revivals or translations of both, and María Bastianes's essay here explores what happens when tragic deaths are transposed through time and space.[28] As we have already set out, even catharsis itself is inflected by its cultural and temporal context: frequently evoked to defend theatre from critiques of immorality, its theories have evolved in conjunction with practice, sometimes prescribing, sometimes describing, and sometimes justifying, always heavily influenced by the theory of emotions that holds sway at any one moment.[29] But these shifting representations and understandings are nonetheless linked by the history of theatre into which they are all written, by the ubiquity of human mortality, and by the limitations and potential of the physical form of the stage and its audience. The spectators are thus key participants in what is a form of shared ritual, in which death can often be a climactic moment. And whilst death and catharsis imply endings, ritual, like re-presentation, implies repetition (night after night, year after year)[30] — a repetition which simultaneously writes these deaths into the cultural and theatrical tradition by which the audience reads them, and subverts the definitive 'sense of an ending' that might be expected. The French revolutionary texts analysed by Cecilia Feilla explicitly play on this notion, whilst Fiona Macintosh identifies both multiple past theatrical deaths and the Greek and Irish mourning traditions as haunting the 'suspended action' that is the moment of dying in Marina Carr's 2007 work, the liminality of this moment mapping neatly onto that tension between ending and ever-repeating that is our focus here.

The double vision (at the very least) required of the spectator of death in the theatre is thus akin to that required for catharsis to take place: they dispassionately acknowledge or admire the manner in which death or dying is (repeatedly) performed (according to particular theatrical norms), whilst also temporarily suppressing the recognition of this repeated art in order to access an emotional response, prescribed by the cultural norms of their context, but at the same time contingent, in that it relies on human presence and experience shared at a very precise moment in time. And the addition of 'repetition' to Curtin's 'nexus of theatre and death' sheds light on further elements relating to the closure — or lack of it — that theatre provides. When deceased individuals are depicted onstage, as in Sarah Burdett's and Jonathan Patterson's chapters in this volume, a life that has ended is made to repeat, dispelling any fiction that we put a full stop to our own stories at the moment of our passing. These recreations of historical figures, literal re-memberances that culminate in re-dyings (in one case, a further dismembering), point to the frailty of the human body, shared by actors, spectators, and characters, but also to the tenacity of humanity as a whole, in surviving to keep telling the story. Indeed, in the unremarkable deaths of modern American drama examined by Julie Vatain-Corfdir it is the dead and not the living who forget, their gentle ending coming not at the moment of crossing the divide between death and life (depicted here as mistily porous), but later, as they drift away from memory, rather than life itself.

And of course, part of that survival of humanity is the survival of theatre itself. Stefano Giannini's essay on Pirandello's *I giganti della montagna* considers how art continues to exist beyond its creators, and the haunting half-living that implies. Barry Murnane's discussion of Brecht's non-tragic deaths, meanwhile, places the emphasis on dying as rebirth, a re-opening to the world of the questions at stake and the story being told, in order that the spectator be engaged and encouraged to take action in the world beyond the stage, whilst Feilla shows similarly how French revolutionary comedies present death overcome and a subsequent renewal of life, love and community, both essays demonstrating how expectations of closure and catharsis are overturned to revitalize the very function of theatre. Theatre about death, then, is often also about theatre itself.

★   ★   ★   ★   ★

Given the polysemous nature of 'catharsis', applied to a genre that by its very nature relies on a high degree of contingency and continually oscillates between theory and practice, it is unsurprising that the plays and authors examined in this book (even the very earliest) deal with notions of death and closure in very different ways, playing with and against expectation and theory in a more or less explicit fashion. The moments at which closure is denied, catharsis (as purgation, purification, or narrative balance) is thwarted, or questions are left unanswered might appear to contradict the claims made by the scholars cited at this start of this Introduction, who posit all theatre (explicitly deathly or otherwise) as a tool for coming to terms with death, for learning to die well.

But in fact, the tension between ending and non-ending we identify throughout perhaps serves to satisfy this function in another way, by encouraging spectators to come to terms not with death, but with life. Human life, ephemeral like a performance, with an inevitable ending that is simultaneously enormously significant (for the individual/that night's audience) and totally insignificant (in the broader scheme of humanity/a long-running production), but which also forms a part of a greater whole, gives its individual components meaning, and perhaps therefore provides them with consolation — at least until that 'last scene of all [...] and mere oblivion'.[31]

Notes to the Introduction

1. References to Shakespeare are taken from *The Arden Shakespeare Complete Works*, 3rd series, ed. by Richard Proudfoot, Ann Thompson and David Scott Kastan (Walton-on-Thames: Nelson, 1998), p. 1038.
2. Cf. Thomas C. K. Rist, 'Miraculous Organ: Shakespeare and "Catharsis"', *SKENÈ Journal of Theatre and Drama Studies*, 2.1 (2016), 133–50.
3. *A Midsummer Night's Dream*, v. 1. 422 (p. 910).
4. For example, in literary studies see Joseph Harris, *Inventing the Spectator: Subjectivity and the Theatrical Experience in Early Modern France* (Oxford: Oxford University Press, 2014), Rebecca Yearling, 'Emotion, Cognition and Spectator Response to the Plays of Shakespeare', *Cultural History*, 7.2 (2018), 129–44, and Logan Connors, *The Emergence of a Theatrical Science of Man in France, 1660–1740* (Liverpool: Liverpool University Press, 2020). For a more sociological approach (audience questionnaires) see Elly A. Konjin, 'Spotlight on Spectators: Emotions in the Theater', *Discourse Processes*, 28 (1999), 169–94 <https://doi.org/10.1080/01638539909545079>.
5. Adrian Curtin, *Death in Modern Theatre: Stages of Mortality* (Manchester: Manchester University Press, 2019), p. 5.
6. Cf. Hélène Cixous's definition of theatre as 'the stage where the living meet and confront the dead', in 'Enter the Theatre (in between)', *Modern Drama*, 42.3 (1999), 301–14.
7. Marvin Carlson, *The Haunted Stage: The Theatre as Memory Machine* (Ann Arbor: University of Michigan Press, 2003). Cf. also Alice Rayner on the recognizable made uncanny in *Ghosts: Death's Double and the Phenomena of Theatre* (Minneapolis: University of Minnesota Press, 2006).
8. Cf. Herbert Blau, on the actor as living person dying (ageing) in front of audience, in 'Universals of Performance or Amortalizing Play', *Substance*, 11.4 (1983), 140–61.
9. Tom Stoppard, *Rosencrantz & Guildenstern Are Dead* (New York: Grove Press, 1968), p. 84.
10. Maggie Vinter, *Last Acts: The Act of Dying on the Early Modern Stage* (New York: Fordham University Press, 2019), p. 1.
11. Linda Hutcheon and Michael Hutcheon, *Opera: The Art of Dying* (Cambridge, MA: Harvard University Press, 2004), p. 10.
12. Curtin, p. 188.
13. Michael Neill, *Issues of Death: Mortality and Identity in English Renaissance Tragedy* (Oxford: Clarendon Press, 1997).
14. Philippe Ariès, *L'Homme devant la mort* (Paris: Seuil, 1977).
15. Stephen Halliwell, *Aristotle's Poetics* (London: Bloomsbury, 1986), Appendix 5, pp. 350–56; Halliwell, *The Aesthetics of Mimesis: Ancient Texts and Modern Problems* (Princeton, NJ: Princeton University Press, 2002), p. 206. See also Patrice Pavis, *Dictionary of the Theatre: Terms, Concepts, and Analysis*, trans. by Christine Shantz (Toronto: University of Toronto Press, 1999), pp. 44–46.
16. Halliwell describes catharsis as homeopathic: the arousal of the emotions in order to change them (*Aristotle's Poetics*, p. 194).
17. In his *Lettre à d'Alembert*, Rousseau echoes the Augustinian view from many centuries before: 'J'entends dire que la tragédie mène à la pitié par la terreur; soit, mais quelle est cette pitié? Une émotion passagère et vaine, qui ne dure pas plus que l'illusion qui l'a produite; un reste

de sentiment naturel étouffé bientôt par les passions; une pitié stérile qui se repaît de quelques larmes, et n'a jamais produit le moindre acte d'humanité' [I have heard it said that tragedy leads to pity via fear; be that as it may, but what is this pity? A fleeting and vain emotion, which lasts no longer than the illusion that produces it; the remains of a natural feeling soon stifled by the passions; a sterile pity which is satisfied with a few tears, and never produced the smallest act of humanity] (Rousseau, *Lettre à d'Alembert* [1758], ed. by M. Launay (Paris: Garnier-Flammarion, 1967), pp. 78–79), my translation. Du Bos gives a more positive version of this argument in his 1719 *Réflexions critiques sur la poésie et sur la peinture*: 'Il n'est pas suivi des inconvénients dont les émotions sérieuses qui auraient été causées par l'objet même seraient accompagnées [...] l'affliction n'est, pour ainsi dire, que sur la superficie de notre cœur, et nous sentons bien que nos pleurs finiront avec la représentation de la fiction ingénieuse que les fait couler' [It is not followed by the inconveniences which would accompany serious emotions produced by the same object [...] the affliction produced is, we might say, merely upon the surface of our hearts, and we are we aware that our tears will end along with the ingenious fiction that makes them fall] (Jean-Baptiste Dubos, *Réflexions critiques sur la poésie et sur la peinture*, 3 vols (Paris: Pissot, 1770 [1719]), I, 30–31), my translation.

18. The same opposition is set up by Serge Tisseron, 'La Catharsis: purge ou thérapie?', *Les Cahiers de médiologie*, 1 (1996), 181–91, and Florence Naugrette, *Le Plaisir du spectateur de théâtre* (Paris: Bréal, 2002), p. 82, though Halliwell says that setting catharsis up as only one or the other is in fact misleading (*Aristotle's Poetics*, p. 198). Another form of purgation that may be linked to catharsis is the idea of watching a play in order to provoke a confession — cf. Rist, p. 148, and also Burdett's chapter in this volume.

19. Emmanuelle Hénin recasts this virtuous catharsis as another form of purgation, via tears, in 'Le Plaisir des larmes, ou l'invention d'une catharsis galante', *Littératures classiques*, 62 (2007), 223–44. Catharsis for her takes place through a shared emotion, passed from author to actor to spectator: it is, therefore, a wholly interior process.

20. Cf. Bradley Rubidge, 'Catharsis through Admiration: Corneille, Le Moyne, and the Social Uses of Emotion', *Modern Philology*, 95.3 (1998), 316–33.

21. Battista Guarini, *A Compendium of Tragicomic Poetry* [1601], cited in translation in Rist, p. 1.

22. See Nicholas Boyle, 'Goethe's Theory of Tragedy', *MLR*, 105.4 (2010), 1072–86. He describes Goethe's version of catharsis as precisely not moralizing: passions are roused and then calmed, and the audience goes home unchanged. The representation of the spectator within Goethe's own dramatic works is presented as evidence of this internality.

23. Nikolaj Lübecker, *The Feel-Bad Film* (Edinburgh: Edinburgh University Press, 2015), p. 13.

24. On the imminence of death for humans see Frank Kermode, *The Sense of an Ending: Studies in the Theory of Fiction with a New Epilogue* (New York: Oxford University Press, 2000).

25. From Molière to Tommy Cooper...

26. Pierre Rémond de Sainte Albine, *Le Comédien* (1747), in *Sept traités sur le jeu comédien et autres textes*, ed. by Sabine Chaouche (Paris: Champion, 2001), pp. 515–670 (p. 579, my translation).

27. Hutcheon & Hutcheon, p. 9; Neill, p. 2.

28. See also Thérèse Malachy, *La Mort en situation dans le théâtre contemporain* (Paris: Nizet, 1982).

29. This is even true of Aristotle, who is answering Plato's critique about the psychological effects of theatre (Halliwell, *Aristotle's Poetics*, p. 184).

30. On repetition see Lee Strasberg, *A Dream of Passion: The Development of the Method* (New York: Plume, 1988), p. 35 and Tzachi Zamir, 'Theatrical Repetition and Inspired Performance', *Journal of Aesthetics and Art Criticism* (2009), pp. 365–73. Carlson's *Haunted Stage* is also relevant here.

31. *As You Like It*, II. 7. 163–65.

CHAPTER 1

❖

Killing Coligny: Staging the Admiral's Death in Sixteenth-Century France and England

Jonathan Patterson

St Edmund Hall, Oxford

Introduction

An act of killing on a theatrical stage represents death as a sensational finality — perhaps all the more so when it is based on historical events still live in the memory of the play's first audiences. So what happens when that finality is undone, when the brutal act of killing is reduced to the barest of allusions? And what will be gained by reinstating the death onstage with quirky violence in a subsequent play? These questions underpin my enquiry which focuses on the repeated spectacle of killing an important military leader, in sixteenth-century tragedy and beyond.

During the 1560s, Gaspard II de Coligny, Seigneur de Châtillon and Admiral of France, emerged as a key player in France's Wars of Religion (1562–98). He became the leader of the Huguenot (Protestant) opposition to the Catholic monarchy; he was declared a state traitor, and was eventually assassinated in 1572. His decease soon provoked multiple and conflicting interpretations. The death of Admiral Coligny was one of very few murders to be represented in two stage plays composed during the Wars of Religion; moreover, during this period, in the years surrounding his murder, the Admiral had been subjected to ritual hanging (twice) and dismemberment. These ritual performances were notorious public events in 1570s France, but modern scholars have yet to enquire how far they shaped theatrical interpretation of Coligny's death. That is my task. I shall begin with the Coligny killings *outside* the theatre, to show how aspects of them were recuperated — to strikingly different ends — in the two plays to feature his gory demise.

Coligny's murder on the night of the Saint Bartholomew Feast (23–24 August 1572) triggered what is now called the Saint Bartholomew's Day Massacre.[1] What began as a wave of mob violence against Huguenots in Paris spread across France and became one of the worst mass killings to have ever been perpetrated on European soil.[2] The historical events of the Saint Bartholomew's Day Massacre are one chapter of Coligny's death. To understand its longer cultural significance, however, we must consider the enactment of criminal proceedings against Coligny before, during and after the Massacre. Thus, Coligny's killing was performed and re-enacted in a series of spectacles of retribution. Each spectacle might be considered a symbolic 'staging' of Coligny's 'death' before a public audience: the people of Paris. The first spectacle was of an effigy of Coligny hanged to assuage Catholic hatred of his treason; this occurred in 1569, some three years before he was physically slaughtered. Once the Saint Bartholomew's Day Massacre was under way, a second spectacle took place: the Admiral's dismembered body (according to some accounts) made a degrading sight as it was dragged off to the gallows of Montfaucon outside Paris, where criminals were strung up to rot. Two months later, a third spectacle of Coligny's death was enacted: this time he was posthumously tried for treason, and another effigy of him was hanged. Details of these spectacles flowed into the pamphlet polemic that engulfed Coligny's posthumous commemoration: did he die as a traitor or as a martyr? Was his death good riddance or a tragic loss?

These questions cried out for theatrical responses — which they duly received in France and England. Coligny's death inspired François de Chantelouve's *La Tragedie de feu Gaspard de Colligny* (1575), and Christopher Marlowe's *The Massacre at Paris* (c. 1593). The Marlowe and Chantelouve plays belonged to an era in which the portrayal of lethal violence in the theatre was haphazardly evolving, incorporating rhetorically charged description of bloodshed, and, in some cases, the enactment of death onstage. In Coligny's France, the leading tragedians, Robert Garnier and Jean de la Taille, followed Horace and Aristotle in their insistence that deaths onstage were unseemly and unbelievable. Others disagreed. Indeed we now know that a good number of late sixteenth-century French tragedians put deadly violence centre-stage in forms that were popular across the Channel, especially in the genre of revenge tragedy: beheadings, bodily mutilation, duels, battles, murder, assassinations, and executions.[3] Thus, the killing of Coligny entered a theatrical environment in which stage violence was an option, but not a necessity, for various different settings: biblical and mythological subjects; ancient and (as in our case) recent history. Chantelouve dramatizes the reporting of Coligny's violent death, which occurs offstage; Marlowe shows Coligny's killing onstage, albeit briefly. In their different ways both dramatists sought to avoid 'overkilling' Coligny. If this avoidance of overkill was not overtly motivated by dramaturgical concerns about decorum and verisimilitude, it does seem to have been a reaction to the vindictive public spectacles (and their attendant pamphlets) that represented Coligny's death prior to its appearance in the theatre.

Coligny's death altered considerably as it was (re)enacted on the street, on the scaffold, on the gallows — and in the theatre. To capture this process of re-enactment over time and in different social spaces, I shall base my analysis on a performance-anthropological model: that of the 'social drama' of conflict conceived by Victor Turner and since developed by others, most notably Richard Schechner.[4] If all the world's a stage for the performance of everyday interactions,[5] then, for Turner, the dramatic phase properly begins at the point when conflicts arise. These social dramas, as Turner named them, are a kind of metatheatre, in which role-playing itself becomes more and more intensely articulated, and integral to the outcome of the conflict.[6] Turner then proceeds to identify four typical phases of public action. The social drama comprises firstly, a flagrant breach of regular societal relations; secondly, a period of crisis (or a succession of crises) widening that breach; thirdly, a phase of redressive action ranging from personal advice and informal arbitration to formal legal machinery. The fourth and final phase may have opposite outcomes — either the social reintegration of the pariah group / individual, or the recognition that the schism between the opposing parties is irreparable. The four phases of the Turnerian model underpin my thinking, but it is the fluidity between them that matters most: the transitions, or, as Turner would say, the liminal — 'that which is betwixt and between' — the many killings of Coligny.

Overkill: Coligny's Death(s) in Paris

Before he died in 1572, Coligny had been at the centre of a social drama highly resistant to closure. He was already 'dead' to a vocal faction of French society — that is to say, from the early 1560s he was despised by numerous Catholics, particularly those siding with the Guise family, the powerful clan leading the charge to eradicate Protestant belief in France. In February 1563, during the first War of Religion, François de Guise was shot by the Huguenot Jean de Poltrot de Méré: some of his confession by torture implicated Coligny, although the latter emphatically denied involvement. Our social drama reached crisis point as the second War of Religion (1567–68) got underway, and the image of Coligny as a Machiavellian villain with regicidal intentions became a staple of Catholic propaganda.[7] By the summer of 1568, Coligny had fled the royal court to play a key role in Huguenot resistance to the Catholic monarchy in a third War of Religion.[8] In September 1569, the Parlement de Paris, France's foremost seat of legal authority, pronounced him guilty of *lèse-majesté* (high treason).[9] Parlement's *arrest* specifies the charge and the redressive action it entailed: Coligny was to be stripped of all honours and titles, then strung up to hang — like a common criminal — on the time-honoured stage of public executions, the Place de Grève.[10] But since Coligny could not be physically apprehended in this case, an effigy would be gibbeted instead.

This practice of execution in effigy was quite common in *Ancien Régime* France. Effigies were free-standing, portable objects: they could be nailed to scaffolds, hung by a noose, or beheaded then burned in a pyre, all ways of symbolizing the destruction of the criminal's body during the punishment process.[11] Early modern execution in effigy could be seen as a form of secular ritual constituting, in the words of Sally Falk Moore and Barbara Myerhoff, 'a declaration of form against indeterminacy', to compensate for the unknown whereabouts of the live criminal, and to legitimate confiscation of his goods and property. It was also a form of liminal performance, simulating the crossing of the all-important threshold from life to death. According to Allie Terry-Fritsch, the effigy was considered 'properly' punished if its form was fully destroyed during the ritual; justice was then seen to have been served and the populace assuaged.[12] Crucially, that is *not* what happened in Coligny's case, as we learn from a contemporary witness, who saw the effigy erected on the Place de Grève — and noted that it was left hanging there for almost a year.[13]

Thinking about this spectacle as a staging of retributive action in the social drama, we have an oddly amorphous performance lacking a dénouement: Coligny the effigy is ceremonially dragged along the streets of Paris — but there is no climatic moment of 'death' on the scaffold signifying the full expenditure of ritual violence. Instead, contrary to the expectations of modern Girardian effigy theory, the sacrificial double here increases rather than displaces violent desire.[14] The lingering post-dramatic presence of the effigy on the Place de Grève was insulting, and more than enough to keep Parisian hatred of the Admiral simmering. In the wider social drama, the effigy hanging prolonged a subplot of grievance enacted by officials: the confiscation of Coligny's property.[15] The real drama, however, was ongoing elsewhere: Coligny was still at large, rampaging his way through villages in the south of France and heading northwards towards Paris.

A pacification edict ratified at Saint-Germain-en-Laye in August 1570 put a stop to these depredations, concluding the third War of Religion. Only then was the Parisian effigy of Coligny taken down. But there was to be a twist in the plot that many found baffling. In 1571, Coligny would be pardoned. He was even received at court with a view to advising the royal council. In the eyes of Catholic Parisians this rehabilitation of a traitor was incomprehensible, and reeked of 'behind-the-scenes' politics.[16] Parisian bewilderment and resentment of these manoeuvres represents another liminal moment in the social drama's phase of redressive action. For partisan Catholics, it was Coligny who, by virtue of his metamorphosis from rebel leader to royal counsellor, epitomized the 'rotten peace' that had to be shattered.[17] Yet Coligny's renewed presence in Paris led many to hope that he *could* be physically killed — and that his death would restore the social and religious cohesion of the community.[18]

The opportunity came when Coligny and other leading Huguenots amassed in Paris to celebrate the royal wedding of Henri de Navarre and Marguerite de Valois on 18 August 1572. Four days later, the Admiral was shot by an assailant as he returned to his lodgings in the rue de Béthisy. Coligny was only wounded, but less than 48 hours later he would be well and truly butchered by a squad sent to his lodgings to finish him off. A decision had been taken at the highest level to eliminate Coligny and the Huguenot leadership, on the pretext that they were plotting together in Paris to overthrow the monarchy. The social drama comes to life gruesome prints such as Fig. 1.1.

This scene captures several stages of the process of overkill that brought about Coligny's physical demise at the beginning of the Saint Bartholomew's Day Massacre: firstly the shooting (on the left), secondly the defenestration (top right), and thirdly, the dragging of Coligny's corpse through the streets (centre) along with other bodies hurled from the surrounding buildings. Historically, what happened next is unclear. Two recurring threads in Protestant sources hold that Coligny's hands and feet were dispatched to the Pope, and that his remains were taken away to the gallows of Montfaucon.[19] Looking at the reactions to Coligny's death in

FIG. 1.1. Frans Hogenberg, *Assassinat de Coligny et massacre de la Saint-Barthélemy* (1572). Reproduced with permission of the Bibliothèque nationale de France.

militant Catholic hymns and pamphlets, the historian Denis Crouzet argues that as the Admiral's body was paraded across Paris over the next three days, as an irresistible wave of sacral violence was unleashed.[20] This, for Crouzet, was *the* liminal moment at which retributive action was 'miraculously' transposed from a human to a divine level. Crouzet's interpretation harmonizes with the Girardian notion that sacral violence operates as a kind of expenditure through which society prolongs its sense of coherence. In Paris, and then throughout the nation, Catholic zealots took Coligny's killing as an eschatological portent: as news rapidly spread, it was reported that the *Dies irae* had begun. God's terrifying vengeance was being unleashed; one could only be caught up in it. Each and every Huguenot became a Coligny to be massacred.

Mystical rapture and the enactment of 'extraordinary' justice (execution without a judicial sentence) do not account for every performative aspect of Catholics' attempts to overkill Coligny and his Huguenot brethren. One should not overlook the irony of recourse to 'ordinary' justice (i.e. bringing Huguenot suspects to trial by the normal legal procedures). Even though Coligny had been massacred, King Charles IX still came under pressure from the Parlement de Paris to foreclose the criminal proceedings that had been instantiated against the Admiral back in September 1569. Thus on 27 October 1572, the remains of the Admiral were judged *post mortem* and again he was declared guilty of *lèse-majesté*. With a strange sense of déjà vu, he was hanged in effigy; then his coat of arms was dragged through the streets of Paris and all his property was confiscated. This repeat ritual was no parodic staging of the original performance three years earlier, at least not in the minds of Parlement's senior magistrates, for whom it regularized the executive political action taken more recently on 23 August 1572 to eradicate Coligny and his alleged co-conspirators.[21] Besides the Coligny effigy, a pair of the Admiral's associates were tried and hanged for treason on 27 October: François de Briquemault and Arnaud de Cavaignes, who (unlike Coligny) had hitherto survived.

So did these judicial rituals constitute a final, 'proper' expending of the public's retributive desire? Niggling indeterminacy remained. Had all the conspirators been eradicated? What further symbolic gain was there in overkill, in conducting a *second* hanging of a Coligny effigy, three years on from the first, and two months after his actual body had been ritually defamed in various Parisian localities? To what extent were these performances of killing Coligny in Paris a distraction from the Massacre that had spread throughout France — and in which many Catholics as well as Huguenots were now losing their lives? These were significant doubts, not least because they spanned the confessional and political divide.[22] Without their persistence in the minds of many French people (and foreign observers), the killing of Coligny could not have made a lasting mark on the theatrical stage.

Underkill: Chantelouve's *La Tragedie de feu Gaspard de Colligny*

By 1575, Catholics, even partisan Catholics, were viewing the death of Coligny in an equivocal manner. Notable among these was François de Chantelouve, an erudite nobleman and a Knight of Malta, who had seen his Order's commanderies in Gascony sacked by Huguenots during the uprisings that had followed the Saint Bartholomew's Day Massacre.[23] Chantelouve was angered by this Huguenot resurgence post-1572, and was all too aware of its wider socio-cultural implications. Fired by idealizations of their martyred leader,[24] the Huguenot faction was putting military pressure on the French monarchy to pardon Coligny's crimes.[25] That, for the likes of Chantelouve, was unthinkable; Catholics must oppose any posthumous legal rehabilitation of Coligny just as they had opposed his rehabilitation at court in 1571. For Chantelouve, Coligny *had* to be remembered as a failed traitor — and yet one whose treachery had proved tragically persistent, despite his certain death. Stage tragedy incorporating some neoclassical elements (five acts, chorus, reported deaths) was the medium through which Chantelouve strove to dramatize this conundrum and thereby create an artefact of cultural longevity.

The play-text of Chantelouve's *La Tragedie de feu Gaspard de Colligny* usually receives a passing mention in historical surveys of French theatre.[26] *Colligny* was hastily ushered into print, probably in Paris, in 1575; no further editions followed until the publication of a scholarly edition in the eighteenth century (which underpins three modern critical editions).[27] *Colligny* may not have had a rich family of printed editions, but that did not stop the nineteenth-century historian Jean-Baptiste Capefigue claiming that Chantelouve's tragedy was performed in cities all over France to popular acclaim in the years following the Saint Bartholomew's Day Massacre.[28] Modern scholars are split on the veracity of Capefigue's claim: Charles Mazouer finds it very plausible, whereas Richard Hillman remains sceptical.[29] Both, however, agree on *Colligny*'s stage potential: it requires but a small cast and entails no complex theatrical machinery; this simplicity would make it viable for the sixteenth-century school stage, at a time when *collège* performances of humanist and neo-Latin tragedies were well documented.[30] My premise is that Chantelouve's play-text allows for performance in schools and private houses; more importantly, the minimal stagecraft necessitates a willingness to imagine what takes place on- and — crucially — offstage.

In Turnerian terms, *Colligny* sits at a crucial threshold between stage and page. In this liminal space, where the reintegration of the villain hangs in the balance, we are afforded a hurried glimpse of the Admiral's death. Chantelouve's tastes are not obviously neoclassical; but he does clearly affirm and then depart from — anti-Coligny polemic. Act v seems at first glance conventionally vituperative, dramatizing Coligny's final demise in two brisk scenes: in the first, the discovery of a wicked plot hatched by the Admiral and his henchmen to assassinate King Charles IX and all his royal line; in the second, the king's severe yet expedient response. Looking more closely at the second and final scene, however, we see a distinctive de-dramatization of the action taken to eliminate Coligny et al. In short, they are *underkilled*. Chantelouve stages their passing with heavy dramatic irony. Not only does he decline to have Huguenots murdered onstage (in stark contrast, as we shall see, to Christopher Marlowe); he moreover refuses to relay a lengthy report of the Massacre taking place offstage. The People of France (several actors who comprise a chorus) desperately want to know what action their king has taken to smash the plot and the plotters (1129–30), but Chantelouve's Messenger gives them just six lines of narrated violence (1135–40):

> En gaignant le devant, il envoya grand force,
> (Tandis que tout Paris és cantons se renforce)
> Qui Piles, l'Admiral, Pardaillan, & Pinos,
> Et autres, envoya souz les stiges flos;
> Bien que Dieu ait permis que Lorges à la fuitte,
> Se soit sauvé bien loing sur sa cavale visite.

> [Taking action first, he despatched a puissant band
> (While having all parts of Paris more strongly manned):
> They sank Piles, Pardaillan, Pinos, the Admiral,
> And others deep down into Styx's gloomy channel,
> Although God permitted Lorges, in desperate flight,
> To ride off on his swift horse with all of its might.][31]

For Richard Hillman, this report 'can hardly help evoking one of the central images of the Massacre, the casting of corpses into the Seine'.[32] And yet, the economy of allusion here is so marked as to suggest a deeply ambivalent act of recollection. Firstly, one might query how Coligny's corpse has ended up in the Stygian channel of the Seine, when other sources insist upon its displacement around Paris. And what of the other three named victims? Only the first bears a firm resemblance to an historical individual (Armand de Clermont, baron de Piles) known to have been killed in the initial wave of massacre.[33] With the advantages of hindsight, Chantelouve sows confusion and then turns our attention to the limitations of the king's 'puissant band' in enforcing extraordinary justice and thereby protecting their monarch. Chantelouve underscores the one Huguenot who got away — 'Lorges', alias Gabriel de Montgomery, who as it happened, already had the tragic distinction of killing a French King (Montgomery had committed involuntary regicide, fatally wounding Henri II in a jousting accident in 1559). Montgomery, as was well known, had escaped the Massacre and taken up refuge in England.[34] A morbid irony of displacement — Montgomery's, not the Admiral's — cuts short what could have been a triumphant narrative of Huguenot insurrection suppressed.

Chantelouve's sparse *récit* of underkill is staged as a sombre tempering of the initial outpouring of Catholic glee soon after the Saint Bartholomew's Day Massacre. Pamphlets such as the *Discours sur la mort de Gaspart de Coligny* (1572) had celebrated at much greater length the agonizing death of the Admiral in a mythological and dramatic register. Here, the Olympian deities, represented by Juno, harangue Coligny's corpse and refuse to bear it aloft to a heavenly resting place. The Seine is a far less accommodating portal to the underworld than she is in Chantelouve's *Colligny*. In this *Discours*, she refuses to admit Coligny through her Stygian gates: he has not yet suffered enough for his crimes, and deserves a still crueller death than either Water or Earth is prepared to grant. So the gods decree that Coligny's headless, handless corpse must remain indefinitely strung up by its feet on the gallows of Montfaucon: a grotesque *point de suspension* in the nation's cultural register of prodigious deaths.

Chantelouve was conversant with this sort of gallows humour. In *Colligny*, the Admiral makes his very first appearance anticipating a noose around his neck (i. i. 5) should he fail in his treasonous plot. For Hillman, this calls for a halter prop which Coligny might have held onstage, or possibly even worn throughout Act i to symbolize his designation as a 'nouveau Judas' [latter-day Judas] (i. 3. 242).[35] It is a parodic reminder, furthermore, of the effigy hangings in 1569 and 1572. Nevertheless, Chantelouve's allusions to the gibbet remain minimal and ambivalent. When Montfaucon is finally mentioned, we hear none of the jubilation that rings out of the *Discours sur la mort de Gaspart de Coligny*. Instead, Chantelouve has his chorus of People briefly relay (v. ii. 1188) how Coligny's body now hangs at the heights of another stage — the tiered criminal scaffold outside Paris. Chantelouve has no time for prolonging the Admiral's suffering in accordance with divine vengeance (1187). Instead he moves towards a different moral outcome: cautionary contemplation. Coligny's demise connotes no revilement in reverse gear as suggested by Huguenot polemicists,[36] no paradoxical, Christ-like honour in a debasing death. As Coligny is raised up on Paris's Golgotha, the People of France are reminded of the saviour and pacifying Christ who Coligny is *not*.

But this dissociation, crucially, serves to remind Chantelouve's audience of 'Ambition des hommes la ruine' [Ambition to whom men's downfall is due] (1145) rampaging across the nation-stage. Therein lies the tragedy: Coligny may have been punished in full sight of all of Paris, but many other ambitious Huguenots remain at large. For Chantelouve, Coligny's fate has only exacerbated the ambition of those powerful individuals, whose will to dominate is irreconcilable with the ideal of 'la modestie d'or' [golden moderation] (1156) for the common good. In Turnerian terms, we are reminded of the schism, the final phase of the wider social drama that shapes *Colligny*, in which Huguenot rebels cannot be reintegrated into the French (Catholic) nation. For some twenty years or more, this would be the finale. Then, in the 1590s, Christopher Marlowe re-opened the wounds, to put the Saint Bartholomew's Day Massacre on the English stage.

Dark Play: Marlowe's *Massacre at Paris*

We have significant albeit patchy details of how *The Massacre at Paris* came into being.[37] The likely first performance was on 30 January 1593 by the Lord Strange's Men at the Rose Theatre in London.[38] Philip Henslowe (the proprietor of The Rose) subsequently records a number of performances by the Admiral's Men in 1594, with generally diminishing returns. *The Massacre at Paris* then seems to have dropped off the London stage repertoire until probable revivals in 1598, and 1601–02, after which Henslowe gives no further records. So what do we make of this play's genesis and its heyday at the turn of the seventeenth century? Modern scholarly reaction to *The Massacre at Paris* has been extremely negative, but there is a gradual shifting away from pointing out structural flaws and aesthetic demerits, with a move towards a deeper consideration of the play's potential for insight in performance-theoretical terms.[39]

The Massacre at Paris is a kind of history play which re-presents Coligny's death, the Saint Bartholomew's Day Massacre, and the high drama of French politics up to 1589. Marlowe compresses some seventeen years of French history into twenty-four scenes of uneven length. The resultant play capitalizes on English fears about French affairs: that England was being sucked into problems of tyranny, succession, and religious fanaticism that had all come to a head in France during the 1580s, culminating in the assassinations of Henri de Guise (1588) and King Henri III (1589). The latter half of *The Massacre at Paris* stages these events. Operating in English espionage, Marlowe had access to a number of pamphlets indicating how the political and theological fault-lines had extended since the Saint Bartholomew's Day Massacre.[40] Furthermore, Marlowe may well have read Chantelouve's *Coligny*, to further his knowledge of topical French crises from the viewpoint of the partisan Catholic milieu. If not, he did an uncanny job of re-inscribing Chantelouve's tragedy, such that Guise wrests from Coligny the role of the godless murderer soon-to-be murdered.[41]

This role-swap, however, does not in itself explain how Marlowe saw potential for further dramatic innovation in staging the death of Coligny. Though over two decades old, the Admiral's murder still had not been *enacted* upon a theatrical stage; thus Marlowe's enactment of it instantiates a vital if awkward stretch of onstage 'action in *The Massacre at Paris* (scenes 6–11). The symbolic significance of these scenes, we shall see, differs noticeably from the instances of overkill and underkill we have hitherto encountered. Marlowe's sense of uncertain disarray in sequencing the murders of Coligny and other Huguenots throws into question the very performativity of death on stage. In an important contribution, Julia Briggs notes that:

> The scenes of the massacre may be viewed either as a subtle [...] analysis of contemporary crowd violence and religious hatred, or as a black comedy that paradoxically invites its audience to laugh at helpless Protestant victims. Either way, it must be conceded that *The Massacre at Paris* is something more than a tract on their behalf.[42]

Briggs certainly has a point, although her analysis calls for further nuances. As well as affording something more than the numerous pamphlet polemicists, and the partisan French tragedy of Chantelouve, Marlowe offers something distinctly *less* than any of these. A closer look at the staging of the massacre scenes reveals Marlowe's art of less-is-more.

Scene 6 stages the famous defenestration of Coligny. It opens with the Duke of Guise and his assassination squadron entering the main stage area, discussing how to make the Admiral their initial victim. Guise, Anjoy[43] and their Swiss mercenaries will guard the street; meanwhile Gonzago[44] leads the rest of the party offstage and into an upper acting area representing the interior of the Admiral's house.[45]

GONZAGO   Where is the Admirall?
ADMIRALL   O let me pray before I dye.
GONZAGO   Then pray unto our Ladye, kisse this crosse.
          Stab him.
ADMIRALL   O God forgive my sins. [*Dyes.*] (6. 27–30)

Blink and you miss it. This killing of Coligny is pared down to the bare minimum of martyrdom.[46] To that extent it speaks of 'a certain slap-dash efficiency' (to quote Neil Carson) in the pre-rehearsal preparation of parts.[47] Gonzago almost immediately confronts Coligny, whose request for a prayerful passing becomes an on-the-spot combination of murder and intercessory sarcasm. The lines are easily memorized, and they speak of an intuition shared by actor and dramatist for morbid religious satire — in moderation. In the act of killing, there is nothing of Marlowe's main source, François Hotman, according to whom the Admiral's main killer is of German (rather than Franco-Italian) descent. Hotman's version is replete with dramatic overkill: the blaspheming assassin Benuese stabs Coligny in the head and thigh, whilst another mercenary shoots him in the breast.[48]

Marlowe follows the Hotman accounts only once Coligny's corpse has been hurled down onto the main stage area (6. 36–48). Even here, the imitation is arrestingly inexact. Hotman had stressed how Guise kept on proclaiming that Coligny's death was the fulfilment of King Charles IX's wishes. Marlowe's Guise instead performs a grotesque victory dance upon a religious and dynastic rival (Coligny, we remember, was accused of assassinating Guise's father in 1563). Still, Marlowe knows when to switch off the grotesque, and he therefore avoids the further display of indecent overkill that his Protestant source invites. Marlowe's Guise orders Coligny to be dragged offstage for ritual dissection (head and hands for dispatch to the Pope), whereas Hotman had described a free-for-all dismemberment of limbs and genitalia (the Admiral's 'secrete partes').

Dismemberment and decapitation both lay within the capability of early modern staging, as Margaret Owens has shown.[49] Indeed, Marlowe himself explored such possibilities in his *Dr Faustus*: the latter's shredded body is eventually scattered in pieces across the stage. So in refraining from such displays in *The Massacre at Paris*, Marlowe is testing the limits of stage violence in a different mode. This mode of experimentation seems attuned to the dynamics of religious mob violence, as Briggs suggests — but its character does not quite fit with what she sees as 'black comedy' inviting laughter upon the Protestant victims of the massacre scenes. Instead, I would venture, Marlowe comes closer to types of 'dark play' theorized by Richard Schechner in *The Future of Ritual* (1993) and latterly by Joseph Roach.[50] Dark play emphasizes risk and the sheer thrill of deceiving; it subverts order and breaks its own rules — so much so that the play itself is in danger of being destroyed. In practice, not all parties know the rules of the game they have entered into, or even that they are playing a game.

Playing dark is a highly suggestive concept for interpreting the mayhem orchestrated by Guise in scenes 6–11 of *The Massacre at Paris*. Guise is the master player — but even he struggles to make an efficacious combination of murder and play. Scene 9 features Guise indulging in an extended mockery of the scholar Petrus Ramus, whose chief crime is to have scoffed at Aristotelian logic (9. 25–38). Guise wants to take down Ramus with scholar's wit ('*Argumentum testimonii est inartificiale*. [*the evidence of testimony is inartificial*] | To contradict which, I say *Ramus* shall dye') — but he also forces Ramus to play along ('How answere you that?'). A bemused Ramus begs to get a word in edgeways — but, unsure of the perverse rules of the game that will certainly end with his death, he takes the risk of declaiming at length against Aristotle and the Sorbonne (41–53). Guise is both delighted and irritated by Ramus's pedantic self-defence, berating his henchmen for not slaying Ramus upon his initial command (38). The gamesmanship jars to a halt and becomes an act of stabbing; any audience laughter is likely to be directed not at the victim but at a situation that has degenerated to the point of absurdity.

Dark play's switch into plain murder is neither fully explicit nor complete. A briefer example comes in scene 7, where Guise encounters a Huguenot preacher and suddenly breaks into liturgical parody: ' "Dearly beloved brother", thus 'tis written. *He stabs him*' (7. 8). This time, for Guise, that little flash of ludic frenzy was enough — but Anjoy, unaware that the game is over, wants to prolong the dark play on liturgy: 'Stay my Lord, let me begin the psalme' (9). Guise refuses to let him. Playing dark in the midst of massacre, Marlowe shows us, tends away from ideological unity and towards private gratification, in which not even co-belligerents are invited to share.[51] Once this level of selfishness has been reached, it affords a hollow laugh at the fleeting pleasures of getting away with murder. Marlowe's original spectators might just have managed a grin at the wasted opportunity for an irreverent parody of psalm-singing (which had replaced the traditional Catholic liturgy in Protestant services).

The fallout from moments of dark play scattered throughout scenes 6–11 is, unambiguously, waste. That is, wasted humans amid other forms of detritus. On Guise's command, dead Huguenots are dragged offstage to be dumped in rivers and ditches. Scene 11 goes further still, offering a curious twist to this very process of wasting. Here we get our final glimpses of what has become of Coligny's body, which has ended up in the hands of two soldiers. By this point, the ritual killing has all but ground to a halt: the soldiers are paralysed with indecision as to how they should properly dispose of the Admiral. The scene reads almost as a parody of the *Discours sur la mort de Gaspart de Coligny*. The Admiral's corpse cannot be burned lest it poison the very air its captors breathe; likewise, it cannot be committed to the Seine lest it corrupt the water, the fish, and all those who consume the fish. In the end, the soldiers opt for what had always been the most popular form of killing Coligny: gibbeting him (9. 10–11) in full sight of the audience.

And yet — as ever — the performance of hanging fails to achieve symbolic closure. It is something distinctly less than a climatic suspension from the gallows of Montfaucon. Nor is there any hint that the Coligny who now hangs before us is Coligny the Protestant martyr, representing Christ 'that hangeth on a tree' (Galatians 3. 13). Instead of spectacles of proper retribution that will bring legal and theological closure upon the drama, Marlowe is staging something quite different — something that modern anthropology would call an ominous performance of waste, a performance that sits on the dangerous cusp of violence and the aesthetic, where people are consumed in catastrophically unproductive acts of expenditure.[52] Coligny's decomposing corpse rankles the nostrils of Guise and the Queen Mother, so the offending body is (once again) ordered offstage: 'Sirs, take him away and throw him in some ditch' (9. 18).[53] No more performative overkill, nor even dramatic underkill: just waste. In the relentless acceleration of historical time that drives *The Massacre at Paris*, Coligny may be killed no more.

★   ★   ★   ★   ★

If we view Coligny's death primarily as an instance of massacre, then it ends as a waste product of fervent civil-religious violence in 1572. Marlowe's play indicated as much. But Marlowe does more: re-inscribing elements of Chantelouve's tragedy, he offers further dark plays on the wider social drama surrounding Coligny's death. This drama played out across the late sixteenth century and became an enduring phenomenon, whose multiple transitions always already left the door open to future interpretation. Each spectacle of retribution — consciously performed within a particular space, for a particular audience — had an essential role in making immediate sense of Coligny's death. But the unscripted open-endedness of these spectacles has necessitated a process of transcultural (re)valorization that has never fully run its course.

Since the mid-twentieth century, there have been sporadic revivals of Marlowe's *Massacre at Paris* in the US, the UK and France. Reviews of these productions have, unsurprisingly, emphasized the stage orgy of murder of the massacre scenes.

Whilst the subtleties of Marlowe's religious-political allusions may have been lost, a convincing performance of death is still greatly prized: 'an ability to be killed and dragged across the stage',[54] without special-effects deficiencies that would add unwanted farcical touches to an otherwise chilling spectacle.[55] To retain that eerie sense of the macabre, one recent production used red strip lighting along the theatre floor, reflecting in a shallow pool to evoke the river Seine flowing red with blood.[56] Patrice Chéreau (whose production ran May–June 1972 at the Théâtre National Populaire de Villeurbanne) sums up what was, and continues to be, the undying dramatic interest unfolding from the killing of Coligny: 'le passage sanglant d'une époque à une autre' [a gory passage from one era to the next],[57] in which a social drama degenerates into a fascination with the act itself of dying. Thus contextualized, the Coligny spectacles of retribution find their place in a much longer narrative of death: that confounding symbol of the never-ending ending and its staging in the Western World.

Notes to Chapter 1

1. The most thorough analysis is Jean-Louis Bourgeon, *L'Assassinat de Coligny* (Geneva: Droz, 1992).
2. The historiography is ever expanding: for an overview, see Barbara Diefendorf, *The St. Bartholomew's Day Massacre: A Brief History with Documents* (Boston, MA, and New York: Bedford/St. Martin's Press, 2008).
3. For the French context, see Michael Meere, *Onstage Violence in Sixteenth-Century French Tragedy: Performance, Ethics, Poetics* (Oxford: Oxford University Press, 2021); Christian Biet and Marie-Madeleine Fragonard (eds), *Le Théâtre, la violence et les arts en Europe (XVIe–XVIIe s.)* (Paris: Champion, 2010); François Lecercle (ed.), *Réécritures du crime: l'acte sanglant sur la scène (XVIe–XVIIIe s.)* (Paris: Champion, 2009). For the English context, see Timothy Reiss, 'Renaissance Theatre and the Theory of Tragedy', in *The Cambridge History of Literary Criticism*, III: *The Renaissance*, ed. by Glyn Norton (Cambridge: Cambridge University Press, 1999), pp. 229–47; Mike Pincombe, 'English Renaissance Tragedy: Theories and Antecedents', in *The Cambridge Companion to English Renaissance Tragedy*, ed. by Emma Smith and Garrett A. Sullivan (Cambridge: Cambridge University Press, 2010), pp. 3–16; and in the same volume, see Tanya Pollard, 'Tragedy and Revenge', pp. 58–72.
4. See principally Turner's posthumous book, *The Anthropology of Performance* (New York: PAJ Publications, 1988), and Schechner's much-revised *Performance Theory* (London: Routledge, 2003).
5. I take performativity as 'the potential for enacting self-awareness, or the possible thematization of an event sequence' (J. Lowell Lewis, *The Anthropology of Cultural Performance* (New York: Palgrave Macmillan, 2013), p. 7). Framed as such, performativity relates either to an event that constitutes a performance proper — a particular sequence of actions witnessed and acknowledged as a spectacle by others — or to an action that is consciously enacted whether or not anyone is watching.
6. Turner, *The Anthropology of Performance*, pp. 74–76. Schechner has applied this model of the social drama to *Romeo and Juliet* (see Schechner, 'Ritual and Performance', ch. 22 of *Companion Encyclopedia of Anthropology*, ed. by Tim Ingold (London: Routledge, 2002)).
7. See Denis Crouzet, *La Nuit de la Saint-Barthélemy: un rêve perdu de la Renaissance* (Paris: Fayard, 1994), pp. 472–73.
8. Coligny became *de facto* leader of the Huguenots upon the death of the Prince de Condé (Louis de Bourbon) at the Battle of Jarnac (13 March 1569).
9. *Arrest de la Court de Parlement contre Gaspart de Colligny, qui fut admiral de France [13 sept. 1569]* (Lyon: M. Iove, 1569).

10. The erstwhile Place de Grève is today the site of La Place de l'Hôtel-de-Ville — Esplanade de la Libération. It was *Ancien Régime* Paris's largest site of criminal executions and it was here that the guillotine was first used in 1792. Sloping towards the Seine, the Place de Grève was a trapezoid esplanade covered in gravel. Up until the reign of Henri IV, it afforded broad and semi-enclosed spectator viewpoints of executions, many of which were conducted upon the gibbet that stood in the centre of the esplanade in full sight of the Hôtel de Ville.

11. Allie Terry-Fritsch, 'Execution by Image: Visual Spectacularism and Icononclasm in Late Medieval and Early Modern Europe', in *Death, Torture and the Broken Body in European Art, 1300–1650*, ed. by John Decker and Mitzi Kirkland-Ives (Farnham: Ashgate, 2015), pp. 191–206.

12. Terry-Fritsch, 'Execution by Image', pp. 191–92.

13. *Mémoires de Claude Haton (1553–1582)*, ed. by Laurent Bourquin, 4 vols (Paris: Editions du Comité des travaux historiques et scientifiques, 2005), II, 286.

14. A classic formulation of effigy theory is Girard's 'monstrous double', in his *La Violence et le sacré* (Paris: Bernard Grasset, 1972); see also Joseph Roach, *Cities of the Dead: Circum-Atlantic Performance* (New York: Columbia University Press, 1996), pp. 39–40.

15. Coligny would later complain about his difficulties in recovering it, particularly the Châtillon abbeys; see Arlette Jouanna, *The Saint Bartholomew's Day Massacre: The Mysteries of a Crime of State (24 August 1572)*, trans. by Joseph Bergin (Manchester: Manchester University Press, 2015), p. 25.

16. See Stuart Carroll, *Martyrs and Murderers: The Guise Family and the Making of Europe* (Oxford: Oxford University Press, 2009), pp. 199–200.

17. Jouanna, *The Saint Bartholomew's Day Massacre*, pp. 87–88.

18. A recurrent theme of clerics; see Barbara Diefendorf, 'Simon Vigor: A Radical Preacher in Sixteenth-Century Paris', *Sixteenth-Century Journal*, 18 (1987), 399–410.

19. The key pamphlets in this regard were François Hotman's *De furoribus Gallicis* (1573) and *Vita Colinii* (1575), both with vernacular translations in English and French.

20. Crouzet, *La Nuit de la Saint-Barthélemy*, pp. 518–19.

21. Jouanna, *The Saint Bartholomew's Day Massacre*, p. 106.

22. See especially Jouanna, *The Saint Bartholomew's Day Massacre*, ch. 4.

23. I use Keith Cameron's edition, *La Tragédie de feu Gaspard de Colligny* [hereafter *Colligny*] (Exeter: University of Exeter, 1971), and Richard Hillman's English translation, *The Tragedy of the Late Gaspard de Coligny / François de Chantelouve; And, The Guisiade / Pierre Matthieu* [hereafter *Coligny*] (Ottawa: Dovehouse, 2005).

24. Especially Hotman's *Vita Colinii*.

25. See further Cameron, *Colligny*, p. viii.

26. For instance: Charles Mazouer, *Le Théâtre français de la Renaissance* (Paris: Champion, 2002), pp. 238–39.

27. Those of Cameron, Hillman, and Lisa Wollfe (the latter's text is in *La Tragédie à l'époque d'Henri III, vol. I (1574–1579)*, ed. by Enea Balmas and others (Florence: Olschki, 1999)).

28. Capefigue, *Histoire de la réforme, de la ligue, et du règne de Henri IV*, 8 vols (Paris: Duféy, 1834), III, 242–23.

29. Mazouer, 'Chantelouve et la Saint-Barthélemy: *La Tragédie de feu Gaspard de Colligny* (1575)', in *Les Ecrivains et la politique dans le sud-ouest de la France autour des années 1580*, ed. by Claude-Gilbert Dubois et al. (Bordeaux: Presses universitaires de Bordeaux, 1982), pp. 129–40 (p. 132); Hillman, *Coligny*, pp. 32–33.

30. See Madeleine Lazard, *Le Théâtre en France au XVIe siècle* (Paris: Presses universitaires de France, 1980), pp. 77–89, 99–104.

31. Hillman, *Coligny*, p. 136.

32. Hillman, *Coligny*, p. 170, n. 167.

33. 'Pardaillan' is presumably a variant of 'Pardaillon', a page of Henri de Navarre, rather than the better-known François de Ségur-Pardaillan (who did escape); 'Pinos' is untraceable — and for Hillman, possibly the name of one of Chantelouve's personal enemies added to the list for a dash of vindictive humour. See Hillman, *Coligny*, p. 170, n. 165–66.

34. Cameron, *Colligny*, p. 69. In 1574, shortly before the publication of *Colligny*, Montgomery was caught and executed; it is unclear whether Chantelouve was abreast of this development.

35. Hillman, *Coligny*, p. 140, n.7.

36. Simon Goulart, *Memoires de l'Estat de France, sous Charles Neufiesme*, 3 vols (Geneva: H. Wolf, 1578), I, fol. 416^r.

37. Modern editors lament the poor state of the text (its 'corruption' owing to memorial reconstruction) and dispute the dating of the play's composition, first staging and first printing. See Edward Esche's introduction to his edition of *The Massacre at Paris*, in *The Complete Works of Christopher Marlowe*, 5 vols (Oxford: Oxford University Press, 1998), V, 309–16; R. Carter Hailey, 'The Publication Date of Marlowe's *Massacre at Paris*, With a Note on The Collier Leaf', *Marlowe Studies: An Annual*, 1 (2011), 25–40.

38. Esche, *The Massacre at Paris*, p. 315, from which I reproduce the subsequent performance details relating to the period *c.* 1594–1602. All quotations are from the Esche edition.

39. See for instance Mathew Martin's re-evaluation of the play's brokenness and disorientation in *Tragedy and Trauma in the Plays of Christopher Marlowe* (Farnham: Ashgate, 2015), ch. 6.

40. For the death of Coligny, Marlowe drew (though not exclusively) upon the English translation of Hotman's *De furoribus Gallicis*. Much material for the second half of the play has been identified as coming from pro-Catholic pamphlets: see Paul Kocher's two articles, 'François Hotman and Marlowe's *The Massacre at Paris*', *PMLA*, 56.2 (1941), 349–68; 'Contemporary Pamphlet Backgrounds for Marlowe's *The Massacre at Paris*', *Modern Language Quarterly*, 8.2 (1947), 151–73.

41. Richard Hillman, *Shakespeare, Marlowe and the Politics of France* (Basingstoke: Palgrave Macmillan, 2002), ch. 4; and Hillman, 'The Admiral, Upside-Down, or Apocalypse Now and Then: Marlowe's *The Massacre at Paris* and François de Chantelouve's *La Tragédie de Feu Gaspard de Colligny* (1575)', in *Les Huguenots dans les îles britanniques de la Renaissance aux Lumières: écrits religieux et représentations*, ed. by Anne Dunan-Page and Marie-Christine Munoz-Teulié (Paris: Champion, 2008), pp. 61–85.

42. Briggs, 'Marlowe's *Massacre at Paris*: A Reconsideration', *The Review of English Studies*, 34 (1983), 257–78 (p. 278). Briggs builds on Natalie Zemon Davis's pioneering work on the rites of Reformation violence.

43. The Duc d'Anjou, later to be King Henri III.

44. Louis de Gonzague, Duke of Nevers and Rethel, a military officer.

45. The model reconstruction of the Rose Theatre at the Museum of London shows that the Rose had two doors at the back of the main stage area; above these doors was an upper tier with a protruding balcony. This balcony space would have been just large enough for the Admiral's bed (as required in scenes 5 and 6) and for his body to have been cast down upon the main stage (scene 6).

46. See further Kristen Poole, 'Garbled Martyrdom in Christopher Marlowe's *The Massacre at Paris*', *Comparative Drama*, 32.1 (1998), 1–25 (pp. 14–15).

47. Carson, *A Companion to Henslowe's Diary* (Cambridge: Cambridge University Press, 1988), shows that for many plays performed at the Rose, pre-rehearsal preparations of a play (studying, annotating, transcribing, licensing, and preparing parts) took only about two weeks (p. 74).

48. Ernest Varamund [alias Hotman], *A True and Plaine Report of the Furious Outrages of Fraunce* (London: H. Bynneman, 1573), pp. 55–56.

49. Owens, *Stages of Dismemberment: The Fragmented Body in Late Medieval and Early Modern Drama* (Newark: University of Delaware Press, 2005).

50. See Roach, 'Deep Play, Dark Play: Framing the Limit(less)', in *The Rise of Performance Studies: Rethinking Richard Schechner's Broad Spectrum*, ed. by James Harding and Cindy Rosenthal (Basingstoke: Palgrave Macmillan, 2011), pp. 275–83.

51. Hence this is no 'Mardi Gras game' in which churchmen are ceremonially mocked (*pace* Briggs, 'Marlowe's *Massacre at Paris*', p. 276). Dark play's inversions are cruelly private, unlike the inversions of carnivals whose agendas are vindictively public (see Schechner, *The Future of Ritual: Writings on Culture and Performance* (London: Routledge, 1993), p. 36).

52. Roach *Cities of the Dead*, pp. 41, 123. Roach elaborates on Georges Bataille's *The Accursed Share: An Essay on General Economy* [1949], trans. by Robert Hurley, 3 vols (New York: Zone Books, 1988).

53. For Thomas Pettit, Guises's instruction is evidence of a company unable to stage a hanging, the requisite stage prop being unavailable ('Formulaic Dramaturgy in *Doctor Faustus*', in *A Poet*

and a Filthy Play-Maker: New Essays on Christopher Marlowe, ed. by Kenneth Friedenreich, Roma Gill and Constance Kuriyama (New York: AMS Press, 1988), pp. 167–91). This may well have been a besetting difficulty in some early productions, but I am not persuaded that it was in every case. An effigy might have served as an expedient prop for this scene, for ease of hoisting the body upon a stage gibbet. This would put grotesque emphasis on Coligny's degraded state, and function as a burlesque of the actual hangings in effigy in 1569 and 1572. A handless, headless effigy-prop is a further option for staging the enactment of Guise's previous instructions in VI. 43.

54. Michael Ferguson's 1963 production at the Chanticleer Theatre, London, as reviewed in the *Daily Telegraph and Morning Post*, 31 January 1963, p. 13.

55. Although the Ferguson production was generally well received, it was criticized for having sawdust rather than stage blood erupt from the stabbings (*The Times*, 3 January 1963, p. 4).

56. James Wallace's 2014 production in the studio theatre adjoining the archaeological site of the Rose, as reviewed in the *Financial Times*, 16 March 2014. Online at <https://www.ft.com/content/81c25de2-ab5e-11e3-aad9-00144feab7de> [accessed 15 April 2021].

57. See Michel Bataillon, *Un Défi en province : Chéreau, Planchon et leurs invités, 1972–1986 : chronique d'une aventure théâtrale* (Paris: Marval, 2005), p. 147.

CHAPTER 2

Corneille's Aggressive Suicides: *Rodogune* and *Théodore*

Joseph Harris

Royal Holloway, University of London

Introduction: Aggressive Suicide

Throughout his long career as a playwright, Pierre Corneille (1606–84) was often attracted to the dramatic potential of powerfully compelling villain figures. From his very first tragedy, the Senecan-influenced *Médée* (1635), at least until *Attila, roi des Huns* (1667), Corneille created a host of dramatically impressive characters whose crimes, as he claims of one of them in his 1660 theoretical writings, are 'accompagnés d'une grandeur d'âme qui a quelque chose de si haut, qu'en même temps qu'on déteste ses actions, on admire la source dont elles partent' [accompanied by a greatness of soul which has something so elevated about it that, even as we detest their actions, we admire the source from which they stem].[1] Yet such villains can pose thorny questions of narrative resolution for a dramatist, and Corneille's villains meet a range of different fates: the sorceress Médée is finally shown triumphant, borne aloft in a chariot pulled by dragons; the scheming Bithynian queen Arsinoé is eventually won over by the hero Nicomède's magnanimity; Sillace seems to slip into the shadows and be forgotten; and, perhaps most notably, Attila dies of an implausible (if historically attested) haemorrhage as he reaches the paroxysms of murderous rage.[2] Only a small handful of Corneille's villains are actually murdered, and only one — Garibalde in his unsuccessful play *Pertharite* (1651) — is killed by the play's heroic protagonist. Indeed, Corneille is aware that removing an antagonist, even an out-and-out villain, through death brings with it its own intractable ethical and aesthetic questions. In his theoretical writings, Corneille claims indeed that dramatists need to 'préserver nos héros du crime tant qu'il se peut, et les exempter même de tremper leurs mains dans le sang, si ce n'est en un juste combat' [preserve our heroes from crime as far as possible, and even prevent them from steeping their hands in blood, unless this is in a fair combat].[3]

If it is problematic to have a villain murdered, then a potentially more attractive solution would be to have the villain die by their own hand. This, indeed, is the solution that Corneille chooses in the two tragedies discussed in this article: the rather melodramatic tragedy *Rodogune, princesse des Parthes* (1644), and the martyr-drama *Théodore, vierge et martyre* (1644/45). Yet suicide is not without aesthetic and ethical problems for a playwright. For a start, as the abbé Dubos would suggest in the early eighteenth century, suicide could appear to be a form of aesthetic compromise or 'cop-out' for dramatists eager to tie up loose plot threads. Being encumbered by too many secondary characters invented to mask his dramatic sterility, a weak playwright — claims Dubos — typically compels his characters 'à se défaire eux-mêmes par le fer ou par le poison sur le premier motif qu'il imagine' [to do away with themselves by sword or poison on the first pretext he imagines].[4] This risk — that a character's suicide might appear to be motivated more by external dramatic necessity than by factors internal to the plot — is perhaps all the stronger when the character is the primary villain or antagonist. Like a sudden conversion or repentance, a villain's suicide might imply a sudden and implausible change of heart. For a related reason, suicide might seem to be too noble or heroic a gesture, as Hippolyte-Jules de La Mesnardière implies in his *Poétique* (1640). Although he recognizes that Christianity condemns suicide 'irrévocablement' [irrevocably],[5] La Mesnardière praises 'spectacles généreux' [noble spectacles], in which a tragic character — such as Seneca's Phaedra — chooses to die in order to expiate some previous crime.[6] A couple of generations later, Corneille's nephew Fontenelle would echo La Mesnardière's suggestions, insisting that the suicidal tragic hero manages to reconcile the spectator's pity and his respect: 'il fait lui-même sa destinée, on l'admire autant qu'on le plaint' [he forges his own destiny himself; we admire him as much as we pity him].[7] It is not difficult to see, therefore, why a villain's suicide might be problematic. It would seem highly inconsistent for a protagonist who has previously dazzled audiences through sheer force of character to suddenly change tack and display either the cowardly desperation or the magnanimous repentance that suicide tends to connote in tragedy. Such a suicide would seem to be motivated more by external, dramatic factors than by the character's internal psychological coherence, and so risks exposing, to the mind of Dubos at least, the author's creative sterility.

Yet other modes of suicide are available. Indeed, as the sociologist Marzio Barbagli points out, suicide can take on quite different forms in different historical and cultural contexts. Barbagli's history of suicide, *Farewell to the World*, draws attention to the largely non-Western practice of what he calls 'aggressive suicide' — that is, suicide conducted 'against' other people.[8] Traditionally, Europeans have long considered suicide (as La Mesnardière does) as an essentially self-directed act: a personal action in which the individual kills him- or herself in order to be released from some private suffering, despair, remorse, or other overwhelming emotion. Yet Barbagli reminds us that suicide can also be targeted as an implicit act of symbolic aggression aimed at other people, or indeed at whole political regimes; one famous example of this might be the self-immolation of Buddhist monks in protest against the South Vietnamese government in 1963.

Barbagli's theory that suicide can be conducted as an attack on others helps shed a new light on some of Corneille's tragedies. The idea is perhaps best demonstrated by the grieving Roman noblewoman Camille in his famous early tragedy *Horace*

(1640). Although Camille's death is not an act of suicide in the strictest sense, she certainly provokes her brother Horace into killing her, thereby compromising his own virtue and staining his glorious reputation with the shameful act of 'parricide'. As part of her lengthy tirade against the oppressive Roman honour code that she so hates, Camille expresses the wish that Horace will commit some act of 'lâcheté' [cowardice] that will forever sully 'Cette gloire si chère à ta brutalité' [this glory that is so precious to your brutality] (IV. 5. 1293–94). Her treasonous wish brings about its own fulfilment as she provokes Horace into drawing his sword and chasing her offstage. By provoking her brother to kill her, Camille thus harnesses her suicidal despair, and turns her own death into a political act that brings shame onto him and compels Rome to reflect — however briefly — on its own values and priorities. This reading of Camille's death here should not, of course, suggest that she is not also deeply distraught at the circumstances — the death of her beloved Curiace — that lead her to provoke her brother into killing her. Rather, her death achieves two goals at once; it frees her from private distress whilst making a powerful political statement. Furthermore, far from bringing the play to an aesthetic close, Camille's death takes place in Act IV and then ushers in a lengthy debate about Horace's punishment that takes up most of the final act. Just as in his previous play, the tragicomedy Le Cid, death interests Corneille here not as a means of dramatic resolution, but rather as a moral issue that itself needs to be resolved. Although the deaths that we shall explore here are crucially different, being genuine suicides conducted by out-and-out villains, they also bequeath a similar moral uncertainty to the survivors. As I shall demonstrate, both villains effectively stage their own suicides — one successfully, the other less so — in order to inflict harm onto other people. Their suicides are emphatically not the end of the story, but rather constitute one final act of aggression.

Rodogune: Pre-empting Divine Justice

The two plays I shall be taking as case studies of aggressive suicide here are both dominated by powerful, villainous female characters — the ruthlessly ambitious Syrian queen Cléopâtre in Rodogune and the savagely vindictive Roman colonial governor's wife Marcelle in Théodore. The two women's eventual suicides show several broad similarities, but also some important differences; indeed, as I shall argue, in an important sense it is only the latter's death that can fully and demonstrably be understood as an 'aggressive suicide'. Perhaps most importantly, both deaths are largely Corneille's invention — a fact that might well make us suspect, on first reading, that their main purpose is to bring about an ethically and aesthetically satisfying dramatic conclusion. Corneille certainly suggests something of this fifteen years later when he explains the changes he made to the historical sources when writing the earlier play. According to the historical sources, he recounts, the Syrian queen Cleopatra had, after killing one of her sons, attempted to poison the other; suspecting the truth, however, her remaining son killed her by forcing her to drink the poison herself. Corneille's rewritten version, instead, has the queen Cléopâtre drink the poison of her own volition. This rewriting,

Corneille explains, gives his Cléopâtre's death two dramatic advantages:

> La punition de cette impitoyable mère laisse un plus fort exemple, puisqu'elle devient un effet de la justice du ciel, et non pas de la vengeance des hommes; d'autre côté, Antiochus ne perd rien de la compassion et de l'amitié qu'on avait pour lui, qui redoublent plutôt qu'elles ne diminuent; et enfin l'action historique s'y trouve conservée malgré ce changement, puisque Cléopâtre périt par le même poison qu'elle présente à Antiochus.[9]

> [The punishment of this merciless mother leaves a stronger example, since it becomes an effect of heavenly justice, and not of the vengeance of men; on the other hand, Antiochus loses nothing of the compassion and friendship that we had for him, which increase rather than diminish; finally, this preserves the historical action despite this change, since Cléopâtre perishes by the same poison that she presents to Antiochus.]

Let us take these two advantages in reverse order. Firstly, as Corneille explains, Cléopâtre's downfall spares her son Antiochus from committing the unforgiveable crime of matricide, and thus forfeiting the audience's goodwill towards him as a main character. If, as we saw earlier, Corneille insists that dramatists should not stain the hands of an otherwise virtuous hero with the ignoble act of murder, murder of kin is still more abhorrent and dramatically problematic. Accordingly, Corneille thus refuses to 'punir un parricide par un autre parricide' [punish one parricide with another parricide].[10] Nevertheless, what Corneille calls the overall 'historical action' is more or less preserved here, because his Cléopâtre, like her model, ends up dying of the poison with which she had attempted to kill her son. The other consequence of Corneille's changes is that Cléopâtre's suicide 'becomes' (in the author's words) an effect of divine judgement rather than of human vengeance. Technically speaking, of course, there is nothing implicit to the sequence of onstage events that directly indicates a divine hand guiding them; there is no flagrant transgression of the normal rules of *vraisemblance* [verisimilitude], for example, that could only be the handiwork of the gods. Yet Corneille proposes that some supernatural intervention is nonetheless discernible to the spectator; indeed, he insists that Cléopâtre's death becomes all the more exemplary precisely because it is not, apparently, administered by human justice.

Interestingly, this interpretation of Cléopâtre's death is not just Corneille's retrospective gloss on events, as sometimes happens in his theoretical writings when he feels compelled to justify decisions he made in his earlier plays. Rather, it was clearly in his mind while he was writing the play itself. Indeed, within the onstage fiction, the ambassador Oronte brings together the same two points as Corneille the theoretician in 1660 when he announces that heavenly justice has preserved both Antiochus's life and his innocence:

> Dans les justes rigueurs d'un sort si déplorable,
> Seigneur, le juste Ciel vous est bien favorable.
> Il vous a préservé, sur le point de périr
> Du danger le plus grand que vous puissiez courir,
> Et par un digne effet de ses faveurs puissantes
> La coupable est punie, et vos mains innocentes.
>
> (*Rodogune*, v. 4. 1831–36)

[Amidst the rigours of such a deplorable fate, my lord, righteous Heaven is very favourable to you. It has preserved you, just as you were about to perish from the greatest danger you could face; by a worthy effect of its powerful favours, the culprit is punished, and your hands innocent.]

Corneille's twofold insistence (both in his theory and in the play itself) on Cléopâtre's death as divine punishment is nonetheless curious. For a start, if audiences do instinctively take Cléopâtre's death as a punishment at the hands of divine justice, as Corneille later implies, then it would presumably be unnecessary for any of the onstage characters to offer Oronte's moralizing gloss on events. Oronte's words are thus in a sense excessive or superfluous, at least for the spectator whom Corneille imagines in 1660. Indeed, his unprompted insistence that Antiochus's hands are innocent is particularly striking. After all, while it is certainly true that Cléopâtre's suicide has taken place without Antiochus's input, Antiochus has never articulated any desire to kill her. Throughout the play, Antiochus has shown himself insistently respectful towards his unworthy mother; even when suspecting her and his bride Rodogune of wanting to kill him, he has defiantly resisted the prospect of killing either of them to preserve his own life. Oronte's curious insistence on Antiochus's continued innocence thus seems to gesture beyond the confines of the fictional onstage world, tacitly acknowledging the extra-textual historical reality that Corneille's very play is counterfactually rewriting. In other words, although it is explicitly addressed to the new king, Oronte's unprompted comment thus seems to be aimed, through the fourth wall, at another audience — Corneille's spectator.

Corneille the theoretician and his intradiegetic mouthpiece Oronte thus treat Cléopâtre's death less as a suicide than as a *deus ex machina* in which supernatural forces restore the moral order. But it is surely a counterintuitive move to understand Cléopâtre's suicide (a deliberate, volitional act conducted in full knowledge of the situation) as somehow the handiwork of a third party (the gods). Perhaps recognizing this, Corneille does what he can as playwright to thematically associate Cléopâtre's death-wish with the question of divine justice some time before the final scene. As I shall suggest, however, he does so not (or not only) to make spectators read her eventual death in terms of divine justice, but rather (or also) to problematize such a reading. In a defiant monologue at the start of Act v, Cléopâtre openly welcomes the most violent of deaths, so long as she never lives to see the Syrian throne pass to another:

> Trône, à t'abandonner je ne puis consentir.
> Par un coup de tonnerre il vaut mieux en sortir,
> Il vaut mieux mériter le sort le plus étrange:
> Tombe sur moi le ciel, pourvu que je me venge,
> J'en recevrai le coup d'un visage remis,
> Il est doux de périr après ses ennemis. (*Rodogune*, v. 1. 1529–34)

[Throne, I cannot consent to abandon you. I would rather depart through a thunderbolt. It is better to deserve the most perverse fate: let the sky fall on me, provided I get my revenge. I will receive its blow with a composed face; it is sweet to perish after one's enemies.]

Cléopâtre's speech here performs various functions. While it foreshadows and hence helps to psychologically motivate her self-destructive actions in the final scene, her talk of a thunderbolt striking her or heaven falling upon her — two over-the-top, implausible, and hence apparently supernatural fates — also subtly prepares the audience to think of her later downfall in terms of divine judgement. Yet by gesturing towards the question of divine judgement so clearly, Cléopâtre simultaneously problematizes her upcoming fate. After all, although she imagines meeting 'the most perverse fate', she explicitly consents to it — even welcomes and pre-emptively relishes it — in exchange for her vengeance. Indeed, although she claims to be ready to deserve this supernatural fate, she clearly does not regard it as the punishment that Oronte the onstage character and Corneille the dramatic theoretician would later have us believe.

Corneille has therefore 'upped' the dramatic stakes in anticipation of the play's climactic conclusion. Being unafraid of death, Cléopâtre apparently has nothing to lose; indeed, once she realizes that suicide is her only course of action, she seizes on it as a means to a further end. A little plot summary is needed in order to bring out the dramatic complexity of *Rodogune*'s final scene. Frustrated by her twin sons' refusal to do her bidding, and anxious to stop the Syrian throne falling into other hands, Cléopâtre decides to kill them both. Having fatally stabbed one son, Séleucus, during the interval, she plans to kill the other, the incumbent king Antiochus, and his bride during an early part of the wedding ceremony, which takes place onstage. The play's final act is imbued with a sense of performance and ritual; indeed, M. J. Muratore compares it to the 'play within a play' of the final act of Corneille's explicitly metatheatrical *L'Illusion comique*.[11] Yet while the wizard Alcandre in the earlier play finally unveils Clindor's apparently tragic death as having been a fiction all along, Cléopâtre aims to do quite the inverse in *Rodogune*: to expose the apparently joyful wedding festivities as something doomed from the start to a tragic end. Having secretly poisoned the wine in the nuptial chalice from which bride and groom will drink, Cléopâtre shows her keen sense of the dramatic. While poison is a very secretive, deceptive means of killing, Cléopâtre decides to use it in an explicitly public situation, in full view of representatives of the Syrians and Parthians (and us, the extradiegetic audience), and as part of the prescribed rites of the wedding ritual itself.

The plan thus amply demonstrates Cléopâtre's cunning in exploiting the ritual nature of the wedding ceremony to her own ends. As it is, however, a succession of timely events and interruptions (not least the report of Séleucus's death) means that the chalice never actually reaches Antiochus's lips. Ironically, indeed, Antiochus fails to drink the wine even when he already suspects that it has been poisoned and wishes to commit suicide rather than have to accuse his mother or bride of killing his brother. Rather than endure more of her son's vacillations, Cléopâtre impatiently grabs the chalice and drinks from it herself, desperately hoping to turn her suicidal act into a triple murder by tricking her rivals into following suit. Her plan, however, fails. Antiochus is again just about to drink when Rodogune notes the physical symptoms that are now affecting Cléopâtre: she sweats, her eyes go wild, and her throat swells. Antiochus recognizes this in time, and his life is spared, even though it is too late to save his mother's.

We can now revisit Corneille's glib claims about heaven's handiwork and try to resolve his paradox that would have us read suicide as divine punishment. Whatever Corneille's theory implies, Cléopâtre's real punishment is perhaps not her death — which, after all, she freely chooses — but rather the fact that her suicide fails in its true purpose, to bring her rivals down with her. This, at least, is what Cléopâtre announces in her final dying speech. As she tells Antiochus, 'le seul déplaisir qu'en mourant je reçoi' [the only displeasure I feel in dying] is that she was not able to 'te perdre avec moi' [bring you down with me] (v. 4. 1813–14).[12] If heaven's hand is discernible at all here, it is not in Cléopâtre's actions themselves but rather in the timing of events; her plans come undone because the symptoms of her poisoning become apparent too soon. Indeed, although she had previously announced that she would face death with a 'composed face', it is — ironically — precisely her facial discomposure that gives away her physical collapse.

By orchestrating events this way, Corneille thus artfully manages to reconcile Cléopâtre's self-willed death with a sense of a divine hand guiding events, thus bearing out to some extent his (and Oronte's) subsequent claims about divine justice. Even so, though, Corneille is not content to wrap things up so neatly. Indeed, Cléopâtre's final speech defiantly troubles such neat conclusions. Although Cléopâtre acknowledges her 'déplaisir' [displeasure] and even her 'disgrâce' [disgrace] (v. 4. 1815), she does not regard herself as being straightforwardly punished; indeed, she insists that she can experience the 'douceur' (v. 4. 1815) of not seeing her rival Rodogune reigning in her place. She uses her dying words, indeed, to remind Antiochus of the succession of crimes that she has committed and on which his royal power now rests, presenting her suicide as the last in a series of deaths that she has conducted in order to help Antiochus take the throne:

> Règne, de crime en crime enfin te voilà Roi :
> Je t'ai défait d'un père, et d'un frère, et de moi. (v. 4. 1817–18)

[Reign, finally you are now king after crimes and crimes; I have rid you of a father, a brother, and of myself.]

Having established Antiochus as the beneficiary of her various crimes, Cléopâtre is now free to escape punishment for them. Indeed, far from regarding her death as a punishment — whether self-administered or divine — for her crimes, she presents herself as escaping a punishment that she hopes will befall her successors:

> Puisse le ciel tous deux vous prendre pour victimes,
> Et laisser choir sur vous les peines de mes crimes,
> Puissiez-vous ne trouver dedans votre union
> Qu'horreur, que jalousie, et que confusion,
> Et, pour vous souhaiter tous les malheurs ensemble,
> Puisse naître de vous un fils qui me ressemble. (v. 4. 1819–24)

[May heaven take you both for its victims, and let the punishment for my crimes fall on you. May you find in your union only horror, jealousy, and confusion — and, to wish you all misfortunes together, may you bear a son who resembles me.]

Whether Cléopâtre intends these second and third curses as extra ones or merely explanatory amplifications of her original curse, it is clear that she has already anticipated and rejected the glib narrative that will see her death as a straightforward punishment. Far from accepting her death as just, she regards it as a way of cheating divine justice, and thus thwarting the heavens of their rightful victim so that it is compelled to cause more havoc by punishing the survivors. The same idea will be played out to still more deadly effect in Corneille's next play.

Théodore: Vengeance Thwarted

For all the rhetorical power of her defiant final speech, Cléopâtre ultimately fails to make her suicide as destructive as she had hoped. Her successor in Corneille's next tragedy, however, is rather more successful in turning her suicide into an aggressive act. Driven to despair by the death of her daughter Flavie, the Roman provincial governor's wife Marcelle embarks on a murderous, vengeful rampage, hoping to cause as much suffering as she can to her enemies, even at the cost of her own life. Unlike Cléopâtre's unsuccessful murder attempts, Marcelle's killing spree takes place offstage; we learn about it through the narration of her servant Stéphanie, who comes onstage to recount events in Act v Scene 8. But even though we do not witness these deaths, Corneille nonetheless manages to make them very dramatic — both for his audience and for their primary witness within the fictional world.

The backstory to Marcelle's vengeance is complex, and I shall only list the salient points here. At the start, Marcelle's bedbound daughter Flavie is literally dying of love for Placide, the son of Marcelle's husband Valens by his first marriage. Placide, however, is desperately in love with the Christian princess Théodore, and his rejection of Flavie has kindled in Marcelle a deadly loathing for the princess. Once Flavie finally dies, Marcelle is driven into a desperate, bloodthirsty rage, and fantasizes about sacrificing all the Christians, and indeed all of Syria, to her dead daughter. Dismissing the advisor Paulin's concerns that she is acting without her husband the governor's approval, Marcelle has the two Christian captives Théodore and Didyme dragged offstage with her by her guards. Her husband Valens now rushes onstage, concerned both about his wife's behaviour and about how his unstable, hot-headed son Placide might respond. Both men recognize Placide's violent nature; indeed, Paulin warns his master that bloodshed of some form will invariably ensue if Théodore's life is under threat: 'pour la secourir | Il périra lui-même, ou fera tout périr' [to save her he will perish himself, or make everything perish] (v. 7. 1777–78). Indeed, Paulin is still more concerned about what might ensue 'Si Marcelle à ses yeux fait périr Théodore' [if Marcelle has Théodore killed before his eyes] (v. 7. 1767).

Paulin's use of the phrase 'à ses yeux' [before his eyes] is surely significant. Whether Paulin suspects this or not, Marcelle has seized the opportunity to stage her murder of the Christian princess as a visual assault on her hated son-in-law. Escorting her Christian captives out of the palace, Marcelle is waylaid at the gates by Placide and an armed group of friends and servants. At this, her own fury exacerbated by her son-in-law's presence, Marcelle draws a dagger and stabs her captives:

> 'Viens, dit-elle, viens voir l'effet de ton secours',
> Et sans perdre le temps en de plus longs discours,
> Ayant fait avancer l'une et l'autre victime,
> D'un côté Théodore, et de l'autre Didyme,
> Elle lève le bras, et de la même main
> Leur enfonce à tous deux un poignard dans le sein. (v. 8. 1801–06)

['Come', she said, 'come and see the effect of your help', and, without wasting time in longer speeches, she moved both victims forward — Théodore on one side and Didyme on the other — raised her arm, and with the same hand thrust a dagger into both their breasts.]

In various ways, Marcelle thus transforms the Christians' deaths into a spectacle for the horrified Placide. The few words she utters neatly cast him not only as the scene's horrified spectator (in her alliterative invitation 'Viens, [...] viens voir'), but also as the effective instigator of a spectacle she claims is the 'effect of your help'. Having realized some time earlier that the devout Christians actively embrace death as a route to martyrdom, Marcelle presses on with the double murder with an eye more to horrifying their passive spectator Placide than to punishing her apparent victims.

Placide's response to witnessing his beloved's murder is perhaps uncharacteristic of him. Rather than being driven to the furious rage that Paulin had expected, Placide plunges into powerless despair, becoming immobile and experiencing symptoms of extreme physical weakness: 'Il pâlit, il frémit, il tremble, il tombe, il pâme, | Sur son cher Cléobule il semble rendre l'âme' [he turns pale, he shudders, he trembles, he falls, he swoons, he seems to die on his dear Cléobule] (v. 8. 1815–16). As the rhyme of 'pâme' and 'rendre l'âme' implies, Placide's physical collapse replicates the very death that he is witnessing. Not unlike the wizard Alcandre, who assaults the father Pridamant with the apparent spectacle of his son's death at the end of *L'Illusion comique*, Marcelle thus manages to transform Théodore's murder into an act of violence conducted against the spectator. For a moment, indeed, it seems that Théodore's death will provoke an identical mimetic response in her distraught suitor.

Yet this is not the only theatrical dimension to Marcelle's vengeance. Indeed, while Marcelle stages the murder as a distressing spectacle for Placide, his own suffering becomes part of a second spectacle that she savours as part of her own private enjoyment:

> Marcelle les contemple à ses pieds expirants,
> Jouit de sa vengeance et, d'un regard avide,
> En cherche les douceurs jusqu'au cœur de Placide;
> Et tantôt se repaît de leurs derniers soupirs,
> Tantôt goûte à pleins yeux ses mortels déplaisirs,
> Y mesure sa joie, et trouve plus charmante
> La douleur de l'Amant que la mort de l'Amante... (*Théodore*, v. 8. 1818–24)

[Marcelle contemplates them as they expire at her feet, enjoys her revenge and, with an eager gaze, looks for its pleasures even in Placide's heart; sometimes she feasts on their last sighs, and sometimes she drinks in his mortal displeasures with her eyes; she measures her joy, and finds the suitor's pain more charming than his beloved's death]

With words such as 'jouit', 'avide', 'se repaître', and 'goûter', Stéphanie presents Marcelle's cruel pleasures here as almost greedily sensual, while her astute comparison of the different characters' sufferings also suggests a degree of perversely aesthetic refinement. Even so, Marcelle is apparently still not satisfied. Although she enjoys watching his 'mortels déplaisirs' [mortal displeasures], she starts to feel frustration that the shell-shocked Placide is still too numb to fully experience the horror of her actions. Accordingly, Marcelle patiently waits until Placide has reawakened from his semi-conscious swoon before drawing her dagger and stabbing herself to death before him, defiantly announcing that 'Je n'ai pas résolu de mourir à ton choix' [I am resolved not to die by your choice] (v. 8. 1830).

Marcelle thus claims her death as a deliberate act of defiance and independence; she robs him of the power to kill her. Once she has dealt the fatal blow, however, Marcelle curiously shifts tack, now ironically presenting her suicide as a favour to Placide and telling him 'Va, traître, à qui j'épargne un crime, | Si tu veux te venger, cherche une autre victime' [go, traitor whom I am sparing a crime — if you want to avenge yourself, seek another victim] (v. 8. 1835–36). With spiteful irony, Marcelle implies that, in taking her own life, she is selflessly sparing Placide the very need to sully his hands with bloodshed. Perversely, she thus adopts much the same logic as Oronte does in *Rodogune*, when he tells Antiochus that the gods have kept his hands clean as a sign of their favour. However, whereas Oronte had presented Cléopâtre's suicide as neatly resolving Antiochus's situation, Marcelle implies that her suicide has now made Placide's predicament definitively unresolvable. Much as she has just done with Théodore's murder, Marcelle thus turns her own suicide into a further implicit attack on Placide, who is now thwarted of any prospect of exacting vengeance on her. To add blasphemous insult to injury, in her final lines, she even claims that heavenly justice has helped her to triumph: 'Je meurs, mais j'ai de quoi rendre grâces aux dieux, | Puisque je meurs vengée, et vengée à tes yeux' [I die, but I can thanks the gods, for I die avenged, and avenged before your eyes] (v. 8. 1837–38).

Even more so than in *Rodogune*, then, the villain's death in *Théodore* does not bring about any conclusive return to order. Indeed, it is surely significant that Marcelle's final words — 'à tes yeux' — again stress the spectacular dimension of her revenge. Even in death, though, Marcelle also continues to retain some visual mastery of the scene. Defiant to the last, she deliberately positions herself in such a way that, while dying, she can savour the carnage she has produced:

> Lors même dans la mort conservant son audace,
> Elle tombe, et, tombant, elle choisit sa place,
> D'où son œil semble encore à longs traits se soûler
> Du sang des malheureux qu'elle vient d'immoler. (v. 8. 1839–42)

[Then, retaining her audacity even in death, she falls, and, falling, she chooses a place for herself from which her eye still seems to drink in, in long gulps, the blood of the unfortunate victims of her sacrifice.]

The last image we have of Marcelle is thus one of perversity, indeterminacy, and excess. She remains a cruel, sadistic, spectating presence. It is unclear whether she is now alive or dead; her hauntingly open eye still seems to be greedily drinking in the fresh blood she has spilled. Her indeterminate status (as living and dead, victim and victor) seems to symbolically express the play's lack of dramatic resolution.

Marcelle's suicide thus forever thwarts Placide's duty to avenge Théodore's death. By killing herself, Marcelle escapes the retributive justice that Placide is both duty-bound and temperamentally inclined to take. Cléopâtre, we recall, had hoped that her suicide would compel heaven to take new victims in her place; Marcelle does much the same thing here, but she calls upon an all-too-human agent of justice, rather than a divine one, to do so. By robbing Placide of his rightful victim, she thus compels him to seek a new victim. But who will this substitute victim be? Stéphanie flees the scene at this point, presumably for fear that Placide will take vengeance on her instead; another potential victim could indeed be Placide's father Valens himself, for his passive complicity in Théodore's death. Both these options, however, turn out to be wrong. When Placide staggers onto the stage, covered in blood, we learn that he has stabbed himself with the very same dagger with which Marcelle has already killed the two Christians and then herself. As the dying Placide explains to his horrified father, he chose to kill himself to forestall the risk of committing the unforgivable sin of parricide: 'je me suis puni de peur de te punir' [I have punished myself for fear of punishing you] (v. 9. 1870). Placide, it seems, can prevent himself from such a terrible deed only by turning his aggression against himself beforehand.

Yet Placide does not mean to spare his father all punishment; indeed, he makes it very clear to Valens that he means his suicide as a direct attack on him:

> Je te punis pourtant, c'est ton sang que je verse,
> Si tu m'aimes encor, c'est ton sein que je perce,
> Et c'est pour te punir que je viens en ces lieux
> Pour le moins en mourant te blesser par les yeux. (v. 9. 1871–74)

[And yet I am punishing you: it is your blood I am shedding; if you still love me, it's your breast I'm piercing, and it is to punish you that I have come here, at least to hurt you, while I die, through your eyes.]

Drawing attention to the emotional and familial bonds (the heart and blood) that link father and son, Placide thus offers his suicide as a symbolic patricide. If kin killing kin is too taboo even for the hot-headed Placide, the still more intimate violence of self killing self might provide a more acceptable replacement.

Placide has, it seems, learned from his stepmother's example that suicide can be harnessed as an act of aggression conducted against its onlooker. Yet this is not the only thing that he seems to have learned from her. He starts his final speech with an ironic allusion to divine justice — 'Rends-en grâces au Ciel, heureux père et mari' [thank heaven, happy father and husband] (v. 9. 1861) — which both bitterly praises heaven for sparing him the crime of parricide while reminding Valens of his double bereavement. Placide not only copies his enemy's suicidal action but also replicates its underlying aggression, directing it this time at his father. Both

Marcelle's and Placide's deaths end with an emphasis on the visual, but in different ways. The dying Marcelle establishes herself as spectator — deliberately positioned so as to savour the spectacle of the bloodshed she has committed with impunity. The dying Placide, in contrast, offers himself as object of Valens's horrified sight, hoping to make him suffer through the visual. Placide's suicide thus confronts his father with the sorry spectacle of a son who has dutifully killed himself rather than disrespect the paternal bond of which he himself has proved so unworthy. The play ends with Placide's dying body being carried offstage while his distraught father tries to calm him.

Conclusion

As we have seen, in *Rodogune* and *Théodore* Corneille develops new solutions to our opening problem: of how to dispose of a villainous antagonist without either sullying the hero's hand with murder or coercing the villain into an uncharacteristic and unconvincing state of repentance. In both plays, Corneille manages to develop new modes of suicide that nonetheless remain largely in character for his villainous figures and so does not break their own psychological *vraisemblance*. Implicitly addressing La Mesnardière's concerns that self-murder, however dramatically impressive it is, remains a sin in the eyes of God, Corneille turns his antagonists' suicides into a further, final crime that consummates rather than expiates their villainous careers.

And this final crime is, in an important sense, theatrical, or indeed even metatheatrical. Echoing Corneille's first great villain Médée, both Cléopâtre and Marcelle show a dramatist's keen eye for orchestrating violence as a cruel spectacle to horrify and traumatize its observers. Yet whereas Médée torments Jason with spectacles of death and violence inflicted on other people (Créuse, Créon, and finally their children), these later villains turn their violence upon themselves as well. They do so, however, in different ways and with different results. Cléopâtre uses subterfuge, hoping her rivals will continue to perform the prescribed rituals of the wedding ceremony and not notice that she has been poisoned until they too have drunk from the nuptial cup. Far from hoping to harm others with the spectacle of her death, she seeks to offer them the deceptive spectacle of her continued health so that they will inadvertently poison themselves. As we have seen, what provides Cléopâtre's 'punishment' is not her death itself but rather its failure, due to a quirk of timing, to achieve her ultimate murderous goal. The curiously unexpected timing of the poison's efficacy leaves open the possibility that her fate is in part the gods' handiwork — an idea leapt upon by Oronte and later echoed by Corneille as theoretician. For the later Corneille, Cléopâtre's death not only spares Antiochus the need to commit a crime, but it also offers a salutary purgative lesson for any spectators who might be tainted with a milder version of the queen's deadly vices.

In contrast, and perhaps ironically for a putatively Christian play, *Théodore* gives little scope for the spectator to see any divine power at work guiding its events. Eschewing any of Cléopâtre's underhand trickery, Marcelle's murder of the Christians and her subsequent suicide are direct, open, and explicit; her suicide achieves precisely what it sets out to do, leaving little room to discern divine intervention. It is this directness that makes Marcelle's death — and, more unexpectedly, that of Placide in turn — a more truly 'aggressive' suicide in Barbagli's sense than Cléopâtre's. Whereas Cléopâtre tries to pretend that she is not dying, Marcelle and Placide dramatically exploit the fact that they clearly are dying; they confront others openly with their bloody, dying bodies, flagging up the short-circuit of justice that their suicide has produced and challenging their survivors to find some new way of restoring moral order. In doing so, however, Marcelle and Placide (and indeed Corneille through them) also challenge and provoke us as spectators and readers in ways that Cléopâtre's death does not.

This is not to say that Cléopâtre's death lacks any moral or aesthetic ambiguity. For example, Corneille's accounts of it in his dramatic theory veer towards the contradictory; he discusses the purgative potential of her death for spectators mere sentences after rehearsing the Aristotelian line that a villain's downfall cannot produce the fear normally deemed necessary for catharsis. Although these inconsistencies seem to reside within Corneille's dramatic theory rather than within Cléopâtre herself, even within the play Corneille is keen to stress her death as somehow incomplete. Most obviously, her final curse on the bridal couple hangs over the denouement, both reminding them of the various crimes that have led them to the throne and threatening them with the prospect of producing a son who resembles his grandmother. Her threats seem to trouble Antiochus in particular; indeed, implicitly dismissing Oronte's naively positivist claims about divine favour and neat resolution, Antiochus continues to be morally unsettled by his mother's fate, and ends up deferring resolution to some later point, hoping that the gods will prove more favourable in future.

Whether threatened by Cléopâtre or acknowledged by Antiochus, however, the ambivalence and irresolution evoked in *Rodogune* are essentially verbal in nature, and do not affect the underlying plot. In *Théodore*, conversely, the ambivalence of the villain's death is evoked above all not through words but through actions. Unlike Cléopâtre's botched attempt to bring her enemies down with her, Marcelle's successfully aggressive suicide cannot be so easily integrated into a narrative framework of crime and punishment. Most strikingly, rather than resolving matters, her death provokes her impetuous spectator Placide to visit a further, copycat, suicide onto his father Valens. Whereas the dying Cléopâtre had merely cursed her survivors, verbally wishing further misfortune onto them, Marcelle thus effectively manages to prolong her actual bloody rampage even after her death, via the suicidal Placide. The conclusion of *Théodore* thus seems to undermine the implicit confidence with which the previous play had sought to restore order. Indeed, Placide's own last words seem to rehearse and parodically undermine Oronte's own glib account of Cléopâtre's death at the end of *Rodogune*. Both men attribute the preceding events to the workings of heaven ('le juste Ciel' [just heaven]),[13] flattering their listeners (Antiochus and Valens) by suggesting that they have been preserved from having to resort to crime by some pagan form of divine grace. Yet, unlike Oronte, Placide expresses these ideas with a deep sense of bitter irony. Presenting his impending death as heaven's handiwork rather than his own, he bitterly tells his father to thank the gods for preserving his own power, dignity, and life untarnished.

Théodore thus ends on a level of ambiguity that is atypical even by Corneille's idiosyncratic standards. In different ways, Marcelle and Placide both stage their suicides as visual, spectacular assaults on their spectators; in so doing, however, they raise a host of metatheatrical questions that undermine any attempt to recuperate their actions into any reassuringly moralizing theoretical framework — even those that Corneille himself will attempt to develop fifteen years later with reference to *Rodogune*. It is perhaps symbolic that our last impressions of both Marcelle and Placide are characterized above all by a deep sense of incompleteness. While we see bloody Placide is carried offstage by Valens and Cléobule, who disagree about whether he is actually dead yet, what perhaps lingers in the mind still more unsettlingly is the unseen, offstage image of Marcelle's corpse — her eye still open, still savouring, even in death, the carnage she has inflicted. Revealingly, perhaps, after Marcelle, Corneille never returns to the suicidal villain; indeed, whereas Cléopâtre and her death recur at key points in his lengthy theoretical writings to illustrate axioms of his dramatic theory, Marcelle goes unmentioned throughout, except in his prefatory 'Examen' to *Théodore*. Paradoxically, by negotiating the aesthetic paradoxes of a villainous suicide so successfully, Marcelle ultimately defies recuperation even into Corneille's own dramatic theory; he chooses to leave her unmentioned rather than attempt to discuss her. If Marcelle's aggressive suicide troubles and distresses her onstage onlooker Placide, leaving his own duties unresolved and unresolvable, it might be no less troubling, on an aesthetic level, for her very creator.

Notes to Chapter 2

1. Pierre Corneille, *Discours du poème dramatique*, in *Œuvres complètes*, ed. by Georges Couton, 3 vols (Paris: Gallimard [Pléiade], 1980–98), III, 115–90 (p. 129). All references to Corneille are taken from this edition. All translations are my own.
2. For discussions of Attila's death, see John D. Lyons, *The Tragedy of Origins: Pierre Corneille and Historical Perspective* (Palo Alto, CA: Stanford University Press, 1996), pp. 154–79, and my own 'Dying of the Fifth Act: Corneille's (Un)natural Deaths', in *French Studies*, 69.2 (July 2015), 289–304.
3. Corneille, III, 160.
4. Dubos, *Réflexions critiques sur la poésie et sur la peinture* (Paris: Mariette, 1739), p. 99.
5. Hippolyte-Jules de La Mesnardière, *La Poétique*, ed. by Jean-Marc Civardi (Paris: Champion, 2015), p. 319.
6. La Mesnardière, p. 315.
7. Fontenelle, *Œuvres complètes*, 7 vols (Paris: Fayard, 1991–2001), III, 143.
8. Marzio Barbagli, *Farewell to the World: a History of Suicide*, trans. by Lucinda Byatt (Cambridge and Malden, MA: Polity Press, 2015), p. 6.
9. Corneille, III, 160.
10. Corneille, III, 160.
11. M. J. Muratore, *Cornelian Theater: The Metadramatic Dimension* (Birmingham, AL: Summa, 1990), p. 63.

12. Curiously, her use of the singular pronoun 'te' here implies that her goal was to destroy her son in particular rather than both him and his bride.

13. *Rodogune*, v. 4. 1832; *Théodore*, v. 9. 1875.

❖

CHAPTER 3

"Tis Gallia's hopeless Queen!': Resurrecting the Dead in John Philip Kemble's *Macbeth* (1794)

Sarah Burdett

St Mary's University, Twickenham

On 21 April 1794, John Philip Kemble's production of Shakespeare's *Macbeth* was staged at the new Drury Lane theatre. The production appeared just six months after the execution of Marie Antoinette, an event which greatly intensified British antipathy to the French Revolution. Building on scholarship that has emphasized the capacity for Shakespearean plays to acquire new meanings when reinterpreted in the context of the 1790s, this essay makes a case for identifying Marie Antoinette's death, and the spectacle surrounding it, as crucial in facilitating an ideologically charged and deeply psychological reading of Kemble's production, in which the living represent the dead, the fictive represents the real, and death is equated not with tragic closure, but antithetically, with the need for such closure in political and cultural terms.[1]

My reading draws on Marvin Carlson's theory of 'ghosting': the haunting replication in the theatre of something previously encountered within an altered context.[2] While Carlson shows performances to be haunted by memories of previous theatrical experiences, such as the performer's embodiment of a prior character in a prior drama, this chapter will show Kemble's *Macbeth* to be ghosted by a figure, or rather, popular representations of such a figure, who played a starring role in a theatrical event which occurred outside the theatre. Marie Antoinette's execution, a key and spectacular scene in the 'monstrous tragic-comic' drama of the French Revolution, haunts Kemble's production.[3] The memory of this event, coaxed into reanimation by the tragedy's oblique allusions to Marie Antoinette as she lived, and finally, to her ghost, prohibits the play's achievement of Aristotelian catharsis, and encourages instead emotional tension, and an active response to such tension, impelled by the longing fostered in theatregoers for the closure that the tragedy, like the Queen's execution itself, fails in Britain to grant.[4]

Marie Antoinette's Spectacular Death

Marie Antoinette was a key player in the theatrical spectacle of the French Revolution.[5] Her execution was performed centre stage in Paris at the Place de Revolution, in a manner shown to combine the theatrical customs of farce and domestic drama.[6] The event was exhibited before a vast public crowd, who responded to the spectacle precisely as they might have done to a good play: a journalist writing for the *Evening Mail* tells how 'the hired mob, which was assembled in the courts and the streets, cried out bravo, in the midst of plaudits'.[7] As Sanja Perovic has outlined, Marie Antoinette's death was required 'to achieve what the trial and execution of the King failed to grant: the definitive end of the Revolution'. That the Queen was still living following the execution of Louis XVI and the creation of the revolutionary calendar 'frustrated the revolutionaries' claims that the new world was in place, and the Revolution over'. Despite the proclamation of new time, the revolution would only reach its ultimate end once 'the genealogical continuity that reaffirmed the King's symbolic presence' was erased 'once and for all'.[8] Given the complications of her ongoing existence, it is significant that the mob's response to Marie Antoinette's execution mimics the ovation conventionally heard at the end of a play: contrasting with the death of Louis in July, which was marked with profound silence, the execution of Marie Antoinette, replicating the French theatrical practice of following a piece of serious theatre — the death of the King — with a closing farce, provided the afterpiece necessary to allow the curtain finally to come down, albeit nine months later than planned, on the drama of the French Revolution.[9]

However, if Marie Antoinette's execution was framed by the French Republic as a definitive break with the past, the alignment of her death with any form of ending was disrupted in Britain by the refusal of monarchical sympathizers to allow the Queen to die: or at least, to die properly. From October 1793, the British public was brought into continual contact with multimedia manifestations of Marie Antoinette's ghost, both metaphorical and literal. Confronted on the one hand with representations of the Queen as she was while she lived — representations which themselves become ghostly following the Queen's demise — the public were exposed concurrently to representations of the Queen as a spectral form having risen from the dead. While the Queen's ghost materializes literally and explicitly in a number of poetical works, this chapter is concerned chiefly with the role played by theatrical spectacle in enabling the potential detection by British audiences of allegorical representations of the late Queen's ghost on stage. And it is here that we turn to Kemble's *Macbeth*.

Political Allegory and Shakespearean Ghosts

Theatre historians have long stressed the capacity and readiness of Georgian audiences to interpret plays as contemporary political commentaries. When theatre censorship escalated in the early 1790s, and playwrights were forced to engage with political affairs using veiled methods, theatregoers keenly sought out surreptitious standpoints, and readily manipulated plays' nuanced meanings to suit their own political agendas.[10] In this context, allegorical readings of dramatis personae as modern-day figures became a popular practice. This was something that the dramatist Frederick Reynolds discovered to his dismay in 1795, when his comedy *The Rage* was perceived by 'the mis-judging million' to present '*living portraits*' of various members of Parliament, making him 'a democrat, without knowing it'.[11]

Performances of Shakespeare were especially prone to this treatment. As David Taylor has shown, the ubiquity of Shakespearean figures within political allegories of the Georgian period meant that plays themselves became rife with allegorical interpretation.[12] Particularly prevalent in the 1790s were allusions to the ghost of Banquo from *Macbeth*, used to signify guilt among those complicit in revolutionary horrors: not just French radicals, but British revolutionary sympathizers too, who came to feel accountable for the deterioration into violence of a movement they had extolled.[13] Alongside the ghost of Banquo, that of Hamlet Senior was equally pervasive. As Dale Townshend identifies, *Macbeth* and *Hamlet*, the most frequently performed of Shakespeare's tragedies during the final quarter of the eighteenth century, provided 'precedents for two distinctive modes of ghost-seeing' which dominated cultural understandings of apparitions in the period's literature: while ghosts modelled on Banquo appeared before the guilty and signified wrongdoing, those fashioned in the image of Hamlet Senior appeared before the virtuous to inspire vengeance against unpunished crimes.[14]

The ghost's dual characterization in 1790s political and literary culture is epitomized in two poetical accounts of Marie Antoinette's ghost published in Britain ahead of Kemble's production. In an anonymously written ballad of 1793, it is the ghost of Banquo to which the Queen's apparition alludes. While the 'murd'rous guilty train' of the revolutionary Convention sit plotting 'bloody deeds', they are confronted by a 'ghastly sight' whose 'locks with blood [are] stain'd'.[15] The ghost expresses her 'pity' for the 'lost' and 'desolate crew' who 'tremble' in her presence, before warning them to 'leave [their] crimes', and issuing the statement:

> Let Antoinetta's hapless fate
> Teach you humanity, tho' late...
> When blunted conscience wake her strings,
> ...Remorse must sure each wretch appal
> If now quite deaf to Mercy's call.[16]

Like Banquo in the banquet scene, Marie Antoinette's apparition returns to earth to 'shake [her] goary locks' at those responsible for her death, with the objective of awakening their 'blunted conscience' by fostering in them horror and guilt.[17]

The following year, in Edward Holland's 'Elegy on the death of the late Queen of France' (1794), it is the ghost of Hamlet Senior upon which Marie Antoinette's apparition is modelled. Reminding readers of the fate of the 'hapless parents' who were 'torn to a scaffold' by their 'murd'rous foes', Holland summons up the royal ghosts to aid his call to vengeance against revolutionary France. He commands:

> European powers now all your force unite
> Apease their ghosts, avenge with all your might;
> Oh may your vet'rans regicides destroy,
> Laying guilty Paris low as ancient Troy.[18]

Reminiscent of Hamlet's father, the appearance of the French King and Queen signifies unrequited vice: the royal spirits are not presently at peace, as the 'foul crimes, done in [their] days of nature' are yet to be chastised.[19] The poem therefore instructs its readers that in order to placate the Queen's 'perturbed spirit' and finally 'end her woes', efforts must be made to punish those responsible for her murder, and to cease the 'mighty triumph' of Jacobinism.[20] I consider this twofold meaning projected onto ghosts in contemporary British culture to play a vital role in intensifying the political poignancy of Kemble's 1794 *Macbeth*. This is perhaps a surprising claim to make, given that Banquo's ghost is omitted from the production, a point to which I will return later. However, I want to argue that the play is not without its own equivocal spectre, whose identification with either one of these Shakespearean archetypes, brought into fruition by theatrical spectacle, allows for the tragedy's re-appropriation as a strikingly powerful anti-Jacobin polemic.

In her study *Ghostly Matters*, Avery Gordon defines the act of haunting as 'an animated state in which a repressed or unresolved social violence is making itself known, sometimes very directly, sometimes more obliquely'. It 'is when the over and done with comes alive', and 'registers the harm inflicted or the loss sustained by a social violence done in the past or in the present'.[21] This conflation of ghosts with unresolved social violence has been identified by theatre scholars as a prevalent theatrical trope. Mary Luckhurst and Emilie Morin, for instance, observe the increasing deployment of the stage ghost as 'a powerful political device', used to force a recognition of the violence produced by acts such as war and terrorism.[22] This theory of the ghost's politicization underpins my reading of Kemble's *Macbeth*. Applied to this performance, the 'unresolved social violence' that the ghost, or quasi-ghost represents, is that of the Terror. Marie Antoinette's execution, that which is 'over and done' with, is brought back into view by a covert allusion to the late Queen of France, which materializes, I suggest, from the surprising yet striking parallels formed between Sarah Siddons's Lady Macbeth and popular representations of Marie Antoinette, both living and dead, circulating in 1790s Britain. Siddons's fluid performance of Lady Macbeth replicates the late Queen's shifting representation in British accounts from controlling monster, to sentimental victim, to plaintive apparition: the haunting experience of coming face to face with the latter forcing audiences to register 'the harm inflicted or the loss sustained' by Jacobin violence. Interpreted in the context of the dual meaning assigned to ghosts in contemporary culture, the quasi-spectre is embellished with the capacity to communicate two contrary, yet equally loyalist meanings: capable on the one hand of inspiring in spectators vengeful sentiments against revolutionary France, it has the simultaneous ability to impel theatregoers of a less clear conscience to identify themselves among the guilty, and to share the heroine's desperation to out the 'damn'd spot' of royal blood.[23]

Embodying Marie Antoinette: From Monster to Victim

My reading of Kemble's *Macbeth* rests upon the audience's recognition of Siddons's double embodiment in the play of both fictional character and historical figure: Shakespearean heroine and late Queen of France. This dual transformation, I argue, is enabled chiefly by the marked parallels between the unique manner in which Shakespeare's well-known heroine was personated and presented in 1794, and the wealth of multimedia representations of Marie Antoinette and her ghost infiltrating British culture. As has been well documented, Siddons departed from the rendition of Lady Macbeth offered by her forerunner in the capital, Hannah Pritchard, by creating two contrasting personae for her heroine. While Pritchard had played Lady Macbeth throughout as a 'kind of angry Hecate', remarks on Siddons's interpretation of Lady Macbeth show Siddons's heroine to shift from 'a masculine sublime subject' to 'a feminine beautiful object'.[24] Starting out as a regicidal 'fiend-like woman' who belongs 'to a darker world, full of evil', Siddons's character later transforms into a 'fair, feminine, nay perhaps even fragile' Queen, whose 'feminine nature' and 'delicate structure' are 'overwhelmed by the enormous pressure of her crimes', and provoke in her 'the sickness and despair of guilty ambition'.[25] While it has been argued that Lady Macbeth's former persona, upheld while she delivers the 'unsex me' speech, identifies her explicitly in 1794 with 'the revolutionary spirit threatening to run amok in Britain', given the prevalent identification of 'unsexed' women with political reformers, it is equally possible to detect in both halves of Siddons's performance allusions to popular delineations of Marie Antoinette, and to view the performance in its entirety as an analogy of the Queen's ameliorative transformation in British representations.[26]

Scholars including Lynn Hunt and Adriana Craciun have identified the threat that Marie Antoinette's gender posed to patriarchal structures. Owing to the 'fundamental anxiety' during the *Ancien Régime* 'about Queenship as the most extreme form of woman's invading the public sphere', misogynistic representations of Marie Antoinette, appearing in Britain and France, depicted her as the 'most notable femme fatale of the period', and as a figure who 'was unsexed'.[27] Aligned with infamous murderesses from the past, including Frédégonde, Messalina and Agrippina, whose merciless schemes and interventions in public life characterized them as unnaturally masculine and monstrous figures who 'have become odious' in eighteenth-century thought, Marie Antoinette was likened simultaneously to literal embodiments of monstrosity:[28] in 1790 Joseph Priestley told how the French had 'discovered [her] snaky hair' and found 'her to be a mere Medusa', and British journalists frequently compared Marie Antoinette to a vampire, describing her as 'the scourge and bloodsucker of the French'.[29] While this reputation aligns Marie Antoinette very much with the 'unsexed' and 'fiend-like' woman exhibited by Siddons in the early half of *Macbeth*, the Queen's notoriety for deceit and dominance can also be detected in Siddons's character early in the play. Echoing criticisms of Marie Antoinette as a woman who 'smiled but to deceive', and whose 'compliments were so artfully adapted to flatter the person she wishes to please or dupe', Kemble's script, consistent with John Bell's earlier adaptation, has Lady Macbeth insist that her husband's 'false face must hide what the false heart doth know', and that he must 'bear welcome in [his] eye, | [his] hand, [his] tongue', and 'look like the innocent flower | but be the serpent under it'.[30] Indicative of Siddons's accentuation of Lady Macbeth's artfulness, one witness, the law professor George Bell, recalls Siddons's heroine masking her character's savage designs by bowing 'graciously and sweetly to the nobles' ahead of Duncan's murder, and Siddons's biographer James Boaden similarly comments on the 'exterior of profound obligation' presented by Siddons's heroine in the presence of the King, which concealed entirely her murderous intent.[31]

As well as sharing the trait of dissimulation, Marie Antoinette and Lady Macbeth are both portrayed early on as the driving forces behind their husband's actions. In summer 1788, the *Morning Herald* expressed the prevalent opinion that too many of Louis's political manoeuvres had been 'forced by the Queen's instigation' and were 'contrary to his will'.[32] Marie Antoinette's perceived dictatorship over her husband's public conduct resonates with Siddons's commanding portrayal of Lady Macbeth. Numerous reviewers note the dominion that Siddons's character exercised over Macbeth preceding Duncan's murder. Boaden describes how 'she assails [Macbeth] with sophistry and contempt and female resolution' and the playwright and actor James Sheridan Knowles correspondingly remarks that 'she reproves her vacillating husband and absolutely shames him into resolution'.[33] The two women are therefore further unified by the ascendancy they hold over their husband's decisions: like the version of Marie Antoinette depicted in the *Morning Herald*, Siddons's Lady Macbeth forces her husband into governmental interventions that oppose his better judgement.

While Lady Macbeth and Marie Antoinette are initially connected by their flaws, the characters of both women are subsequently redeemed. As Katherine Binhammer has traced, though criticized in the 1780s and early '90s for her dissimulative and domineering tendencies, post-1793 the Queen appeared in sympathy-inducing portraits as a loyal and devoted wife and frail victim of despair.[34] Following the death of Louis XVI and the Queen's own imprisonment and execution, British loyalists sought to emphasize the barbarity of French radicalism by enhancing the virtue and innocence of its victims. Thus it was that formerly derisive accounts of Marie Antoinette had to be softened.[35] During this epoch, emphasis shifted onto Marie Antoinette's familial sentiments. Images depicting the King's execution, including Isaac Cruikshank's *The Last Interview between Louis XVI, King of France, and his Family* (1793) and Mather Brown's *The Final Interview of Louis the Sixteenth and his Family* (1795), show Marie Antoinette surrounded by her family, visibly distraught at the prospect of her husband's departure.[36] Literary depictions enforce this familial and domesticated characterization. In Mary Robinson's 'Monody on the Late Queen of France' (1793), the Queen's 'domestic virtues' are seen 'glitt'ring round the throne', and in John Bartholomew's tragedy *The Fall of the French Monarchy* (1794), Marie Antoinette indicates her 'domestic turn' by declaring it her ambition to 'soothe and solace her lov'd King', before suffering from a 'broken heart' which 'melts [her] soul' when she is informed of her husband's imprisonment.[37]

These same spousal sentiments are exhibited by Siddons in the latter half of *Macbeth*. While Pritchard's Lady Macbeth had consistently displayed 'indignation, and contempt' for her husband, Siddons perceived the dynamic between the two characters to alter after Duncan's death.[38] She wrote in her 'Remarks on the Character of Lady Macbeth' that while the heroine of the early scenes 'appears to have known no tenderness' for her husband, she later 'devotes herself entirely to the effort of supporting him'.[39] In the banquet scene, writes Siddons, 'we behold for the first time striking indications of sensibility, nay tenderness and sympathy'. Lady Macbeth knows 'the torment which [Macbeth] undergoes and endeavours to alleviate his sufferings' by listening 'to his complaints with sympathising feelings'.[40] Corroborating the actress's execution of these dramatic intentions, Prof. George Bell notes of this scene that in place of Lady Macbeth's former ambition, it is now 'intense love of her husband' which 'animate[s] every word'. Her 'contemptuous reproach' gives way to 'sorrow and sympathy with [Macbeth's] melancholy', and when her husband is startled by the hallucination of Banquo's ghost, she 'comes up to him and catches his hand'.[41]

Depictions of Marie Antoinette as a devoted and domestic wife were accompanied from 1793 by accounts of the Queen's imprisonment, which showed the extremity of her grief to have resulted in physical and mental affliction. Songs delivered at the theatres of Covent Garden and Haymarket in 1793, and a poem printed in *The Gentleman's Magazine* that same year ('Stanzas supposed to be written whilst the late Queen of France was sleeping'), all present Marie Antoinette as a 'victim of anguish and despair', who conveys a 'haggard face', 'wan [and] wasted cheek', and 'fever'd brain'.[42] In each portrayal, Marie Antoinette's mental anguish is shown to manifest itself in 'ghastly shapes' and 'haggard phantoms' which 'haunt the midnight calm' and prevent the Queen from sleeping.[43] At Covent Garden, the figure of Marie Antoinette, embodied by actress and vocalist Anna Maria Crouch, experiences 'frantic wild affright' while 'fancy paints [her] murder'd Lord' and she sees 'th'assassin's blood stain'd sword'.[44] Correspondingly, in 'Stanzas', the Queen is startled by the ghostly vision of her 'headless husband, spouting gore'.[45] Though seemingly acknowledging, through these Banquo-esque spectres, the perception that the King 'might have saved his life by regulating his future politics' had his wife not acquired such 'unbounded sway' over his decisions, the verses seek not to create animosity for the Queen, but to elicit compassion, by emphasizing her repentance, sensibility, and piety.[46] Crouch's Queen 'heaves 'the penitential sigh' as tears fall from her 'streaming eye', and her 'suppliant hands' are 'to Heav'n [...] spread'.[47] Similarly, in 'Stanzas', Marie Antoinette's heart 'throbs with cureless woe', she conveys 'bitter streams of agony', and she too prays to 'thy sainted Lord' that she might soon hear the 'heav'nly harmonies' that will lead her to 'happier slumbers'.[48] By offering these sentimental depictions of the Queen's suffering and contrition, the verses exonerate Marie Antoinette from her past failings, and leave audiences and readers lamenting her deterioration into sickness and madness.

These moving portraits of a devout, mad, and ailing Queen, tortured by phantoms during the night, correspond strikingly with Siddons's performance of the sleepwalking Lady Macbeth, a figure whose conscience is analogously plagued

FIG. 3.1. George Henry Harlow, Mrs Siddons as Lady Macbeth, sleepwalking scene, Act v, from *Macbeth* by Shakespeare (1814). Courtesy of the Garrick Club, London.

during the night by the sight of 'so much blood'.[49] Indicative of Siddons's replication of the piety bestowed on Marie Antoinette in contemporary works, a painting by George Henry Harlow shows Siddons's sleepwalking Lady Macbeth standing with her hands clasped together and her eyes raised upwards as if in prayer (Fig. 3.1). Moreover, Prof. Bell describes Siddons's character as appearing 'feeble now', as though 'preparing for her last sickness and final doom', and notes her enactment of a 'convulsive shudder' accompanied by 'a tone of imbecility' which was 'audible in [her] sigh'.[50] Extending these parallels further, Siddons recalls her intention to exhibit a 'wan and haggard countenance' in this scene, while her character's 'ever restless spirit wanders in troubled dreams'.[51] By the final act of Kemble's production then, Siddons's character presents a perceptible likeness to sympathetic depictions of Marie Antoinette: while the two women were aligned previously by their exertions of power and vice, they are united now by their correspondent displays of spousal sentiments, religious appeal and mental and physical infirmity.

Lady Macbeth and the Ghost of Marie Antoinette

Not quite as simple however as a straightforward transition from sublime to beautiful, monster to victim, Siddons's evolving personation of Shakespeare's heroine maintains to the end some of the fear-inducing qualities that it presented early on. As Heather McPherson has illustrated, Siddons's final scene on stage as Lady Macbeth 'absolutely horrified' her audience on account of the 'preternatural aspect' that accompanied her appearance.[52] Emphasizing the terror aroused by Siddons during the sleepwalking scene, Sheridan Knowles reports:

> Though pit, gallery and boxes were crowded to suffocation, the chill of the grave seemed about you when you looked on her; — there was the hush and damp of the charnel house at midnight; [...] your flesh crept and your breathing became uneasy.[53]

Sheridan Knowles extends this use of deathly tropes when, alluding to Act v Scene 3 of *Richard III*, he exclaims that 'the tithe of horror that attends the silent woman, Lady Macbeth, walking in her sleep' is as great as that excited by 'the ghostly group that enter the tent and surround the couch of Richard'.[54]

Such imagery of death and supernaturalism dominated contemporary reports of Siddons while sleepwalking: Edwin Mangin described her as having a 'corpse-like aspect'; Leigh Hunt said she was 'deathlike'; Boaden claimed that she embodied 'the majesty of the tomb'; and William Hazlitt recalled how 'she glided on and off the stage almost like an apparition'.[55] These reviews attest to the stark resemblance between Siddons's sleepwalking heroine and the contemporary stage ghost: a figure that, though rare in 1794, appears in literal and perceived form in two plays debuting in London in the months either side of *Macbeth*.[56] Writing of the ghost depicted in his gothic drama *Fontainville Forest* (1794), indebted to Ann Radcliffe and premiering at Covent Garden in March, Boaden notes that 'the great contrivance' was to 'convert the moving substance into a gliding essence', a preference recalled in the published play script, which describes how '*the phantom here glides across the*

FIG. 3.2. Henry Pierce Bone, *The Sleepwalking Scene in Macbeth* (1797)
© Yale Center for British Art, Paul Mellon Fund

dark part of the chamber.[57] Two months later, in *The Sicilian Romance* (1794) by Sarah's son Henry Siddons, also adapted from Radcliffe and staged at Covent Garden, Martin is fooled into believing Alinda to be a ghost when she *'comes down with a taper'* and presents Martin with the sight of 'a figure all snow! [...] pale as death!' and illuminated by 'a light!'[58] These depictions of ghosts and quasi-ghosts strongly recall Siddons's sleepwalking Lady Macbeth: appearing, as Boaden describes, wrapped in a 'quantity of white drapery', she glides around the stage carrying *'a taper'*.[59]

The 'white drapery' worn by Siddons is important not only in enhancing her character's ghostliness, but in furthering the allusion to Marie Antoinette. The new clothing designed for the sleepwalking scene in 1794, which Boaden here describes, seems to have been captured in the aforementioned painting by Harlow, and a further by Henry Pierce Bone (Fig. 3.2), both of which show the sleepwalking Siddons enveloped from head to foot in a flowing and loose-fitting white gown and veil. Popular images depicting Marie Antoinette's captivity and trial, including those by Robert Sayer (Fig. 3.3) and Domenico Pellegrini (Fig. 3.4), show Marie Antoinette dressed in comparable clothing.[60] Allegorically, the veil's significance is twofold: not only was Marie Antoinette often depicted wearing a veil in portrayals of her trial, the veil serves also to hide Siddons's long dark hair and to give the illusion of a pure white mane. The whitening of Marie Antoinette's hair, accelerated by distress, was frequently commented on in sympathetic accounts: Crouch's Marie Antoinette laments that 'grief has changed [her] flowing hair', and Robinson likens the Queen's hair to 'the Alpine snow'.[61] At this point in the play then, Siddons's heroine looks not only like a ghost, but fundamentally, she presents physical features likening her to Marie Antoinette in her widely documented final moments of life. In performances of *Hamlet* staged right across the eighteenth century, it is precisely the physical likeness between the ghost and the image of Hamlet's father before he died that confirms the ghost's identity: Horatio knows the ghost to be Hamlet's father, because he appears dressed in 'the very armour he had on' while he lived, and presents the same 'fair and warlike form'.[62] Judging by this well-known logic, and by the parallels formed between Lady Macbeth and Marie Antoinette up to this point in the play, it is not unreasonable for audiences to detect in the play's quasi-spectre subtle allusions to Marie Antoinette's spirit.[63]

The likelihood of this conflation is amplified by the analogies detectable between the sleepwalking Lady Macbeth and representations of Marie Antoinette's ghost circulating offstage. In 1793, a poetic account of the Queen's ghost, signed with the name 'Eliza', appeared in *The Gentleman's Magazine*. The poem describes Marie Antoinette's apparition in the following terms:

> And soft! What ghastly shade attracts my sight!
> Skims o'er the glade with looks of wild affright!
> [...]
> Oh! My full heart; 'tis Gallia's hopeless Queen!
> Distraction, grief and horror in her mien!
> [...]
> See the poor mourner wildly stare around,
> talk to the walls and madly strike the ground!
> [...]

The DEATH of MARIE ANTONIETTE QUEEN of FRANCE and NAVARRE.

FIG. 3.3. Robert Sayer, *Death of Marie Antoinette Queen of France and Navarre* (1794). French Revolution Digital Archive <http://purl.stanford.edu/qm057nd2026> [accessed 12 March 2015]

FIG. 3.4. Mariano Bovi, engraving after Domenico Pellegrini, *The Trial of Marie Antoinette Queen of France October 14, 1793/Proces de Marie Antoinette Reine de France Octobre 14, 1793* (1796). French Revolution Digital Archive <http://purl.stanford.edu/wy288rs0618> [accessed 11 March 2015]

> the quivering lip, short breath and stretched out arm,
> starting convulsive at each dread alarm.
> View in terrific forms before her eyes
> A headless group of shrieking forms arise!
> [...]
> Oh I am sick! — sick! — sick! — and worn with grief.[64]

The poem could almost have been written to describe Siddons's character sleepwalking: like 'Gallia's hopeless Queen', Lady Macbeth's 'heart is [so] sorely charged' that she too produces 'convulsive shudders' and 'horrible' sighs.[65] She too 'talk[s] to the walls' when instructing her absent husband to 'wash [his] hands', and 'look not so pale'.[66] She is similarly haunted by the 'terrific forms' of 'bleeding victims', which are 'for ever present' in her mind, and she too resembles a 'ghastly shade' as she 'skims o'er' the stage.[67] While Siddons's Lady Macbeth is ghosted from the outset of the tragedy then by popular representations of the living Marie Antoinette, her behaviour and appearance at this point in the play allow for the production's quasi-ghost to itself become ghosted by the literal spectre of the late

Queen of France.[68] Haunted by Marie Antoinette's apparition, Siddons's character acquires the potential to communicate to theatregoers two fiercely monarchical meanings: both of which supplant tragic catharsis with emotional unrest, and implore active participation from theatregoers in the crusade against Jacobinism.

Complicating Dramatic Closure

Recognition of Siddons's Lady Macbeth as an allegorical representation of the deceased Queen of France endows theatregoers with an active role in Kemble's drama: they are cast as ghost-seers, and, by extension, as either Macbeth or Hamlet. To theatregoers of former or current revolutionary sympathies, it is the role of Macbeth that is offered most persuasively. Kemble's greatest innovation in his 1794 production was the physical removal of Banquo's ghost from the banquet scene. In his diary, the artist Joseph Farington recalls Kemble's declaration that he was 'decidedly not for introducing the figure of Banquo in the feast scene', as the vision ought to be recognized 'as the image of [Macbeth's] disturbed imagination'.[69] Reviews of the tragedy confirm the achievement of this desired effect. One journalist described the apparition's physical absence as confirmation that 'the troubled spirit [is] visible only to the mind's eye of the guilty and distracted tyrant', while the theatre commentator W. C. Oulton insisted that 'it is the ghost of the mind, and the appearance of it to the audience' would have 'absolutely destroy[ed] the visionary effects of a guilty conscience'.[70] As the reviews demonstrate, by refusing to have an actor depict the ghost on stage, Kemble encouraged audiences to recognize the spectre as a mental apparition which is visible only to 'the guilty and distracted'. Theatregoers appreciate that they do not see Banquo's ghost as they hold no responsibility for Banquo's death. Only the guilty see ghosts, and as the audience were innocent spectators of Banquo's murder, they lack Macbeth's troubled conscience, and do not share his haunting vision.

By interpreting ghosts as signifiers of guilt, the production's pseudo-ghost, visible to all spectators, can be read as a figure serving to awaken in revolutionary sympathizers a degree of compunction similar to that experienced by Macbeth. Imitating the ghost of Banquo, the spectral image offers a quasi-projection of the spectator's own tormented conscience. The spectacular allusion to Marie Antoinette's ghost forces theatregoers of reformist affiliations, either past or present, to accept implicit culpability for her death. Acknowledging her murder as the repercussion of a movement they had extolled, audiences are imbued with contrition and self-reproach, and are impelled to distance themselves entirely from revolutionary principles. Perceived this way, the fusion of Lady Macbeth and Marie Antoinette enables Siddons's character to function in the sleepwalking scene both as a manifestation of guilt and as a representation of the guilty: Lady Macbeth haunts the audience through her likeness to the deceased Queen of France, while she herself is haunted by the blood of a murdered monarch. She therefore both prompts and mirrors the emotional experience encountered by the theatregoer: rather than passively observing her display of mental grievance, audiences actively partake in the heroine's desperation to out the 'damned spot' of royal blood, as they are made to recognize, by the heroine's very image, that their 'hands are of [her] colour'.[71]

To theatregoers of a clearer conscience, there is a variant meaning on offer. Exemplifying the contemporary alternative to the mental apparition, of which Banquo is the prototype, Boaden's *Fontainville Forest* establishes its ghost immediately as a prompt to the virtuous for 'a great' and 'mighty vengeance'.[72] Marie Antoinette's pseudo-apparition can similarly be understood, like Hamlet's father, as a catalyst for revenge. Unlike Boaden's ghost however, she inspires vengeance not against an individual, but against a nation. While Kemble's tragedy was being performed, England was at war with revolutionary France. Enthusiasm for the war was not unanimous, and British loyalists were under pressure to ensure the continued enlistment of troops.[73] Siddons's allusion to Marie Antoinette's ghost potentially contributes to this purpose. Like the restless spirits depicted in Holland's 'Elegy', Marie Antoinette appears 'doom'd' to 'walk the night' as her murderers are yet to be reprimanded for their crimes.[74] The play's supernatural spectacle consequently acts as a call to arms against revolutionary France: in order to pacify the ghost of Marie Antoinette, revenge must be sought against Britain's neighbouring nation, and the surest way to enact such revenge is to defeat the country at war.

Read in the context I have proposed, Kemble's *Macbeth* becomes a tragedy that fosters in theatregoers strong anti-Jacobin sentiments using an extremely poignant means of coercion. Freighted with surprising allusions to the late Queen of France, both living and dead, Siddons's character complicates intended and expected forms of closure, both political and theatrical. Contesting the finality attached to Marie Antoinette's death by the French Republic, the spectacular resurrection of the Queen's ghost before the British public demands a revised denouement to the drama of the French Revolution, in which closure is equated not with the death of the monarchy, but with the defeat of Jacobinism and its followers. It does so by denying *Macbeth*'s audiences the anticipated experience of tragic catharsis, and rousing instead emotional tension, and a desire to relieve such tension, which implores theatregoers to contribute to the defeat of Jacobinism in one of two ways: either, they must 'revenge [the Queen's] foul and most unnatural murder' by supporting the war effort, or they must 'wash the blood clean from their hands' and 'cleanse the foul bosom of that perilous stuff | which weighs upon the heart', by retracting their radical sympathies.[75]

Notes to Chapter 3

1. See Frans de Bruyn, 'Shakespeare and the French Revolution', in *Shakespeare in the Eighteenth Century*, ed. by Fiona Ritchie and Peter Sabor (Cambridge: Cambridge University Press, 2012), pp. 297–313; David Taylor, *The Politics of Parody: A Literary History of Caricature, 1760–1830* (New Haven, CT: Yale University Press, 2018), pp. 71–139; Jonathan Bate, *Shakespeare and the English Romantic Imagination* (Oxford: Clarendon Press, 1986); Bate, *Shakespearean Constitutions: Politics, Theatre, Criticism, 1730–1830* (Oxford: Clarendon Press, 1989); Mary Jacobus, ' "That Great Stage. Where Senators Perform": *Macbeth* and the Politics of Romantic Theatre', *Studies in Romanticism*, 22.3 (1983), 353–87; and Fiona Ritchie, *Women and Shakespeare in the Eighteenth Century* (New York: Cambridge University Press, 2014), pp. 110–40.

2. See Marvin Carlson, *The Haunted Stage: The Theatre as Memory Machine* (Ann Arbor: University of Michigan Press, 2003), pp. 1–15.

3. Edmund Burke, *Reflections on the Revolution in France* (London: J. Dodsely, 1790), p. 11.

4. On challenges to Aristotelian catharsis caused by 'overliving' see Emily R. Wilson, *Mocked with Death: Tragic Overliving from Sophocles to Milton* (Baltimore, MD: Johns Hopkins University Press, 2004), pp. 10–15.

5. On theatricality and the French Revolution see Marie-Hélène Huet, *Mourning Glory: The Will of the French Revolution* (Philadelphia: University of Pennsylvania Press, 1997); Paul Friedland, *Political Actors: Representative Bodies and Theatricality in the Age of the French Revolution* (London: Cornell University Press, 2002); and Susan Maslan, *Revolutionary Acts: Theater, Democracy, and the French Revolution* (Baltimore, MD: Johns Hopkins University Press, 2005).

6. See Sanja Perovic, *The Calendar in Revolutionary France: Perceptions of Time in Literature, Culture, Politics* (Cambridge: Cambridge University Press, 2012), pp. 127–41.

7. 'Execution of the Queen of France', *Evening Mail* , 22–24 October 1793, p.5

8. Perovic, *The Calendar*, pp. 132, 130, 133.

9. Perovic, *The Calendar*, pp. 134–41.

10. See esp. Gillian Russell, *The Theatres of War: Performance, Politics and Society, 1793–1815* (Oxford: Clarendon Press, 1995); Susan Valladares, *Staging the Peninsular War: English Theatres, 1807–1815* (London: Routledge, 2015); George Taylor, *The French Revolution on the London Stage, 1789–1805* (Cambridge: Cambridge University Press, 2000), pp. 97–126; and John Barrell, ' "An Entire Change of Performances?" The Politicisation of Theatre and the Theatricalisation of Politics in the mid 1790s', *Lumen*, 17 (1998), 11–50.

11. Frederick Reynolds, *The Life and Times of Frederick Reynolds*, 2 vols (London: Henry Colburn, 1826), II, 181.

12. See Taylor, *Politics of Parody*, pp. 71–139. See also Valladares, *Staging the Peninsular War*, pp. 59–105.

13. See Matthew S. Buckley, *Tragedy Walks the Streets: The French Revolution in the Making of Modern Drama* (Baltimore, MD: Johns Hopkins University Press, 2006), pp. 96–109; and Steven Blakemore, *Crisis in Representation: Thomas Paine, Mary Wollstonecraft, Helen Maria Williams, and the Rewriting of the French Revolution* (London: Associated University Press, 1997), pp. 103–72.

14. See Dale Townshend, 'Gothic Shakespeare', in *A New Companion to the Gothic*, ed. by David Punter (Malden: Wiley-Blackwell, 2012), pp. 43–49. See also Townshend's 'Gothic and the Ghost of Hamlet', in *Gothic Shakespeares*, ed. by John Drakakis and Dale Townshend (Abingdon: Routledge, 2008), pp. 60–97.

15. Anon., *A Ballad on the death of Louis the unfortunate [...] and A description of the appearance of Marie Antoinette's ghost* (Bristol: John Rose, 1793), pp. 20, 22, 28.

16. Anon., *Ballad*, 23–24.

17. John Philip Kemble / William Shakespeare, *Macbeth: written by Shakespeare. As Represented by Their Majesties Servants on Opening the Theatre Royal Drury Lane* (London: C. Lowndes, 1794), III. 4. 40.

18. Edward Holland, *A Poetical Miscellany* (Cork: J. Connor, 1794), p. 39.

19. William Shakespeare, *Hamlet, Prince of Denmark. A Tragedy. Taken from the manager's book, at the Theatre Royal, Drury Lane* (London: Rachael Randall, 1787), I. 5. 15.

20. Holland, *Poetical Miscellany*, p. 39.

21. Avery F. Gordon, *Ghostly Matters: Haunting and the Sociological Imagination* (Minneapolis: University of Minnesota Press, 2008), p. xvi.

22. Mary Luckhurst and Emilie Morin, 'Introduction: Theatre and Spectrality', in *Theatre and Ghosts: Materiality, Performance and Modernity*, ed. by Luckhurst and Morin (New York: Palgrave Macmillan, 2014), p. 1.

23. Kemble, *Macbeth*, v. 1. 56.

24. James Boaden, *Memoirs of Mrs Siddons: Interspersed with anecdotes of Authors and Actors*, 2 vols (London: H. C. Carey & I. Lea, 1827), II, 263; Laura Rosenthal, 'The Sublime, the Beautiful, the Siddons', in *The Clothes that Wear Us*, ed. by Jessica Munns and Penny Richards (Newark: University of Delaware Press, 2003), pp. 56–80 (p. 74). See also Laura Engel, 'The Personating

of Queens: Lady Macbeth, Sarah Siddons and the Creation of Female Celebrity in the late Eighteenth Century', in *Macbeth: New Critical Essays*, ed. by Nick Moschovakis (London: Routledge, 2007), pp. 240–57 (pp. 251–52); Frederick Burwick, 'The Ideal Shatters: Sarah Siddons, Madness, and the Dynamics of Gesture', in *Notorious Muse: The Actress in British Art and Culture, 1776–1812*, ed. by Robyn Asleson (New Haven, CT: Yale University Press, 2003), pp. 129–50; and Marvin Rosenberg, *The Masks of Macbeth* (Berkeley: University of California Press, 1978), pp. 160–65.

25. Boaden, *Memoirs*, II, 259; William Hazlitt, cited in Marvin Rosenberg, 'Macbeth and Lady Macbeth in the Eighteenth and Nineteenth Centuries', in *Focus on Macbeth*, ed. by John Russell Brown (London: Routledge and Kegan Paul, 1982), pp. 73–86 (p. 77); Sarah Siddons, 'Remarks on the Character of Lady Macbeth', in Thomas Campbell, *Life of Mrs. Siddons*, 2 vols (London: Effingham Wilson, 1834), II, 11, 22, 33; H. C. Fleeming Jenkin, 'Mrs Siddons as Lady Macbeth and as Queen Katherine' (1878), in *Papers on Acting*, ed. by Brander Matthews (New York: Hill & Wang, 1958), p. 79.

26. See John Drakakis and Dale Townshend, 'Unsexing Macbeth: 1623–1800', in *Macbeth: A Critical Reader*, ed. Dale Townshend (London: Bloomsbury, 2013), pp. 172–204.

27. Lynn Hunt, 'The Many Bodies of Marie Antoinette: Political Pornography and the Problem of the Feminine in the French Revolution', in *Marie Antoinette: Writings on the Body of the Queen*, ed. by Dena Goodman (New York: Routledge, 2003), pp. 117–36 (p. 123); Adriana Craciun, *Fatal Women of Romanticism* (Cambridge: Cambridge University Press, 2003), pp. 78, 10.

28. 'Trial of Marie Antoinette, Queen of France', in *The Scots Magazine*, 55 (November 1793), p. 21.

29. Joseph Priestley, *Letters to the Right Honourable Edmund Burke* (Dublin: J. Shepherd, 1791), p. 16; 'Trial of the late Queen of France', in *Walker's Hibernia* (November 1793), p. 460; and 'Authentic trial at large of Marie Antoinette', in *The Weekly Entertainer*, 22 (2 December 1793), p. 543.

30. Mary Wollstonecraft, *An Historical and Moral View of the Origin and Progress of the French Revolution* (London: J. Johnson, 1794), pp. 131, 134. See also *Monthly Museum* (March 1814), p. 232; Kemble, *Macbeth*, I. 7. 21; I. 5. 17. On Kemble's script revisions see Charles Beecher Hogan, *Shakespeare in the Theatre, 1701–1800* (Oxford: Clarendon Press, 1957), p. 363.

31. Jenkin, 'Mrs Siddons', p. 84; Boaden, *Memoirs*, II, 136.

32. 'Change in the French Cabinet', *Morning Herald*, 1 September 1788, p. 3.

33. Boaden, *Memoirs*, II, 258; James Sheridan Knowles, *Lectures on Dramatic Literature: Macbeth* (London: Francis Harvey, 1875), p. 20.

34. Katherine Binhammer, 'Marie Antoinette was "One of Us": British accounts of the Martyred Wicked Queen', *Eighteenth Century: Theory and Interpretation*, 44 (2003), 233–54 (p. 234). See also Craciun, *Fatal Women*, p. 81.

35. See Binhammer, 'Marie Antoinette was "One of Us", pp. 233–56.

36. Both images can be viewed via the British Museum. See <https://www.britishmuseum.org/collection/object/P>_1878-0511-1411 and <https://www.britishmuseum.org/collection/object/P>_1987-1003-24 [both accessed 19 April 202].

37. Mary Robinson, *Monody to the Memory of the Late Queen of France* (London: T. Spilsbury, 1793), p. 5; John Bartholomew, *The Fall of the French Monarchy; or, Louis XVI. An historical tragedy. In five acts* (London: E. Harlow and W. Richardson, 1794), I. 3. 9; II. 2. 27; IV. 5. 76. On Robinson's poem see Amy Garnai, '"One Victim from the Last Despair": Mary Robinson's Marie Antoinette', *Women's Writing*, 12.3 (2005), 388–94.

38. Thomas Davies, *Dramatic Miscellanies: consisting of critical observations on several plays by Shakespeare*, 3 vols (Dublin: S. Price et al., 1784), II, 106.

39. Siddons, 'Remarks', pp. 34, 24.

40. Siddons, 'Remarks', pp. 22–23.

41. Jenkin, 'Mrs Siddons', pp. 91, 93.

42. 'Captivity: Supposed to be sung by the Unfortunate Marie Antoinette during her Imprisonment in the Temple', in *The Hampshire Syren: or Songster's Miscellany* (Southampton: T. Skelton, 1794), p. 121; see also the rival performance at Haymarket, 'The Captive: Sung by Master Walsh', in *The Scots Magazine*, 55 (February 1793), 89; 'Stanzas supposed to be written whilst the late Queen of France was sleeping', in *The Gentleman's Magazine*, 74 (October 1793), 941. On the songs see

Harriet Guest, *Unbounded Attachment: Sentiment and Politics in the Age of the French Revolution* (Oxford: Oxford University Press, 2013), p. 56. For similar depictions see John Barrell, *Imagining the King's Death: Figurative Treason, Fantasies of Regicide, 1793–1796* (Oxford: Oxford University Press, 2000), pp. 55–58.

43. Crouch, 'Captivity', p. 122; 'Stanzas', p. 941.

44. Crouch, 'Captivity', p. 122.

45. 'Stanzas', p. 941.

46. Wollstonecraft, *Historical and Moral View*, p. 135.

47. 'Captivity', p. 122.

48. 'Stanzas', p. 941.

49. Kemble, *Macbeth*, v. 1. 56.

50. Jenkin, 'Mrs Siddons', pp. 95, 96.

51. Siddons, 'Remarks', pp. 33, 31.

52. Heather McPherson, 'Masculinity, Femininity, and the Tragic Sublime: Reinventing Lady Macbeth', *Studies in Eighteenth-Century Culture*, 29 (2000), 299–333 (pp. 313, 316).

53. Knowles, *Lectures*, pp. 21–22.

54. Knowles, *Lectures*, p. 21.

55. William Hazlitt, 'Mrs Siddons', in *The Examiner* (16 June 1816), reprinted in *A View of the English Stage, or, A Series of Dramatic Criticisms, by William Hazlitt*, ed. by W. Spencer Jackson (London: George Bell and Sons, 1906), p. 217.

56. On stage ghosts in the 1790s see Michael Gamer, *Romanticism and the Gothic: Genre, Reception and Canon Formation* (Cambridge: Cambridge University Press, 2000), pp. 127–31; and Robert P. Reno, 'James Boaden's *Fontainville Forest* and Matthew G. Lewis's *The Castle Spectre*: Challenges of the Supernatural Ghost on the Late Eighteenth-Century Stage', *Eighteenth-Century Life*, 9 (1984), 95–103.

57. James Boaden, *Memoirs of the Life of John Philip Kemble, Esq.*, 2 vols (London: Longman, Hurst, Rees, Orme, Brown and Green, 1825), II, 117; Boaden, *Fontainville Forest: A Play, in five acts* (London: Hookham and Carpenter, 1794), III. 4. 40.

58. Henry Siddons, *The Sicilian Romance: Or, the Apparition of the Cliffs* (London: J. Barker, 1794), III. 2. 36, 37. On these plays see Nathalie Wolfram, 'Gothic Adaptation and the Stage Ghost', in *Theatre and Ghosts*, ed. by Luckhurst and Morin, pp. 46–61; and Diego Saglia, ' "A Portion of the name": Stage Adaptations of Radcliffe's Fiction, 1794–1806', in *Ann Radcliffe, Romanticism and the Gothic*, ed. by Dale Townshend and Angela Wright (Cambridge: Cambridge University Press, 2014), pp. 219–36.

59. Boaden, *Memoirs*, II, 263; Kemble, *Macbeth*, v. 1. 56.

60. See also William Hamilton's *Marie-Antoinette conduite à son exécution, 16 Octobre 1793* (1794). On these images see Guest, *Unbounded Attachment*, pp. 57–60.

61. Crouch, 'Captivity', p. 121; Robinson, *Monody*, p. 9. On Marie Antoinette's hair see Garnai, '"One Victim", p. 391; and Judith Pascoe, *Romantic Theatricality: Gender, Poetry and Spectatorship* (Ithaca, NY: Cornell University Press, 1997), p. 106.

62. Shakespeare, *Hamlet*, I. 1. 4.

63. On *Hamlet*'s role in popularizing understandings of the ghosts' appearance see 'A Curious and Whimsical Dissertation on Ghosts', *The New Wonderful Magazine*, 3 (1 April 1794), 137–38.

64. 'An Elegy. Written on Reading the Melancholy separation of the Dauphin from the Queen of France', in *The Gentleman's Magazine*, 63 (November 1793), 1037–38. On this poem see Pascoe, *Romantic Theatricality*, pp. 111–13.

65. Kemble, *Macbeth*, v. 1. 57; Jenkin, *Mrs Siddons*, p. 313.

66. Kemble, *Macbeth*, v. 1. 56, 57.

67. Boaden, *Memoirs*, II, 261.

68. Visual similarities to the sleepwalking Siddons are also observable in *Ballad*. See pp. 19–21.

69. *The Diary of Joseph Farington*, ed. by Kathryn Cave, 16 vols (New Haven, CT: Yale University Press, 1983), XI: *January 1811–June 1812*, p. 4029.

70. 'Theatre', *The Times*, 22 April 1794, p. 2; W. C. Oulton, *A History of the Theatres of London*, 2 vols (London: Martin & Bain, 1818), I, 93.

71. Kemble, *Macbeth*, II. 1. 26.

72. Boaden, *Fontainville Forest*, IV. 2. 43. For further examples see Townshend, 'Gothic and the Ghost of Hamlet', pp. 60–97.

73. See Emma Vincent Macleod, *A War of Ideas: British Attitudes to the Wars against Revolutionary France, 1792–1802* (Aldershot: Ashgate, 1998), pp. 187–95; and Philip Shaw, *Romantic Wars: Studies in Culture and Conflict, 1793–1822* (Aldershot: Ashgate, 2000), pp. 4–6.

74. Shakespeare, *Hamlet*, I. 5. 15.

75. Shakespeare, *Hamlet*, I. 5. 15; Kemble, *Macbeth*, II. 1. 25, V. 2. 59.

CHAPTER 4

❖

Crypts, Corpses, and Living Tombs on Stage during the French Revolution: Crises of Burial and Mourning

Cecilia Feilla

Marymount Manhattan College, NY

The only production of Sophocles' tragedy, *Antigone*, to take the stage during the French Revolution — an adaptation by Marmontel at the Paris Opera in 1790 — proved an unmitigated failure, closing after only two performances. Greek tragedies were a staple of lyric theatre and the manager at the Opera, hoping to repeat the success of an earlier *Antigone* (1787) by Doigny at a rival theatre, had commissioned the young Italian composer Zingarelli to write a score for Marmontel's script.[1] A review in the *Mercure de France* attributed the play's poor reception to its subject matter: 'en raison de la moindre importance pour les modernes de l'inhumation [...] le sacrifice d'Antigone ne parlerait pas aux gens du temps' [because burial is of the least importance among moderns [...] the sacrifice of Antigone cannot speak to people today].[2] Another review, in *L'Esprit des journaux français et étrangers*, similarly took issue with the subject of burial, claiming that 'le sentiment de la *piété fraternelle* pour un cadavre privé de la sépulture [...] pouvoit être très-vif chez les anciens: mais il est nul pour nous' [the sentiment of *fraternal piety* for a cadaver deprived of burial [...] might be very strong among the ancients: but it is nothing to us].[3] Rather than faulting this particular performance or production (the music and acting of which both reviewers praise), they focus instead on burial as a dramatic subject which could never succeed with contemporary audiences.[4] '[T]outes les fois qu'on a mis ce sujet au théâtre, chaque spectateur a pu se dire: *Peu m'importe que Polynice soit enterré ou non*' [Every time this subject was put on in the theatre, each spectator could say to himself: *What does it matter to me if Polynices is buried or not*].[5] Both reviewers also cited the unfortunate changes Marmontel had made to the last act of Sophocles' play, namely, Antigone does not die. Instead, Marmontel had added a final scene in which Creon liberates her and his son Hémon from the tomb before they can commit suicide, and then grants honourable burial to Antigone's brother.[6] Such bowdlerized endings to well-known tragedies were commonplace during the Revolution — indeed expected by convention in the 'lyric' genres in the eighteenth century — yet audiences at Marmontel's *Antigone* found the changed ending risible.[7]

Antigone would, of course, become the emblematic tragedy for a number of thinkers and writers across Europe in the wake of the French Revolution, most notably Hegel, for whom Antigone's choice of death embodies the tragic dilemma of the modern self.[8] George Steiner dates the prominence of *Antigone* in Western culture from roughly 1790 to 1905, attributing the 'exaltation of Sophocles' heroine' directly to the Revolution and its ideals.[9] How then should we understand the exceptional failure of *Antigone* in 1790 in France, and its absence from the dramatic repertory throughout the Revolutionary decade? Was the subject of burial bound to flop with contemporary sensibilities, as the reviewers suggest? What role did shifting conventions and expectations around genre play in its poor reception?[10] This essay seeks to answer these questions by focusing on burial storylines on stage during the French Revolution. Although the reviewers were correct to state that burial rites were 'of the least importance' in eighteenth-century France by comparison with Ancient Greece, an examination of the Revolutionary repertory shows that, as a subject in theatre, crises of burial actually proved quite popular with audiences: not only is burial a recurrent theme, plotline, and spectacle in numerous plays of the era, but several of the most successful (and most often anthologized) works of the Revolutionary period dramatize a crisis of burial akin to the one found in *Antigone*. From commemorative plays about revolutionary heroes and martyrs to spectacular melodramas in which victims are buried alive, death and the dead are employed in Revolutionary theatre to address the era's most pressing questions and anxieties regarding political, social, ethical, and religious life. Indeed, death finds new life on the Revolutionary stage, mainly in comedies — comic farces and comedies of manners but also in the popular *drames* of the era ('comédies où l'on pleure' [comedies where one weeps], according to theatre historian Charles Félix Lenient) — which were popular in spite of, or because of, their focus on the signs, spaces, and rites of death.[11]

Moreover, the supposed indifference of the public toward burial did not mean that burying the dead was not a constant issue in France during the Revolution. The overcrowding of common graves in particular caused recurrent health crises in Paris; already on the eve of the Revolution, the state undertook the vast exhumation and transfer of the graves at the Cimitière des Saints-Innocents to the catacombs for reasons of public safety. The guillotine brought further crisis several years later when, according to Michelet, the city's graveyards could not accommodate the daily corpses brought for burial.[12] As Margaret Field Denton notes, during the Revolution:

> disregard for the dignity of burial and the appalling conditions of cemeteries provoked intense protests. For while perfect order and devotion governed the enactment of communal funerary festivals for Revolutionary heroes like Jean-Paul Marat, there was only anarchy and indifference when it came to the individual. Protests appeared in pamphlets, poems, and periodicals throughout the 1790s.[13]

Protests also appeared in plays of the period, one of which will be discussed below. By the end of the decade, burial was considered enough of a problem, and of sufficient importance, that the government sponsored a national essay contest on the topics, 'Quelles sont les cérémonies à faire pour les funérailles?' [What ceremonies should be performed at funerals?] and 'Quel est le règlement à adopter pour les lieux de sépulture?' [What rules should be adopted for places of burial?].[14]

Taking the reviews of *Antigone* in 1790 as my starting point, this essay will explore death on stage through examination of two burial plays from the Revolution, one an obscure anticlerical comedy, *L'Office du Mort, ou le mariage du bas clergé de France* [*The Funeral Service, or the Marriage of the Lower Clergy of France*] (1790), and the other one of the most successful dramas of the period, *Les Victimes cloîtrées* [*The Cloistered Victims*] (1791), by Boutet de Monvel. Although profoundly different in style and genre, both works can be seen as responses to the 'anarchy and indifference' that attended burial in 1790s France. I will argue that both plays offered contemporary audiences a symbolic space both temporal and spatial in which anxieties about the disorder and indignity of death are allayed through the harmonious resolution of conflict between the political-civic and religious-ritual spheres. *Antigone* will serve as a touchstone for comparison, particularly through Jacques Lacan's notion of *l'entre-deux-morts*, or *the between-two-deaths*, which he develops in his extended discussion of *Antigone* in *The Ethics of Psychoanalysis* (1959–60). For Lacan, *l'entre-deux-morts* is not the space between life and death or between the living and the dead, but between two deaths: physical death and symbolic death.[15] Symbolic death concerns the rites by which the community acknowledges and recognizes the person as dead and represents the individual's transition from living to dead. As Jane Gilbert explains, symbolic death 'is seen as the ceasing to be one kind of person and becoming another, as altering but not destroying the social roles and relations of the person'.[16] Significantly, this symbolic death can precede corporeal death — as it does for Antigone who enters *l'entre-deux-morts* through the symbolic death she chooses when she joins her fate with her brother's in the tomb.[17] Although I will not be pursuing a Lacanian reading *per se* of the plays under discussion here, *l'entre-deux-morts* will nonetheless provide a useful theoretical frame and counterpoint for clarifying the specificity of the Revolutionary context and how burial plays in the Revolutionary theatre represent an inversion of classical tragedy and catharsis, wherein death becomes communal celebration.

Burial Plots: Performing the Rites/Rights of the Dead

> Dans notre riche et fastueuse capitale, nous n'employons, pour les funérailles, que quatre ais de sapin. On en fait, avec quelques clous, un coffre oblong où l'on renferme le corps de son parent, empaqueté dans un mauvais drap; on le transporte ensuite, sans convoi, à l'extrémité d'un faubourg […] où l'on a creusé une fosse vaste et profonde. C'est dans ce barathrum qu'on le précipite pour jamais, au milieu d'une foule de morts de tout sexe et de tout âge.

> [In our rich and haughty capital, we employ for burial only four boards of fir. With them, and a few nails, one makes an oblong coffin to enclose the body of their relative, packed in a mess; then transports it without a convoy to the edge

of the neighbourhood . . . where one hollows a vast and deep pit. It is in this cesspit that one throws it forever, among a crowd of dead of all sexes and ages.][18]

Such were the burial customs in 1790s Paris according to the novelist Bernardin de Saint-Pierre, although even the humble wood coffin he describes was a luxury most could not afford. 'Rien de plus rare à Paris que le luxe d'un coffre' [Nothing rarer in Paris than the luxury of a coffin], says the Sexton (Sacristain) in the play, *L'Office du Mort*, a three-act comedy by an unknown author who signs his name 'the Hermit of Mont-Perdu'.[19] The play's story is based on actual events that became a *cause célèbre* in the provinces in 1789 when a humble carpenter named Claude Perrot (citizen Guilhot in the play) was denied burial because the family could not afford the fee for a funeral service.[20] In the play the deceased's relatives have spent their last pennies on a coffin and have nothing left to give the Pastor for the ceremony. 'Pourquoi lui a t-on donné un coffre à lui?' [Why was he given a coffin?], asks the Sexton; 'pour la petite c'est un met d'archevêque' [for common folk it is the get-up of an archbishop] (p. 19). The Sexton is the religious officer charged with maintaining the church grounds, including its graveyard. For him, Guilhot's death is not a spiritual matter so much as an administrative one. He is annoyed that Guilhot did not die at the hospital, and that his widow and children chose the extravagance of a coffin; had they not, Guilhot would have been buried at no cost: 'Mort, veuve, enfans, font bien peu économes: ils ont tort, réellement tort' [The deceased, the widow, the children, made no economies: they were wrong, really wrong] (p. 19). To be sure, attitudes toward death had undergone a radical secularization over the course of the eighteenth century. According to Jacqueline Thibault-Payen, death went from being 'seen in a Christian perspective' to 'seen in an administrative perspective' by the century's end.[21] This process was accelerated during the Revolution as the Church and its property came under the control of the state and as new legislation that required the Civil Oath of the Clergy and the closing of parish churches disrupted the customary rituals of burial.[22] In one striking incident in 1790, distraught parents in Strasbourg were barred from burying their two children in the church cemetery because a nonjuring priest had performed their baptisms.[23] In *L'Office du Mort*, the protest at the heart of the play is against the indifference and avarice of Church officials, represented by the Pastor and the Sexton, who refuse to perform the ritual for the dead. Caught between two value systems and two jurisdictions — sacred and secular — Guilhot's unburied body exposes the shifting customs, laws, and practices surrounding death during the Revolution. In their desire to honour the deceased, the family and the community demand dignity of burial for the humble Guilhot. The coffin catalyses the burial crisis. To the clergy it is a sign of luxury beyond the means of the lowly poor; to the family and compatriots of Guilhot, it shows respect for an honest citizen and patriot. The coffin remains on stage throughout the action, a visible marker of death and the crisis it provokes at the individual, institutional, and collective levels. Despite the serious subject matter, the mood of the play is comic and ribald, involving puns, buffoonery, and farce. It expands the facts of the original Perrot case to portray a colourful cast of types representing the people and their perspectives on burial, the

Revolution, and the Church. As such, *L'Office du Mort* takes its place alongside the many anticlerical plays or *pièces monacales* of the period, especially its pointed criticism of the clergy. The comedy's episodic action and humour stem from the anarchy of forms and meanings (social, religious, national) that reign in the interstice between Guilhot's death and his burial. The other characters reflect on the need for an end to this disorder: calls 'À l'ordre!' [Order!] supply a constant refrain from the soldiers and townswomen, while the Commander's wife (La Commandante) observes that order is necessary because the aristocracy 'n'a vécu, ne s'est conservé, n'a prospéré que dans le désordre' [only lived, conserved itself, and prospered in disorder] (p. 6). The arbitrary power and unequal justice under the Old Regime must cede to the new order if the people are to live and prosper. As the old order is dismantled, the comedy asks what the rites and rights of the dead should be in a republic.

The play seeks to balance the people's religious beliefs with the Revolution's new civic ideals of liberty, equality, and fraternity. The action opens with several townswomen gathering to discuss what they can do to help the family of the deceased. The latter sit silently around the coffin at the back of the stage as friends and compatriots come to pay their respects. At one point, a Young Pilgrim with whom Guilhot had made a pilgrimage to Saint-Jacques-de-Compostelle arrives to attend the funeral. 'N'a pas qui veut pareil honneur' [No one deserves such honour more [than him]], he says (p. 8). However, when he learns that there will be no funeral service, he remarks that:

> [L]es routes célestes sont applanies pour un pélérin. Cependent il faut qu'on le mette en terre dans toutes les formes: nos coquilles, nos bourdons en font une loi sacrée, & cette respectable dépouille est le seul salaire du célebrant.

> [The celestial roads are levelled for a pilgrim. Nonetheless one must inter him according to form: our shells, our walking sticks make it a sacred law, and this respectable spoil [*dépouille*] is the only pay for the celebrant.] (p. 9)

Guilhot's soul might ascend unimpeded to heaven due to his piety, but his body must descend into the earth. The duty to bury the dead follows from 'sacred law' and from nature, explains the Young Pilgrim, whose puns on the shells (*coquilles*) and walking sticks (*bourdons*) of pilgrims combine the two in order to highlight that the crisis is also physical: the body cannot remain among the living, but must be interred, according to nature and custom.[24] The pun on 'dépouille,' which can mean both cadaver and spoils or plunder, points to the church's material rather than spiritual concerns in the affair and the violation to the natural, social, and religious order that results.

The offence to Guilhot and to the community is compounded by the fact that the deceased was a hero who participated in the liberation of the Bastille. 'Guilhot étoit au siège de la Bastille, l'immortel siège de la Bastille; nous portons des trophées patriotiques & religieux sur son cercueil' [Guilhot was at the siege of the Bastille, the immortal siege of the Bastille; we bring patriotic and religious trophies for the coffin] (pp. 12–13), says the Sergeant of the Guards. Guilhot's memory is honoured with symbols of his victory and piety. Tied to the 'immortal' events of 14 July, the tributes over his coffin serve to instil patriotism in the mourners and attach the citizen to his country. The initial question of what Guilhot's family owes the Pastor to perform the obsequies quickly shifts here to what compatriots and authorities owe to their citizen-heroes. Despite the honour and adornments placed on the coffin, one of the townswomen, La Doyenne, expresses concern that it will nonetheless remain unburied: 'je gagerais que l'on l'oubliera, ou qu'on ne l'emportera pas seul & de jour pour le grand trou' [I would bet that it [the coffin] will be forgotten, or will not be carried alone and in time to the gravepit] (p. 8). Even as Guilhot and his deeds are remembered by the community, the crisis of burial persists. However, another townswoman, La Commandante, sees it differently and replies: 'Tu perdrois. L'habitué en veut à la fille: le pasteur n'a pas oublié la mère. Tiens que l'office du mort sera gratuit et solemnel' [You would lose [that bet]. The novice wants the daughter, the pastor hasn't forgotten the mother. You'll see that the funeral service will be free and solemn] (p. 8). In other words, the Novice and the Pastor have taken a romantic interest in the grieving daughter and widow respectively. La Commandante sees in this development the happy resolution of the dual dilemmas for the Guilhot family — the fate of the corpse and the fate of the poverty-stricken survivors — as the funeral service will now be expanded to include a wedding service as well ('épithalame', p. 34). The play thus unites the story of Guilhot's burial with the topical subject of the marriage of ecclesiasts announced in the subtitle of the play, 'the marriage of the lower clergy of France'.

L'Office du Mort is of special interest here as an illustration of *l'entre-deux-morts* on stage. Guilhot is dead, physically, but what remains uncertain and what the community collectively seeks over the course of the play is the symbolic death. The unburied body, silent and still on stage within its wooden casement, remains in limbo. The play dramatizes the temporal and physical space the corpse must traverse from the first to the second death; this space stands as a breach in the norms that must be righted. Indeed, Guilhot's unburied coffin stays ever-present to the spectator's eye, the sign of the physical death and a constant reminder of the symbolic death that eludes it. In the interstice between Guilhot's two deaths, the actions of the community affirm and transform the norms of burial to align with the Revolution's ideals of liberty, equality, and fraternity. The staging of the play further underscores the symbolic dimension of the action: throughout the first two acts, Guilhot's widow and daughter sit in the humble granary at the back of the stage, while the foreground is filled with the comings and goings of the diverse types who come for the funeral; in between the two spaces lies the coffin.

It is in the third and final act that the scene changes and the characters collectively bear the coffin to the doors of the church where they confront the Pastor. The transition from physical to symbolic death occurs in the physical crossing of the threshold into the sacred space of the church, as various characters 'portant le cercueil pénétrent dans le temple' [bearing the coffin enter the temple] (p. 38). The crowd successfully extracts a promise from the Pastor to perform the holy rite of burial for Guilhot. This second symbolic death completes Guilhot's transition from living to dead, a process that in effect brings the symbolic transformation of Guilhot's identity in the community and reinscribes him into the life of the community in a new way.

His death in turn becomes the occasion for the transformation of other identities in the play as well. The crisis of burial now resolved, the action immediately turns to the marriages of the clergy. In the shift from burial to nuptial ceremony, the widow will become a wife again, the daughter will become a 'femme' [woman/wife], and the Pastor and Novice will become husbands and citizens. The Pastor not only, marries the widow, but as the Old Pilgrim explains, 'on transfère au pasteur le nom & les armes du défun' [one transfers to the pastor the name and the arms of the deceased] (p. 34). That is, he will assume Guilhot's identity and property. 'Le pasteur endossera les coquilles du défunt' [The pastor dons the shell of the deceased] (p. 34), affirms the Young Pilgrim, punning again on the multiple meanings of *coquilles* (as a shell or hide, the ornaments of a pilgrim, and a written substitution). The Pastor also becomes a father when he is forced to recognize his illegitimate son (p. 53). The transformations continue with a courtesan who becomes wife to a rabbi (the latter agrees to work on Saturdays in order to fulfil his duty to the nation and the courtesan agrees to become a mother). Death cedes to the libidinal and productive forces of nature and comedy. In the rhetoric of the Revolution, all are made 'utile[s]' [useful] (p. 4) citizens of the nation in the process.

The death of Guilhot therefore proves to be of great importance to the community as an occasion for the rebirth of several characters into new patriotic identities. In Lacanian terms, the imaginary of the play makes the community whole again by substituting the Pastor for Guilhot, the living for the dead.[25] This transformation of identities is heralded earlier in the play when the Sergeant of the Guards says: 'Au moment qu'on prit la Bastille, sauf nos clercs, tout devint François' [At the moment the Bastille was taken, except for our clercs, all became Frenchmen] (p. 37). La Doyenne replies: 'Au moment qu'ils auront femmes, nos clercs aussi seront François' [At the moment they have wives, our clergy, too, will be Frenchmen] (p. 37).[26] In other words, the clergy will be assimilated into the life of the nation as (re)productive citizens when they marry. The funeral becomes a marriage, tragedy becomes comedy, the 'inutile' [useless] clergy become useful Frenchmen and citizens, and Guilhot lives again in the person of the Pastor. The initial failure of burial has forced the community to express its values and identity, and in the completion of the funeral it is able to return to life. The physical death disturbed a settled vision of the world; the symbolic death restores order (religious and civic) and assures equality and dignity in death to all.

We can see in this play how much theatre audiences had changed after 1789, bringing a return to forms of the comic grounded in the popular. Unlike *Antigone*, the clash of laws and values in *L'Office du Mort* is not between an individual (Antigone representing the family) and the collective (Creon representing the state). Rather, the conflict is between the people and its institutions. The Pastor's selfish interest runs up against the 'loi sacrée' [sacred law] of burial, which Guilhot's compatriots see righted over the course of the play. Significantly, the widow and daughter do not speak for the deceased or petition for his burial; rather they remain silent alongside the coffin. It is the townspeople who besiege the clerics and carry the coffin to the church door, and who scheme to achieve the marriages that resolve the crisis of Guilhot's burial. The play represents regeneration from death — a second symbolic death for the deceased, but also a second life for the living. The carnivalesque ending further brings the overturning of the power of the high for the low, a reversal of values, a symbolic end to Old Regime church privileges and hierarchies, and the beginning of a new order of liberty, equality, and fraternity.

In a metatheatrical moment in the last act, the Sexton addresses a troupe of actors who have entered the scene: 'Autrefois vous avez joué Tartuffe: aujourd'hui Charles IX. Bientôt le Folliculaire vous enverra d'Enfer le mariage du clergé que vous jouerez aussi' [Formerly you performed Tartuffe: today Charles IX. Soon the Writer will send you from Hell the marriage of the clergy which you will perform, too] (p. 54). Having mounted works by Molière and Marie-Joseph Chénier, the actors will next put on the comedy we are watching, 'The Funeral Service, or the marriage of the lower clergy', which the Folliculaire [Writer] is finishing. The Sexton's choice of plays is, of course, pointed: the first two concern the hypocrisy and crimes of the Church. By contrast, the third play is about the clergy's integration into civil society through marriage. Theatre, too, is thus transformed in the process. No longer the high comedies and tragedies associated with the Old Regime — wherein the clergy profit from aristocratic disorder — the popular theatre depicts the triumph and tastes of the common folk in the new democratic order. This episode reframes the action of the play in relation to its representation, a gesture both to the real-world events upon which *L'Office du Mort* is based and to its real-world publication and performance. The Folliculaire's script thus provides a mirror image in which the fragmented society and identities are made whole, and in which the characters (and by extension the audience members) come to recognize themselves as 'françois' [Frenchmen] and 'frères' [brothers].[27] Emphasizing transformation and survival of the community, the comedy presents an interdiction of mourning. 'Point de larmes sur le cercueil d'un homme qui s'est trouvé au siège de la Bastille, point de larmes!' says the Sergeant; 'seulement n'oubliez pas des trophées' [Shed no tears over the coffin of a man who was at the siege of the Bastille, no tears! [...] just don't forget the trophies] (p. 17). Do not mourn, but remember to honour virtue and heroism. The comedy rejects tragedy and catharsis to embrace celebration and transformation instead. The two pilgrims close the action as they hurry from the wedding banquets to the next feast — this time, in celebration of their own nuptials to come. 'Allons, frère, allons' [Let's go, brother, let's go], the younger pilgrim says; the time for mourning is over. 'Le folliculaire a tout hâté' [The writer has hastened everything] (p. 58).

Deliverance from the Tomb: *Antigone* Inverted

Boutet de Monvel's proto-melodrama, *Les Victimes cloîtrées*, was the runaway hit of 1791 and remained in production through the end of the decade and well into the nineteenth century.[28] The play's immense popularity was undoubtedly due to its spectacular staging, melodramatic subject and situations, and references to contemporary Revolutionary events. However, the drama is also of interest here as a burial storyline which stages *l'entre-deux-morts* in a different way from *L'Office du Mort*. If the coffin dominated the latter as a reminder and protest for the rights of the dead, in *Les Victimes cloîtrées* the crypt and tomb take centre stage as sites of both hidden crimes and sentimental scenes of mourning. In brief, the play tells the story of the virtuous young lovers Eugénie and Dorval. When the play begins, Dorval is mourning Eugénie, whom he believes died a year earlier after being forced into a convent by her parents to prevent the youths from marrying. The bereft Dorval now decides to join the monastery adjacent to the convent where Eugénie has been laid to rest so that he may 'vis auprès de son cercueil' [live near to her coffin] (p. 46). '[L]a solitude et la tombe, voilà mon seul espoir' [solitude and the tomb, those are my only hope], he explains (p. 38). However, on the eve of taking religious vows, Dorval discovers the truth: Père Laurent imprisoned Eugénie in an underground crypt for rejecting his sexual advances then falsely reported her death to the family. Père Laurent now throws Dorval into a hidden vault below the monastery as well. Unbeknownst to the youth, his cell shares an adjoining wall with that of Eugénie. In the play's sensational climax, Dorval claws through the wall to unite with his beloved in the crypt. A crowd is now heard at the door: the youths fear it is Laurent, but when the door flies open, the republican mayor, Francheville (Eugénie's uncle), enters with National Guard soldiers, Eugénie's parents, and others who help secure the couple's release. The play ends with the joyous reunion of the lovers and family, as all celebrate Eugénie's miraculous return to life.

The family initially accepts the false report of Eugénie's death because of their trust in the religious authority of Père Laurent, but also because he performs a sham funeral service over an empty coffin to convince them of it.[29] Hers is therefore a symbolic death: through the fake ritual she is recognized as dead, removed from the world of the living, and buried alive in the recesses of the cloister. She thus occupies the liminal space of *l'entre-deux-morts* between her symbolic death and the physical death she awaits in the tomb. Eugénie's living death is not revealed on stage until the fourth act when the entire theatre is spectacularly transformed into the subterranean crypts of the monastery.[30] Deprived of food, light, and society, she laments her fate and hopes for nothing but death: 'l'espoir de la mort, voilà tout ce qui me reste ... et quand viendra-t-elle cette mort tant souhaitée? Hélas! l'ordre de la nature n'existe plus pour moi' [the hope of death, that is all that remains to me ... and when will it come, this much wished-for death? Alas! The natural order no longer exists for me!].[31] This space and time *between-two-deaths* represents a breach in the natural order. Here Eugénie contemplates her life from the place where it is already lost, where she is already on the other side lamenting everything refused her in life. Eugénie recalls the phony *office du mort* that Laurent performed to dupe her family: 'J'ai vu jusqu'au cercueil trompeur qu'on allait exposer aux regards, à la compassion, aux regrets de ceux qui m'ont aimés' [I saw all the way to the false coffin that they were going to expose to the eyes, the compassion, the regrets of those who loved me] (p. 64). While they mourned an empty coffin, she says: 'je descendais vivante dans cette asyle de la mort' [I descended alive into this asylum of the dead] (p. 64). Her predicament represents the ultimate gothic nightmare of burial alive, immobility, and loss of identity. The innocent victim of Laurent's libertine greed and lust, but also of her parents' credulity, Eugénie's undue suffering stands as an indictment of the unnatural and unjust power of the Old Regime aristocracy and priesthood.

The false representation of Eugénie's death and funeral by Père Laurent is contrasted in the play with the true likeness of her that Dorval painted while she was living. This portrait of her hangs in Francheville's office and serves to keep her memory alive. As Francheville says while looking upon it in Act I: 'le temps et la distance ne vous ont point effacés de ma mémoire' [time and distance have not effaced you from my memory] (p. 15). The painting also becomes the occasion for proving the love and goodness of Eugénie's mother when she is moved to tears by it and repents having forced her daughter into the convent (p. 37).[32] Interestingly, the representation is far removed from the tomb where Eugénie's remains are supposedly buried.[33] However, Dorval is not content with representation alone, and seeks to collapse the distance between himself and the departed by choosing to inhabit 'à jamais un lieu, voisin de celui qui renferme la cendre de l'objet qu'il aime encore' [forever a place next door to the one that encloses the ashes of the object I love still] (p. 11). That is, Dorval decides to enter the monastery neighbouring the convent where Eugénie is buried. The monastery and the tomb are equated throughout the play, as when Francheville asks Dorval: 'Pourquoi t'ensevelir vivant dans ces tombeaux?' [Why bury yourself alive in these tombs?] (p. 44). Like Antigone, Dorval joins his fate with that of his deceased loved one in the tomb. He thus chooses symbolic death, rejecting the right to life and liberty by entering into the time and space of *l'entre-deux-morts*. Indeed, Dorval hopes to meet his corporeal death at Eugénie's side, believing that 'la mort réunira ce que la mort a séparé' [death will reunite what death has separated] (p. 38). Upon leaving the others for the last time, he says: 'Adieu, je meurs au monde' [Goodbye, I die to the world] (p. 50). His choice embodies the protest of one who dares to act according to his heart rather than social conventions. '[J]e veux briser les barrières qui nous séparent,' he says; 'je veux mourir en baignant avec mes larmes les restes inanimés de mon amante' [I want to break the barriers that separate us, I want to die while bathing with my tears the inanimate remains of my lover] (p. 36). For Lacan, *l'entre-deux-morts* is characterized by such a breaking of barriers; it is a double encroachment, 'a death that crosses over into the sphere of life, a life that moves into the realm of death'.[34] Dorval imagines himself perpetually mourning at Eugénie's coffin: 'Je vis auprès de son cercueil, je suis encore près d'elle, et je mourrai près d'elle' [I live beside her coffin, I am still near her, and I will die near her] (p. 46). The coffin is the dual sign of death and life: the material proof and container of her (supposed) remains as well as the object that keeps her alive in the memory of the living. Her tomb stimulates a morbid melancholy in Dorval consistent with the sentimental 'cult of tombs' that flourished in the last decades of the eighteenth century.[35] As Bernardin de Saint Pierre implied in his description of burial practices in Paris, mass graves did not allow for the sentimental mourning at a tomb or gravesite that people desired. In 1791, the same year *Les Victimes cloîtrées* premiered (and a year after *Antigone* failed), a deputy to the National Convention, Charles Villette, expressed admiration for the ancient Greek tradition of respect for the dead and by contrast lamented contemporary burial customs in France: 'Que nous sommes loin de connaître cet art sentimental qui perpétue le souvenir de ce qu'on aime! Quoi de plus révoltant que nos hideux cimitières!' [How far we are from knowing this sentimental art that perpetuates the memory of the one we love! What is more revolting than our hideous cemeteries!].[36] The play revives this 'sentimental art' of grieving at a tomb. Not only does Dorval express the desire to reside with the dead and devote himself entirely to honouring Eugénie's tomb and memory, but also the *mise-en-scène* brings the tombs visibly on stage in the final act such that the theatre itself becomes a collective space of mourning and remembrance of the dead.

However, once Dorval is incarcerated against his will in the underground crypt, desire for life and liberty is reborn in him and he searches his cell for an exit. In the dim light Dorval recognizes two tombs. 'Une pour moi... C'est-là que tout finit... tout' [One for me... It is there that all ends... all] (p. 71). He tries to read the words engraved on the lid of one and discovers an unburied cadaver at his feet. Repulsed by the 'décombres' [debris] (p. 70), he nonetheless recognizes among the fragments a letter written in blood left by the previous prisoner.[37] These words from the dead spell salvation for Dorval: they direct him to a lever in the wall that lifts a stone concealing the hole dug by the deceased captive. Instead of a gravepit, it is an exit from death into life, achieved through the heroic effort of another. With a single burst of force, Dorval breaches the wall and reunites with Eugénie, who collapses unconscious in his arms. He has torn down the obstacles (both literal and figurative) to their union. 'Tu vis!' [You live!] (p. 73) he cries upon recognizing her. However, the two are still symbolically dead; their liberty and transformation back into life will require the actions and consent of the community. In a final scene remarkably similar to the one Marmontel added to *Antigone* in 1790, the political leader, Francheville, arrives with a crowd of soldiers, townspeople, clergy, and nobles to throw open the tomb and rescue the young lovers from death. The evil Père Laurent, the figure of tyranny and libertinism in the play, is forgotten, not heard from again after Act III. He is replaced here by the virtuous mayor, Francheville, who ushers in a new set of democratic social relations based upon 'l'heureuse égalité qui règne à présent entre nous' [the happy equality that reigns at present between us] (p. 21). Francheville's forceful rescue of the incarcerated youths is in accord with the new laws of the Revolution that abolished religious orders and monastic vows.[38] He thus supplies a foil to both the priesthood and aristocracy. As a servant in the play explains, the reign of equality reflects a return to the natural order: 'il est certain que la nature nous a tous faits les uns comme les autres, ni plus ni moins' [it is certain that nature has made us all one like another, not more nor less] (p. 2). The order of nature is restored as the corrupt past crumbles into dust and a new order rises from its ashes.

The play thus enacts a dramatic movement from captivity to freedom, from darkness to light, and from death to life. Peter Brooks, drawing on the psychoanalytic theory of Sigmund Freud, interprets the opening of the tomb at the end of the play as a re-enactment of the 'primal scene' of the liberation of the Bastille which releases what has been hidden, and shines light into the repressed areas of the Old Regime.[39] This repetition of the founding act of the Revolution (itself serially repeated in each performance of the play) joins past and present in a joyful and continuous triumph of virtue and liberty. Indeed, as Sophie Marchand points out in her introduction to the play, when the legally sanctioned crowd invades the convent crypt, it is as if contemporary life suddenly intrudes upon the drama: the scene propels the action from the injustices and spaces of the Old Regime to the present moment of liberation and celebration.[40] However, rather than viewing this as a breaking of the fourth wall, as Marchand does, and the rush of reality into the frame of representation — or as an eruption of the unconscious into consciousness and legibility, as Brooks does — I would offer that Lacan's *l'entre-deux-morts* reveals instead that, remaining within the order of the Imaginary, the play's ending represents not reality but a fantasy of wholeness and unity that signals the birth of a new Revolutionary imaginary from death.[41] That is, the ending represents not just the euphoria of liberty and broken chains but also dramatizes the founding of a new symbolic order and a new time based on nature and reason. In an inversion of the dramatic structure of *Antigone*, death is averted and the 'dead' are miraculously resurrected; the time and space of *l'entre-deux-morts* thus resolves, not with the second physical death, but with a second life and the rejuvenating transformation from one kind of society to another. *Les Victimes cloîtrées* celebrates the transgressive force of the Revolution, harmonizing nature and culture, and liberating youthful desire from the repression of arbitrary authority in order to create society anew.

Conclusion

In the process of exposing the abuses of church officials regarding the sacred rites and obsequies of death, the communities in both *L'Office du Mort* and *Les Victimes cloîtrées* successfully bring about the symbolic transformation from death to life. Whether it is Guilhot living again in the person of the Pastor or Eugénie and Dorval walking out of the tomb, these revolutionary plays begin with death and crisis but conclude with the promise of marriage and new life, as death is transformed from a terrible event into a powerful affirmation of life. The plays make sense of death by placing it within an aesthetic framework that reflects the new political, social, ethical, and religious norms governing death's meaning and practices for the community. The focus on the survival of the community through a process of transformation and renewal — from individual death to collective life — helps explain why Marmontel's *Antigone*, despite its changed ending, failed in 1790. As one of the reviewers cited earlier protested in response to the opera: '*Peu m'importe que Polynice soit enterré ou non*' [*What does it matter to me if Polynices is buried or not?*]. By contrast, in *L'Office du Mort* and *Les Victimes cloîtrées* the burials do have importance for the lives of the spectators: the deaths at their centre provoke both a religious and civic crisis in which all citizens share. For the critic Jean Duvignaud, the final tableau of *Les Victimes cloîtrées* coalesces a sense of a 'nous' [us] in the public, a communal identity out of their differences through which spectators in the theatre come to recognize in the victims on stage their own oppression thrown off as a new society opens to them.[42] Significantly, as we have seen above, this communal identity is constituted around the space and time of the tomb.

Yet the un-tragic endings of *L'Office du Mort* and *Les Victimes cloîtrées* require us to adjust Lacan's notion of *l'entre-deux-morts* which for him is the essence of tragedy. If tragedy represents a breach of limits, a transgression of the borders of life and death, then comedy plays at the limits and expands the borders as the characters overcome obstacles and barriers both real and imagined. Comedy binds death to life. The Revolutionary plays explored here transform *l'entre-deux-morts* into what we might call instead *l'entre-deux-vies*, or *the between-two-lives*.[43] The happy rather than tragic endings of *L'Office du Mort* and *Les Victimes cloîtrées* represent a postponement or rejection of death and an end to mourning in the playful suspension of time through repetition. Just as the characters on stage face death and return to life, so too the audience members return to their lives at the end of the performance. Revolutionary theatre thus offered spectators, in the provisional and temporary experience of the dramatic performance, a space and time of mourning — of *l'entre-deux-vies* — that allowed the community to face death and return to life transformed.

Notes to Chapter 4

1. Jean-François Marmontel, *Antigone* (music by Nicolas-Antoine Zingarelli) premiered 30 April 1790 and was performed a second and last time on 4 May 1790. In addition to Doigny du Ponceau's *Antigone, ou la Piété Fraternelle* (1787), which had inspired Zingarelli, Vittorio Alfieri also published an *Antigone* in 1783 (rev. 1789).

2. *Mercure de France*, 138.20 (15 May 1790), 111–18. All translations are mine unless otherwise specified. Robert Garland in *The Greek Way of Death* (London: Duckworth, 1985) explains that while the modern Western view is that death occurs in an instant, 'in ancient Greece by contrast, death was not seen so much as an event as a process' (p. 13). This process began when death was imminent and lasted a month after death when the thirty-day rites (*triakides*) were performed at the tomb (p. 19).

3. *L'Esprit des journaux français et étrangers*, 6 (June 1790), 305–07. Emphasis in original.

4. For a discussion of the institutional context of the closing of *Antigone* in 1790, see Mark Darlow, *Staging the French Revolution: Cultural Politics and the Paris Opera, 1789–1794* (New York and Oxford: Oxford University Press, 2012), pp. 250–51. Darlow attributes its failure to the poor integration of the music and drama and its simplistic emotion, drawing on reviews from the *Moniteur*. However, the *Moniteur* also notes that whereas for ancient Greeks the play's subject of burial might be 'd'un fort grand intérêt; il ne sauroit avoir le même dans nos mœurs' [of very great interest; it will not have the same in our mores]; *Le Moniteur universel*, 2.122 (2 May 1790), 494.

5. *L'Esprit des journaux*, 305. Emphasis in original.

6. The *Mercure* describes the final scene as follows: 'Créon arrive suivi d'un peuple nombreux, & ordonne qu'on rende les honneurs funèbres à Etéocle & à ceux qui sont morts en servant la Patrie' [Creon arrives followed by many people, and orders that funeral honours be rendered to Eteocles and others who died serving the country] (p. 115).

7. For example, Cordelia and Desdemona survive in Ducis's translations of Shakespeare's *Roi Lear* (1784) and *Othello* (1792) respectively, and Virginie does not drown in the 1794 comic opera based on Bernardin de Saint-Pierre's popular 1788 novel *Paul et Virginie*. This was largely in keeping with the conventions of musical drama (*le genre lyrique*). See Feilla, *The Sentimental Theater of the French Revolution* (Aldershot: Ashgate, 2013; Abingdon: Routledge, 2016), pp. 1–35.

8. In the *Aesthetics*, Hegel calls *Antigone* 'one of the most sublime and in every respect most excellent works of art of all time' (*Aesthetics: Lectures on Fine Art*, trans. by T. M. Knox (Oxford: Clarendon, 1975), p. 232). Hegel also discusses the play in the *Phenomenology of Spirit* (1807) and *Philosophy of Right* (1820). For the performance history of *Antigone* in France, see Frank Jones, 'Scenes from the Life of Antigone,' *Yale French Studies*, 6 (1950), 91–100.

9. George Steiner, *Antigones: How the Antigone Legend Has Endured in Western Literature, Art, and Thought* (New Haven, CT, and London: Yale University Press, 1996 [1984]), p. 10: 'the French Revolution *is*, one feels, key'. He also notes occasional comparisons drawn between Antigone and Charlotte Corday.

10. An essentially aristocratic form, tragedy had already begun to lose ground in the 1760s as society and tastes shifted; the genre's precipitous decline after 1789 is one of the more remarkable developments of Revolutionary drama. See Matthew Buckley, *Tragedy Walks the Streets: The French Revolution in the Making of Modern Drama* (Baltimore, MD: Johns Hopkins University Press, 2006).

11. Cited in Sophie Marchand, *Théâtre et pathétique au XVIIIe siècle: pour une esthétique de l'effet dramatique* (Paris: Champion, 2009), p. 64. See, for example, *Commemorating Mirabeau: 'Mirabeau aux Champs-Elysées' and other texts*, ed. by Jessica Goodman (Cambridge: MHRA, 2017).

12. See Marie-Hélène Huet, *Mourning Glory: The Will of the French Revolution* (Philadelphia: University of Pennsylvania Press, 1997), pp. 97–148; and Antoine de Baecque, *La Gloire et l'Effroi: sept morts sous la Terreur* (Paris: Grasset, 1997).

13. Margaret Fields Denton, 'Death in French Arcady: Nicolas Poussin's *The Arcadian Shepherds* and Burial Reform in France c. 1800', *Eighteenth-Century Studies*, 36.2 (2003), 195–216 (p. 205). See also Philippe Ariès, *The Hour of Our Death*, trans. by Helen Weaver (New York: Knopf, 1981) and John McManners, *Death and the Enlightenment: Changing Attitudes to Death among Christians and Unbelievers in Eighteenth-Century France* (New York: Oxford University Press, 1981).

14. Cited in Denton, 'Death in French Arcady,' p. 205.

15. Jacques Lacan, *The Ethics of Psychoanalysis, 1959–1960: The Seminar of Jacques Lacan: Book VII*, ed. by Jacques-Alain Miller, trans. by Dennis Porter (New York: Routledge, 1992), pp. 241–87.

16. Jane Gilbert, *Living Death in Medieval French and English Literature* (New York; Cambridge: Cambridge University Press, 2017), p. 19. See also Camille Dumoulié, 'L'Entre-deux-morts: Jacques Lacan entre philosophie, littérature et psychanalyse', *Princípios*, 10.13 (2003), 191–206. Antigone seeks proper burial of the corpse of her brother Polynices in order to fulfil the symbolic death denied him by the state; until this second death is complete, he remains in the interstitial zone between two deaths.

17. Her struggle for her brother's symbolic death thus leads her to a complementary or mirror position to Polynices, caught in between two deaths, as she defies the norms of her society. She thereby establishes, according to Lacan, a 'zone' between two deaths as a place of the ethical, which is also a no place (pp. 280–83). For Hegel, this was the conflict of two laws and two rights: that of the *oikos*/home/private and that of the *polis*/state/public, which Luce Irigaray will later read in terms of gender in her book *Être Deux* (Paris: Grasset, 1997).

18. Bernardin de Saint-Pierre, *Les Harmonies de la Nature*, 3 vols, in *Œuvres complètes de Jacques-Henri Bernardin de Saint-Pierre*, 12 vols, mises en ordre et précédées de la vie de l'auteur par Louis-Aimé Martin (Paris: Méquignon-Marvis, 1818), I (VIII), p. 197.

19. *L'Office du Mort, ou Le Mariage du Bas Clergé de France*, comédie en trois actes & en prose dans le genre du Théâtre espagnol ([n.p.]: [n.pub.], May 1790), p. 19. Page numbers from this edition will be cited parenthetically within the text.

20. See Suzanne J. Bérard's introduction to the play in *Le Théâtre révolutionnaire de 1789 à 1794: la déchristianisation sur les planches* (Nanterre: Presses universitaires de Paris Ouest, 2009), pp. 228–29. The main elements of the comedy follow from the facts of the scandal: the coffin exposed at the door of the deceased's garret, the pastor's refusal to perform the burial service, the protest of the friends and neighbours who carry the coffin to the church and besiege the Pastor, and the cantor who refuses to sing and fears he will be hanged.

21. Cited in Huet, *Mourning Glory*, p. 127.

22. According to Richard Etlin, the French Revolution brought, 'a new order in burials' such that

'the customary rituals were gravely disrupted' (*The Architecture of Death: The Transformation of the Cemetery in 18th-Century Paris* (Cambridge, MA: MIT Press, 1984), p. 229).

23. See Suzanne Desan, *The Family on Trial in Revolutionary France* (Berkeley: University of California Press, 2006), p. 53.

24. Pilgrims to Saint-Jacques-de-Compostelle affixed a shell (*coquille*) to their capes and hats (hence the origin of the term *coquille Saint Jacques*), but *coquille* also signifies a typographical error in which one letter is substituted for another. *Bourdons* are long walking sticks that pilgrims carried; *bourdon* also means a drone bee (or an aural drone in music) and a typographical error in which the copyist omits several words of the original text.

25. Death is part of what Lacan names the Real, one of the aspects of life that cannot be mastered. The Real lies at the heart of human culture, although culture by definition excludes it. Representing death figuratively on stage thus involves the Imaginary order of image and imagination, which Lacan associates with the illusion of wholeness, synthesis, autonomy, duality, and similarity. Thus the imaginary is not the Real but rather a response to and placeholder for it. By representing death, it gives it a form, a figuring that is also a disfiguring.

26. The *bas clergé* refers to the lower clergy of the Catholic Church during the Ancien Régime, such as the curates and vicars who lived off the resources of their parish, and who had little power.

27. The terms appear ten and fourteen times respectively in the play. Mona Ozouf notes the prominent parallel between revolutionary fraternity and Christian brotherhood in the early phases of the Revolution, which facilitated the integration of the clergy into the body politic. See *A Critical Dictionary of the French Revolution*, ed. by François Furet and Mona Ozouf, trans. by Arthur Goldhammer (Cambridge, MA: Belknap Press of Harvard University Press, 1989), pp. 694–703.

28. See the introduction to *Monvel, Les Victimes cloîtrées*, ed. by Sophie Marchand (Cambridge: MHRA, 2011).

29. When the play was revived in 1796, audiences found this aspect of the play lacking verisimilitude; see Marchand, *Monvel, Les Victimes cloîtrées*, p. 23.

30. See Annelle Curulla, *Gender and Religious Life in French Revolutionary Drama*, Studies in The Enlightenment (Oxford: Voltaire Foundation, 2019), for an in-depth discussion of the innovative 'double scene' staging (pp. 65–98).

31. Monvel, *Les Victimes cloîtrées*, drames en quatre actes et en prose; nouv. ed. (Paris: Barba, 1796), p. 46. All future page references to this edition will be cited parenthetically in the text.

32. This sentimental redemption of the mother's aristocratic leanings in Act II, Scene 7 represents, for Sophie Marchand, the pedagogical thrust of revolutionary theatre and its belief in the reformative power of representation (p. 18).

33. Mark Deming notes that in the eighteenth century it was seen as 'improper' for sarcophagi, and depositories of human remains, 'to be associated with the honorific likenesses'; cited in Huet, *Mourning Glory*, p. 136.

34. Lacan, *The Ethics of Psychoanalysis*, p. 248.

35. This cult of tombs coincided with the erosion of Church authority and the shift from death being seen as 'a religious crisis in which all the faithful share,' in the words of John McManners, to the view that death was 'an intense, introverted family affair' (*Death and the Enlightenment*, p. 229).

36. *Lettres choisies de Charles Villette sur les principaux événemens de la Révolution* (Paris: Clousier, 1792), p. 139.

37. Curulla notes that corpses became increasingly popular in French theatre from the 1750s on, under the influence of English drama (*Gender and Religious Life*, p. 92).

38. In November 1789 the National Assembly nationalized church property, approved the sale of church lands, and abolished the tithe. Three months later, in February 1790, the deputies of the Assembly abolished monastic vows, suppressed all orders and congregations, and encouraged monks and nuns to return to private life on state pensions and to marry.

39. Peter Brooks, 'The Opening of the Depths', in *The French Revolution, 1789–1989: Two Hundred Years of Rethinking*, ed. by Sandy Petrey (Lubbock: Texas Tech University Press, 1989), p. 50. For Brooks the play blends the topical subject matter (contemporary scandals involving the Church,

new legislation abolishing monasteries and religious vows) with archetypal Gothic narratives found in the contemporary novels of Sade and Ducray-Duminil, forging a link between political oppression and sexual repression by means of the incarceration of innocent bodies.

40. Marchand, *Monvel, Les Victimes cloîtrées*, p. 21.
41. For Lacan, humans choose culture over nature. He sees desire as caught up in the fantasy version of reality that forever dominates our lives after our entrance into language.
42. Cited in Marchand, *Monvel, Les Victimes cloîtrées*, p. 21. Thus, according to Duvignaud, Revolutionary theatre was witness to, as much as a catalyst for, an ideology in the process of taking shape.
43. My thanks to Fiona Macintosh for this insight.

CHAPTER 5

❖

Twilight for a Myth: Images of Death in Luigi Pirandello's *The Mountain Giants*

Stefano Giannini

Syracuse University, NY

In contrast with the theatre of the late nineteenth century, in which bourgeois drama often ended with suicide, Luigi Pirandello's theatre put interpersonal violence back on the stage. His characters are capable of perpetrating violence through dramatically scripted scenes that often highlight an inborn hesitation to commit that very violence. Despite those hesitations, some characters achieve catharsis through acting on their violent instincts. Corrado Alvaro, one of the most perceptive readers of Pirandello's work, suggests that many of Pirandello's characters bring with themselves a modicum of Hamlet's traits. Alvaro singles out Enrico IV as a direct heir to Hamlet, seeing similarities such as indecisiveness, the fight between reason and the unpredictability of instinct, and the literal act of murder.[1]

In his late theatre, Pirandello shifts his attention. While violence remains, the figure of the hesitant and identifiable culprit disappears, and the plurality of individuals become both executors and victims. Together with what seems to be an indictment of the civil values of contemporary society, Pirandello inserts a dramatic reflection on the relationship between art, which does not die, and his fear of death. The clash between the perpetual life of art and the mortal destiny of its author finds a powerful testimony in Pirandello's *The Mountain Giants* [MG], his last play, which remained incomplete after more than eight years of assiduous work between 1929 and 1936. The incomplete status of *MG* mirrors the opposition between art and life that occupied Pirandello's thoughts throughout his long artistic journey. It seems logical that the play that sets out Pirandello's final and most profound reflections on art as life becomes the occasion for reflection on death, as it stands opposed to life, and makes it tangible.

The Play

In a space and time left undefined, 'al limite tra la favola e la realtà'[2] [on the border between fable and reality][3] the otherwise extremely detail-oriented script of *MG* narrates the vicissitudes of the theatre company of the Countess and lead actress

Ilse. Ilse is the artistic leader of the company financially backed by her husband, the
Count, who tours with them. Believing the company has been called to perform in
a local theatre, they arrive at a secluded villa, invited by Cotrone, the leader of the
seven *Scalognati* (out-of-luck fellows) who live there in self-exile. To the company's
dismay, they discover there is no theatre in town. Ilse is particularly distraught
because she has an inescapable desire to act in and endlessly stage *The Fable of the
Changeling* ['La favola del figlio cambiato', henceforth *TFC*],[4] the work the Poet
wrote for her. In love with Ilse, the Poet — never seen in the play — has killed
himself because of her unrequited love, leaving her only with his fable. The feeling
of guilt and the mission to propagate what she sees as the inherent and indispensable
human need for Art pushes Ilse to stage the Poet's work continuously. Cotrone
offers a solution to Ilse's need to perform. He tells them that the wealthy Giants
who own the land and the economic activities around the villa could be approached
about a performance. Two of their young scions are about to get married, and *TFC*
could be the highlight of the nuptial party. Pirandello's manuscript ends with the
frightening sound of the thundering horses of the Giants riding down into the
valley to celebrate their children's wedding. He never completed the play. Stefano
Pirandello, Luigi's son, subsequently wrote the ending that his father recounted
to him on his deathbed.[5] According to Stefano's prose account, the Giants decline
to have the play performed for them, but fund the performance for the benefit
of their servants. The play is not welcomed by the unprepared audience, which
was expecting something similar to a vaudeville show. During the performance,
violence erupts, and Ilse and two actors are killed by the brutish mob. Sorrowful,
the Giants tell their major-domo to offer compensation to the widower Count,
who proclaims that he will erect a funerary monument in Ilse's memory. The play
is divided into three numbered sections, plus the prose account that would have
formed the third act of the theatrical piece that Pirandello defined as one of his
myths.[6]

Foreboding of Death and the Beginning of the Mountain Giants

The many letters Pirandello wrote to his artistic muse Marta Abba reveal how
much he invested emotionally and professionally over eight years of working on
MG. As he describes to her his painful solitude away from her and Italy in self-
imposed exile in Berlin, Pirandello details the writing process:

> Ho ripreso a lavorare con tanto fervore! *I giganti della Montagna*, Marta mia,
> saranno un lavoro veramente gigantesco. Ho pensato cose... cose... Ma non so
> come faranno a farsi rappresentare, non dico in Italia, ma anche qua... Cose
> grandi! prodigiose! Ho preso la favola del *Figlio cambiato* e l'ho trasformata
> magnificamente per servire da dramma: quel dramma che l'eroica Contessa
> va portando in giro, a prezzo della sua vita. La trasformazione è venuta così
> bene, che anche questa volta, come per il *Come tu mi vuoi*, debbo forzarmi a
> vincere la tentazione che ho di farne un lavoro a sé: verrebbe magnifico! Te
> ne parlerò domani. Ma altre e altre cose ho anche pensate e vado pensando! Se
> dovessi morire, sarebbe un vero peccato in questo momento. Ma non morrò,
> non morrò! Faccio le corna![7]

[I started again to write with so much fervor! *The Mountain Giants*, my Marta, will be a truly gigantic work. I have thought things... things... But I don't know how they can be produced, I don't say in Italy, but even here ... Great things! Prodigious! I took the story of *Il figlio cambiato* and I transformed it splendidly to serve as drama: the drama that the heroic countess is carrying around, at the price of her life. The transformation has come out so well that also this time, as for *As You Desire Me*, I must force myself to overcome the temptation to make out of it a work by itself: it would come out magnificent! I'll talk to you about it tomorrow. But I have thought and I am thinking of many other things. It would be a real pity if I should die right at this moment! But I'll not die, I'll not die, knock on wood!][8]

From its inception, Pirandello associates *MG* with the foreboding idea of an impending death that will end the artistic discourse. Its central character, the 'heroic countess' Ilse, is ready to accept any risk, even death ('at the price of her life'), to disseminate the cardinal idea that Art is central to a life worth living. In the same letter of 17 April, Pirandello twice repeats his wish not to die, reinforcing this desire with the description of an apotropaic gesture ('It would be a real pity if I should die right at this moment! But I'll not die, I'll not die, knock on wood!'). The intertwining of the two motifs: the announcement of Ilse's sacrifice, and the disappointment at an untimely arrival of death that could cut short the conceptualization of his art, will reverberate throughout the whole *MG*, to show the magnitude of Pirandello's effort and investment in a work that he wanted to be the summit of his legacy. According to his vision, *MG* will encompass everything Pirandello wants to say, sublimated in the purest art form:

C'è tutto, è l'orgia della fantasia! Una leggerezza di nuvola su profondità d'abissi: risa potenti che scoppiano tra le lagrime, come tuoni tra le tempeste: e tutto sospeso, tutto aereo e vibrante, elettrico: nessun paragone con quello che ho fatto finora: sto toccando l'apice, vedrai! Ma sei Tu, sei Tu che lo tocchi, Marta mia! Tu con tutta la tua anima, che esulta in me e mi fa dentro quest'aria favolosa in cui tutti i personaggi respirano, e le parole sbocciano come fiori che pajono loro stessi stupiti d'esser nati. C'è qualcuno, Marta mia, che sta vivendo la Tua vita, e Tu non lo sai. La Tua *vera* vita![9]

[It has everything, it's an orgy of fantasy! The lightness of a cloud passing over the depth of an abyss; powerful laughter exploding among the tears, like thunder in the midst of storms; and everything suspended, whatever I have done so far; I am touching the peak, you'll see! But it's you, only you who are touching it, my Marta! With all your soul, which rejoices in me and creates inside me that sense of a fable in which all the characters breathe, and the words bloom like flowers that seem astonished at being born. There is somebody, my Marta, who is living your life, and you don't know it. Your true life!][10]

There is an eerie quality to the last two sentences of the letter. Pirandello admits that everything he is writing is a vicarious activity that exists only because Marta Abba is supplying him the words to shed light on the past myths, to recreate them.[11] However, it also seems that Pirandello foists his will on her, that is she is a character that lives the life Pirandello is writing for her, and that 'true' life — in the play one must assume — is the real life, opposed to the mortal quality of any human being.

The chilling juxtaposition propels forward his artistic endeavour, contrasting the life that the actress lives and the life written for her by the playwright.

The premonition of tragedy is felt early in the play. Already in the first act, Ilse says to her husband: 'Stai tranquillo, che finirà, sento che siamo alla fine...' (p. 200) [Don't worry, it will be over soon enough, I can feel we're near the end (p. 142)]. Her words are almost an echo of Pirandello's letter to Marta Abba: 'sarà forse il mio ultimo lavoro drammatico' [perhaps it will be my last dramatic work].[12] An atmosphere of mourning suffuses the pages of the play, which are filled with descriptions of eerie light games, nocturnal settings, and the villa itself, which seems something like a magic castle where spirits, ghosts and puppets transition from stillness to life and back again. The play is stippled with references to spirits, suffering and death: mysterious apparitions, magic spells, Ilse's desire for martyrdom, allusions to the Poet's suicide, premonitions of death, accounts of homicides, and images of the afterlife, like the vision of one hundred marching souls of the Purgatory led by Angel One Hundred-and-One.[13]

The accumulation of images reveals an opening into a hitherto impervious territory defined by a contiguity between what is considered dead or alive.[14] The grey area is identified by the character of Cotrone — a Pirandellian alter ego — who writes: 'Siamo qua come agli orli della vita, Contessa. Gli orli, a un comando, si distaccano; entra l'invisibile: vaporano i fantasmi' (p. 212) [Here, Countess, it's like being on the borders of life. At a word, those borders dissolve, and the invisible enters in: phantoms loom in the mist (p. 149)]. Ilse does not understand Cotrone's words, and her confusion grows when she is approached by Sgricia, a member of the *Scalognati* who asks her: 'Tu forse ti credi ancora viva?' (p. 216) [Do you by any chance think you're still alive? (p. 152)]. When Ilse seeks reassurance from Cotrone of what she thinks is Sgricia's delirium ('Si crede morta? [Does she think she's dead?]), Cotrone counters:

> COTRONE.   In un altro mondo, Contessa, con tutti noi...
> ILSE (*turbatissima*).   Che mondo? E queste voci?
> COTRONE.   Le accolga! Non cerchi di spiegarsele! Potrei... (p. 216)

> [COTRONE.   In another world, Countess, along with all of us.
> ILSE (*very disturbed*).   What world? And these voices?
> COTRONE.   Accept them. Don't try to explain them. I could...] (p. 152)

As a matter of fact, Cotrone — increasingly showing overlapping traits with Pirandello — attempts to explain the world he inhabits, the true one according to him, in which the actors and the *Scalognati* must fulfil one mission. While 'voi attori date corpo ai fantasmi perché vivano — e vivono!' (p. 219) [you actors take phantoms and give them your bodies so that they can live — and they do live! (p. 154)], Cotrone and his friends make phantoms of their bodies. 'Basta farli uscire da noi stessi' (p. 219) [it's enough to just draw them out of ourselves (p. 154)], says Cotrone, giving as an example the phantasm of the Poet who killed himself for love, who is in Ilse and whom only she can bring out.

The Ghost of Previous Stories

Marvin Carlson has demonstrated how '[e]verything in the theatre, the bodies, the materials utilized, the language, the space itself, is now and has always been haunted' by the 'ghosts' of their previous apparitions.[15] This image of the ghosts of previous characters plays out in two ways in Pirandello's work: these ghosts exist both as intertextual presences, following Carlson's strict definition, and as characters who are phantoms that assume life literally to haunt the 'real' characters, in this case Ilse's company.

In the former case, Pirandello's *œuvre* is a glaring example of the Barthian observation regarding the endless assemblage of previous texts to create a new one.[16] He is an author who consistently adapts elements (characters, plots, scenes) that have already appeared in previous works of his, usually his short stories, but also his theatre. For example, *Sei personaggi in cerca d'autore* draws on the short stories 'Personaggi' (1906), 'La tragedia di un personaggio' (1911), 'Colloqui coi personaggi' (1915), and contains the staging of his play *Il giuoco delle parti*. Hinkfuss, the director protagonist of Pirandello's play *Questa sera si recita a soggetto* [Tonight We Improvise] attempts to stage 'Leonora, addio!', one of his short stories. In the case of *MG*, from the beginning of the play, the life–death juxtaposition harks back to the same theme in his past short stories, novels, and plays,[17] whilst the short story 'Il figlio cambiato' is the text behind *TFC*, the fable contained within the myth that animates Ilse's obsessive desire to perform.

In the latter case, haunting in *MG* is a visible and recurring literal presence. Phantoms and spirits populate every part of the stage, in an atmosphere that repeatedly conjures up their appearance. Spizzi, the company's young actor, has a suicidal nightmare that is reminiscent of the deaths of the young boy and the little girl in *Six Characters*. Indeed, we see in *MG* the reverberations of the 'fantasmi' of the 'Colloqui coi personaggi': 'Da anni aspettavo qua gente come voi per far vivere altri fantasmi che ho in mente' (pp. 224–25) [For years I have been waiting for folk like you to give life to other phantoms that I have in mind (p. 158)]. But now, the six characters' search for their author has reversed. The characters of *MG* do not search for their maker. Instead, it is Pirandello who searches for a new society that seems to him increasingly impossible to find, even under the Nietzschean auspices of the necessity of myth as the condition to create a healthy civilization. Pirandello identifies the margins of Cotrone's secluded society as the ideal model of a new society.[18]

The Crisis of Grief

Funerary rites are the paramount example of the establishment of a civilization. Pirandello's short story 'I pensionati della memoria' (1914) problematizes the issue of death between the materiality of the funeral and the sorrow that accompanies a family death, along with the uncomfortable truth of practical problems that a dead body brings with it:

> [I]l morto — diciamo la verità — con quella gelida immobile durezza impassibilmente opposta a tutte le cure che ce ne diamo, a tutto il pianto che gli facciamo attorno, è un orribile ingombro, di cui lo stesso cordoglio — per

quanto accenni e tenti di volersene ancora disperatamente gravare — anela in fondo in fondo a liberarsi.

[The dead person — let's be honest — with that icy motionless hardness, unperturbably opposed to any sort of care we might feel, to all the our crying around him, is a horrible encumbrance, of which the very same grief — as much as it shows of still wanting to burden itself with it — yearns, ultimately, to get rid of it [the dead body]][19]

The word 'cordoglio' is in this context translatable by 'grief', and recalls Ilse's mourning in *MG*. As a consequence of the Poet's suicide, she goes through an endless grieving process from which she cannot escape. The concept 'crisi del cordoglio', crisis of grief, is set out in the studies of the Italian anthropologist Ernesto de Martino (1908–1965). In his *Morte e pianto rituale nel mondo antico*, de Martino articulates a complex discourse on the rituals that civilization has elaborated to control the potentially destructive grief that accompanies the loss of a loved one. Within the long and variegated rituals he studies, de Martino explores how different communities process grief and pain. Ilse does not experience grief for the loss of a family member. However, the Poet was so influential in the artistic dimension Pirandello frames for Ilse that her crisis explodes after the Poet's suicide. In her case, she does not pursue the extremes of grief described by de Martino such as motionless hebetude, self-inflicted physical wounds, homicide, desecration of the corpse, or even necrophagy.[20] Instead, not believing she deserves reprieve, Ilse decides to process the Poet's death by incessantly staging his magisterial work. Ilse is so completely invested in her mission that she seems unable to break character, often starting to recite her lines without warning in a completely different context. Her actors and the Count sustain her by responding with actions or lines from the play that they have memorized by dint of repetition. Pirandello sets the tone of Ilse's behaviour in her very first lines, upon the company's arrival at the villa. As soon as the cart that carries Ilse approaches the entrance of the villa, the *Scalognati* are concerned for her health:

MILORDINO.   Oh Dio, com'è pallida...
MARA-MARA.   Pare morta... (p. 188)

[MILORDINO.   My God, how pale she is!
MARA-MARA.   She seems dead.] (p. 134)

But then Ilse raises her body and her first words are the words of 'her' play, *TFC*:

ILSE (*dopo un momento, levandosi a sedere sul carretto, dice con profonda commozione*).
    Se volete ascoltare
    questa favola nuova,
    credete a questa mia veste
    di povera donna (p. 188)

[ILSE (*after a moment's pause, sitting up on the cart and speaking with deep emotion*).
    If you would stay to hear this tale,
    Not heard before,
    Look on these rags and mark them well,
    Wretched and poor.] (p. 134)

The rest of the company replies as per the script.

Pirandello depicts Ilse as a physically and emotionally exhausted character who progressively distances herself from reality. According to de Martino, detachment and acceptance after a loss are signs of a controlled elaboration of grief that results in a wistful adaptation to the new reality. However, de Martino also notes negative outcomes, specifically, pathological delusions brought on by the negation of loss. In this scenario, loss precipitates the survivors into a centrifugal reorganization of their emotional lives until there is a detachment from reality. De Martino observes that this scenario produces a dissipation of rational and physical energies that lead to no way out of emotional misery. Ilse's attitude towards her goal of forever enacting the dead Poet's *TFC* progressively pushes her toward taking risks that at first jeopardize the financial soundness of her company, and eventually trigger her inability to see the dangers that face her. This is exemplified by her decision to perform in front of the Giants' servants. In this case, unlike de Martino's observation of forgetfulness as an observed solution for the crisis of the mourners, Ilse does not forget the trauma. In fact, she painfully relives the unconsummated relationship with the Poet, and assumes the guilt of his fateful decision, to the point where she embraces her sacrifice in front of a brutish audience. The dead Poet is the overarching yet invisible character in *MG*, the one who has the power to direct Ilse's actions.[21]

Repetition of Art

Pirandello recreates the actor-audience interplay entirely on stage, where characters are actors who play characters in the play (*TFC*) within the play (*MG*) to the never-seen audience of the Giants' servants. In other words, in the most meta-theatrical of Pirandello's plays, viewers see the staging of the theatrical discovery of the repetition of art in theatre. Such repetition reinforces the centrality of art, as it calls on memory to recover past stage events. Caught between tradition and innovation, viewers in the audience of *MG* are asked to continuously adapt to the next contexts that the plays stages.[22] Ilse performs the Poet's *TFC* in a manner that does not meet the expectations of her audience made up of the *Scalognati* and her acting company. The cathartic ending — understood as the cleansing of one's toxic emotions — is not reached in *MG*. In Ilse's case, she never processes her guilt for the Poet's suicide. Her unbending desire to perform is tantamount to the elaboration of a repressed emotion whose pain is temporarily eased only by insisted repetition. This specific form of short-lived catharsis is for her character alone. Meanwhile, the violent deaths of Ilse and two of her actors generate only anxiety and interior conflict for the audience rather than providing them with a cathartic outburst of repressed emotion. In the excess of passionate feelings captured by *MG*, Pirandello leaves audiences without the means to release the emotions that belong only to the background story of the play, and thus leaves them stuck in a circularity that only death will break.

Death overshadows the effort to bring the myth of Art before an audience, as *MG* does. To overcome distress at the sight of the ultimate work of art, one from which the creator, a mortal human being, will remain excluded,[23] Hinkfuss, the character/director of *Tonight We Improvise*, believes renewed life can be brought under one condition:

> Ogni scultore (io non so, ma suppongo) dopo aver creato una statua, se veramente crede d'averle dato vita per sempre, deve desiderare ch'essa, come una cosa viva, debba potersi sciogliere dal suo atteggiamento, e muoversi, e parlare. Finirebbe d'essere statua; diventerebbe persona viva. Ma questo patto soltanto, signori, può tradursi in vita e tornare a muoversi ciò che l'arte fissò nell'immutabilità d'una forma; a patto che questa forma riabbia movimento da noi, una vita varia e diversa e momentanea: quella che ciascuno di noi sarà capace di darle.[24]

> [Every sculptor (I don't know this, but I assume it's true) after he has created a statue, if he really believes he has given it eternal life, must wish that — as a living being — it could free itself from its pose, and move about, and speak. It would cease being a statue; it would become a living person. There's only one way, ladies and gentlemen, in which something that art has fixed in the immutability of a form can come back to life and move about again. It must take back its life from us, a life that is various, diverse, and momentary; the life that each one us is able to give it.][25]

The obstacle to the survival of the characters turns out to be the survival of their creator: the maker of the statue or, in Pirandello's case, the writer, responsible for injecting life into his page. Overcome by concerns, he confesses to Marta Abba that without her presence in his life, his hand will turn into stone.[26] We can discern here a close sequence of synecdoche-metaphor: her absence would bring his body to the stillness of death. The demise of his body is the event that triggers the not-ending of his art, which becomes a perpetual source of aesthetic elevation.

Statues That Crumble

The tight and problematic relationship between creation and death is synthetically summed up by Giovanni Macchia. In his *Pirandello, o La stanza della tortura* (1981), Macchia describes the manifold meanings death assumes in Pirandello's prose:

> è morte sociale; è morte vera, fisica; morte apparente o presunta; morte della ragione; è morte avvenuta non si sa per quale misterioso disastro, di cui non si conosceranno mai le cause. Ma queste morti sono volute, cercate, esaltate perché possa essere portato sulla scena, nei modi della certezza e della più evanescente illusorietà, il grande 'teatro del ritorno', il ritorno del personaggio dinanzi agli occhi allibiti degli spettatori.

> [It is social death; it is real death, physical; apparent death or alleged; death of reason; it is death that arrived through some unknown disaster, whose causes will always remain unknown. But these deaths are wanted, looked for, intensified so that the great 'theatre of comeback', the comeback of the character, can be brought to the stage, in a manner to ensure certainty and the most evanescent illusion, in front of the stunned eyes of the spectators.][27]

Macchia captured Pirandello's goal to stress the unavoidable centrality of the character and of the author/maker as the enabler of characters' artistic eternal life.

The narrator of the short story 'Pensionati della memoria' confirms it: characters have 'la consolazione di viver sempre, finché vivo io. E se n'approfittano! V'assicuro che se n'approfittano' [the consolation of living forever, as long as I live. And they take advantage of it. Believe me: they take advantage of it].[28] The stress on the moment of artistic creation onstage evolves with Pirandello's play *Trovarsi* [To Find Oneself] (1932), where Donata, the protagonist, passionately declares her humanistic credo: 'E questo è vero... E non è vero niente... Vero è soltanto che bisogna crearsi, creare! E allora soltanto, ci si trova' [And this is true... and nothing is true... What is true is that we really need to create ourselves, create! And only then, do we find ourselves].[29] The line between the author Pirandello and his characters is both emotionally taut and blurred. Pirandello dedicates his *Trovarsi* to Marta Abba with the following words: 'A Marta Abba. Per non morire' [To Marta Abba. So as not to die]. The wish is certainly powerful and moving, but also imprecise enough to leave readers undecided as to whether the omen is for Marta, the author, or both. Pirandello is still willing to conflate the pair author/character to pursue art that can incessantly renew itself, in a space where his characters unfailingly show their inability to accept the possibility of their demise.

Reference to a statue is an indication of an enduring doubt in Pirandello. What is the meaning of the ability to complete a work of art? Pirandello had already linked the juxtaposition of life and death to the image of an unfinished work. In his *Diana e la Tuda* (1926), the first play that starred Marta Abba, the sculptor Sirio Dossi cannot bring himself to finish the statue of Diana, modelled after Tuda, his muse and wife. In the play, art (the statue Dossi obsessively works on), and life (Tuda, the young woman Dossi marries to serve as a unique model for his statue) battle for a supremacy that is impossible to achieve. Dossi is made aware of his limitations: 'non la finirà mai quella statua' [he will never finish that statue],[30] whilst Tuda, emotionally broken, stresses her imperative for him to finish it. As Dossi tells Giuncano, his older friend who questions the validity of his desperation, he is ready to pay the ultimate price to see his statue completed. Dossi attacks Tuda because he thinks she wants to destroy the statue, while instead, in a fit of delirium, she wants to hold it and become one with it. The quick series of misunderstandings has tragic consequences: Giuncano, afraid for Tuda's life, attacks Dossi and strangles him. In turn Tuda, without art becomes, as she exclaims: 'niente... più niente' [nothing... nothing].[31]

Conclusion

A myth draws its force from the rites it replicates. Repetition is key to Pirandello's modus operandi. The six characters of the celebrated play want to live; that is, be staged, because for them, as characters, performance is true life. However they are condemned to repeat incessantly the tragedy that they, and only they, can perform flawlessly. In *Enrico IV* (1922), after his homicidal madness, the title character condemns himself to a life of repetition of the rituals he envisioned as proper for a medieval emperor. Ilse too, to expiate the guilt she feels for the Poet's suicide, and devoted to the mission of art, seeks relief in the unending representation of *TFC*. Unlike the two previous works, the representation of *TFC* in *MG* ends with Ilse's murder and, as indicated in the notes of Pirandello's son, the cycle within the play is interrupted. When the Giants' Major-domo financially compensates the company for the havoc created by their servants, the stage directions stress a sense of relief for the Count in the now justified reason to end the performance of *TFC*:

> Ma si sentirà che egli, pur piangendo e protestando i suoi nobili sensi di fedeltà alla morta Poesia, s'è a un tratto come alleggerito, come liberato da un incubo; e così è Cromo, con gli altri attori (p. 264)

> [But one senses that although he weeps and protests a noble fidelity to the dead spirit of Poetry, he feels suddenly relieved, as if freed from a nightmare; and the same is true of Cromo and the other actors] (p. 185)

Maybe the Count's reaction represents the acceptance of the failed artists-to-audience message, since the 'fanatical servants of art' decide to not understand their audience, the 'fanatical servants of life' (p. 185) whom Pirandello had long recognized as the root of all problems impeding the appreciation of the arts:[32]

> non è che la Poesia sia stata rifiutata; ma solo questo: che i poveri servi fanatici della vita, in cui oggi lo spirito non parla, ma potrà pur sempre parlare un giorno, hanno innocentemente rotto, come fantocci ribelli, i servi fanatici dell'Arte, che non sanno parlare agli uomini perché si sono esclusi dalla vita (p. 264)

> [it is not that poetry has been rejected, but only this: the poor *fanatical servants of life*, in whom the spirit does not speak today but may yet speak someday, have in their innocence broken, like rebellious puppets, the *fanatical servants of art* who are incapable of speaking to men because they have withdrawn from life] (p. 185)

Exile in an isolated villa was the solution for Crotone, and so it was for the author, who pushes aside the option of re-creating a worn-out channel of communication with his audience. From *Six Characters* and *Enrico IV* onwards, Pirandello chooses to create imaginary lives with the aim not of mirroring daily reality to capture the truth, but rather of capturing it in art, in fiction (or in myth), as the only activity that allows for the continuous interpretation of human actions. His art is therefore an attempt to comprehend time and space in relation to the life of human beings, whose capability to comprehend is perforce limited by their personal beliefs and illusions. After all, the characters of *MG* perfect the sketches that Pirandello created in his novel *The Late Mattia Pascal* (1904), in which Mattia Pascal feigns his demise, and eventually resurfaces as alive for a society that is no longer ready to accept him. In *MG*, the poet is dead, with no possibility of coming back to life; the ghosts indulge themselves in fun with oneiric images of the actors; and Ilse dies a violent death. The corpses of her two actors undergo so much violence that they cannot be retrieved. However, the fact that the bodies are not seen does not make for a simplistic cliff-hanger to close an imaginary first part of the play. The story of the theatre company is really over, destroyed by the violent rage of the Mountain Giants' servants. What remains is the written text, the consequence made explicit by Cotrone:

> COTRONE: E il miracolo vero non sarà mai la rappresentazione, creda, sarà sempre la fantasia del poeta in cui quei personaggi son nati, vivi, così vivi che lei può vederli anche senza che ci siano corporalmente. (p. 246)

> [COTRONE: And the real miracle will never be the representation, believe me, but always the imagination of the poet where those characters were born alive, so alive that you can see them even when they are not there in the flesh.] (p. 174)

MG is like the unfinished statue in *Diana e la Tuda* that Sirio Dossi knew he would never be able to finish. Until his art and that of Marta Abba are recognized, Pirandello seems to engage in a battle against the formal completion of what he senses is his last work: 'Forse è l'ultimo incendio di idee che mi divorerà!' [Perhaps this is the last flaming of ideas that will devour me];[33] 'sarà forse il mio ultimo lavoro drammatico' [perhaps it will be my last dramatic work].[34] That is, *MG* can be kept in balance only without formally completing it.

Yet, in a moment of involuntary clairvoyance, Pirandello seems to sense the approaching of a threshold: 'Spero ardentissimamente, Marta mia, d'aver poco ormai da vivere: non lo desidero più, veramente. Mi sento mancare ogni voglia e tutto, il mio stesso corpo, m'è ingombro' [I must fervently hope, my dear Marta, that I have little time left to live: I truly do not wish to prolong it. I feel every desire vanishing from me, and everything, my very body, is a burden to me].[35] In September 1936, Marta Abba left Italy for the US. Pirandello's personal relationship with her was causing him increased emotional hardship, and on 21 November 1936 he wrote to her:

> Non faccio più nulla, Marta mia, sto tutto il giorno a pensare, solo come un cane, a tutto ciò che avrei da fare, ancora tanto, tanto, ma non mi pare che metta più conto di aggiungere altro a tutto il già fatto; che gli uomini non lo meritino, incornati come sono a diventare sempre più stupidi e bestiali e rissosi. Il tempo è nemico. Gli animi avversi. Tutto è negato alla contemplazione, in mezzo a tanto tumulto e a tanta feroce brama di carneficina. Ma poi, nel segreto del mio cuore, c'è una più vera e profonda ragione di questo mio annientarmi nel silenzio e nel vuoto. C'era prima una voce, vicino a me, che non c'è più; una luce che non c'è più ...[36]

> [I do not do anything anymore, my Marta, I spend the whole day thinking, alone like a dog, about everything I still should be doing, so much — yet it doesn't seem to me worthwhile to add anything anymore to all that I've already done; people do not deserve it, pigheaded as they are becoming more and more — stupid, beastly, and quarrelsome. Our times are against us: people are ill disposed. Meditation is impossible amidst so much turmoil and such fierce longing for slaughter. But then, in the secret depths of my heart, there is a more real and profound reason for my self-annihilation into silence and emptiness. There was once a voice, close to me, that is no longer there; a light that is no longer there...] [37]

For Pirandello, Marta Abba's departure was not only going to mean physical separation. As she embarked on a new chapter of her life, an emotionally drained

Pirandello probably realized that Marta Abba's role as Ilse could be sacrificed on the altar of art. Without Marta Abba nearby, engaged in performing a play that remained incomplete, Pirandello reveals an emotional inertia that no longer pushes him to write the ending, indicating that *MG* certainly discusses the destiny of the arts and of theatre, but also that it tells the story of Pirandello. After all, *MG* embodies the coexistence of the push toward a solution to Ilse's need to play her drama, and the risk this solution posed of undermining the aesthetic and ethical impulses that had led Pirandello towards his creation. His late novel *Uno, nessuno e centomila* [One, No-One and One Hundred Thousand] (1926) stresses the inability to close. Vitangelo Moscarda, its protagonist, muses:

> La vita non conclude. E non sa di nomi, la vita [...] muojo ogni attimo, io, e rinasco nuovo e senza ricordi: vivo e intero, non più in me, ma in ogni cosa fuori.[38]

> [Life knows no conclusion. Nor does it know anything of names. [...] I am dying every instant, and being born anew and without memories: alive and whole, no longer in myself, in everything outside.][39]

MG constitutes Pirandello's supreme message about art and the manifestation of his decision of how to advocate for it — albeit in an expected manner — despite the audience's rejection of his message, as portrayed in the play itself. To counter his fear, *MG* provided a feeble reason to hope. One can cling on the future tense in 'potrà pur sempre parlare un giorno' (p. 264) [may yet speak someday (p. 185)], as the possibility that art might at some future point communicate with the 'servants of life'. Ilse/Marta must perform, not only to pay homage to the dead Poet, but in order to break out of her small role in society and, with her sacrifice, live forever as a character. As Cotrone maintains the primacy of imagination over reason, his villa radiates light, but it is a spectral light that does little to contain the ghosts that inhabit it. With his play, Pirandello gives voice to the unsaid, the often-neglected element that animates the phantoms of human beings' life, who reach for help, and are often silenced and rejected, except in literature that gives them voice. With the ghosts of *MG*, Pirandello asserts his role in modernity. The apotropaic function of *MG* ends with Pirandello's death, and the villa is the cenotaph he built for himself.

Pirandello never saw his play staged. It premiered in 1937, directed by Renato Simoni in the Florentine Boboli Garden setting.[40]

Notes to Chapter 5

1. Corrado Alvaro, *Scritti dispersi 1921–1956* (Milan: Bompiani, 1995), p. 462.
2. Luigi Pirandello, *La nuova colonia, Lazzaro, I giganti della montagna*, ed. by Marziano Guglielminetti (Milan: Garzanti, 1995), p. 176. Henceforth, page numbers for this Italian edition are given in the text.
3. Luigi Pirandello, *Three Plays*, trans. by Anthony Mortimer (Oxford: Oxford University Press, 2014), p. 126. Henceforward, page numbers for this English edition are given in the text.
4. *TFC* was based on Pirandello's 1902 short story 'Il figlio cambiato'. As an independent work with music by Gian Francesco Malipiero, *TFC* opened separately from *MG* in Braunschweig, Germany, on 13 January 1934. Its Italian debut in Rome on 24 March was attended by Mussolini, who harshly criticized it, and prohibited further performances.

5. Pirandello began writing *MG* in 1929 and, as his son Stefano witnessed, kept thinking about it until the eve of his death in December 1936, when he told his son how to finish the story. His notes are now added to the text of the play that Pirandello never saw published in its entirety. Cf. Susanna Barsella, 'Il silenzio dei *Giganti*: arte e parola nell'ultima opera di Pirandello', *Italian Quarterly*, 38 (2001), 37–51, for discussion on the inclusion of the notes. The first part of *MG* was published in *Nuova Antologia*, 359 (16 December 1931), 475–501; the second part in *Quadrante*, 19 (November 1934), 13–25.

6. With 'myths', Pirandello intended to probe what he defined as archetypical truths of the meaning of life to sustain, in Nietzschean terms, the foundations of new civilizations. He wrote about myths in a note to 'Fantasmi', the first part of *MG*, published in 1931: 'Questo lavoro è stato scritto nei primi mesi del 1931. Un solo accenno verso la fine fa arguire che l'azione proseguirà, ma del resto è compiuto, e può stare a sé. Fa parte de *I giganti della montagna*, che è il terzo dei miei miti moderni. Il primo (religioso) è il *Lazzaro*, il secondo (sociale) è *La nuova colonia*; questo è il mito dell'Arte' [This work was written in the first months of 1931. A single allusion toward the end lets one deduce that the action will continue, but after all it is complete, and it can stand alone. It belongs to *The Mountain Giants*, which is the third of my modern myths. The first one (religious) is *Lazarus*, the second (social) is *The New Colony*; this is the myth of Art]. *Nuova Antologia*, 16 December 1931, p. 475. My translation.

7. *Lettere a Marta Abba*, ed. by Benito Ortolani (Milan: Mondadori, 1994), pp. 395–96; henceforward *Lettere*.

8. Pirandello to Abba, Berlin, 17 April 1930, in *Pirandello's Love Letters to Marta Abba*, ed. and trans. by Benito Ortolani (Princeton, NJ: Princeton University Press, 1994), p. 124; henceforward *Letters*.

9. *Lettere*, p. 648.

10. Paris, 16 February 1931, *Letters*, p. 175.

11. In a 1936 interview, Pirandello used the word 'abyss' in discussing Nietzsche's essay on the birth of the tragedy: 'Nietzsche diceva che i Greci alzavano bianche statue contro il nero abisso, per nasconderlo. Sono finiti quei tempi. Io le scrollo invece per rivelarlo' [Nietzsche said that the Greeks raised white statues against the black abyss, to hide it. Those times are over. I shake them, to uncover it]. Nino Borsellino, *Ritratto e immagini di Pirandello* (Bari: Laterza, 1991), p. 112. My translation.

12. Castiglioncello, 7 July 1933, *Lettere*, p. 1099.

13. Ilse's martyrdom (pp. 136, 202); the Poet's suicide ('The fellow who killed himself', p. 129; 'that poor devil wouldn't have killed himself', p. 140; 'He killed himself because he was with her!', p. 141); and Ilse's ensuing guilt ('I loved him, you see. And I made him die', p. 142); premonition of death (Ilse: 'I'm dying of it', p. 143; 'I feel practically dead', p. 162; Spizzi: 'Let me go. I can't take it any more. I'm off to finish it', p. 170); recounting of homicides (Cotrone: 'the story, Countess, of a carter who gave a lift one night to a small boy [...] Hearing two or three coppers jingling in the child's pocket, he killed him in his sleep and took the cash to buy some tobacco', p. 151); images of the after-life as the one hundred marching souls of the Purgatory led by Angel Hundred-and-One ('I am the Angel Hundred-and-One and these who have escorted you thus far are souls from Purgatory. As soon as you [Sgricia] arrive, set yourself right with God, for before midday you will die', p. 152; 'Two columns of the souls in Purgatory file past in the form of winged angels and in their midst on a majestic white horse rides the Angel Hundred-and-One', p. 164).

14. Cf. Paolo Puppa, 'La scena e i suoi fantasmi: dai Sei personaggi ai Giganti della montagna', *Rivista italiana di drammaturgia*, 6 (1977), 71 — 102 (p. 82); Giovanni Macchia, 'Spiriti e personaggi', in *Pirandello, o La stanza della tortura* (Milan: Mondadori, 1981), pp. 54–62.

15. Marvin Carlson, *The Haunted Stage: The Theatre as Memory Machine* (Ann Arbor: University of Michigan Press, 2003), p. 15. Cf. also Adrian Curtin, *Death in Modern Theatre: Stages of Mortality* (Manchester: Manchester University Press, 2019), pp. 5–19.

16. Many elements contribute to Pirandello's elaboration of *MG*, traced both in numerous accounts of theatrical life and his own past literary productions. In a play defined as the strongest example of *magnetismo intertestuale* (Lucio Lugnani, 'In margine ai *Giganti*', in *Pirandello e il teatro. Atti del*

XXIX Convegno Internazionale, ed. by Enzo Lauretta (Milan: Mursia, 1993), 117–29 (p. 126)), many scholarly investigations have identified influences derived from Pirandello's youth in Germany, his experience as director of his theatre company (between 1925 and 1928), his clashes with the political establishment, and contemporary theatrical events more broadly. For example, it is known that Ilse is mainly calqued on Olga de Dieterichs, an actress married to count Mario Ferrari, who financed de Dieterichs's theatre company, an artistic endeavour that, similarly to Pirandello's theatre company, was short lived. Cf. Giulia Tellini, 'Pirandello e i Giganti: persone e personaggi', *Antologia Vieusseux* XXII, 64 (2016), 5–23 (pp. 9–12). Cornelia Klattke identifies another model for Ilse in the popular *Pole Poppenspäler*, a short story by German author Theodor Storm. The children Lisei, of which Ilse is the likely reformulation, and Paul Paulsen are the protagonists; cf. Cornelia Klettke, 'Il teatro onirico di Pirandello alla luce della sua ricezione di Nietzsche: *I giganti della montagna*, in *La Germania di Pirandello tra sogno e realtà*', ed. by Klettke (Berlin: Frank & Timme, 2019), pp. 169–94 (pp. 179–85).

17. Pirandello's artistic output has also been defined as an 'Anthology of Spoon River' for the continuous presence of several death motifs: 'Tutta la novellistica che precede, accompagna, segue la scena pirandelliana, non fornisce allora solo temi al suo teatro, ma è un'immensa, sterminata sceneggiatura cimiteriale, una sorta di Antologia di Spoon River di vocazione narcisistica all'epitaffio, "Sentirsi incompiuti nella vita e aspirare ad integrarsi sulla scena" significa pertanto installarsi sulla scena come luogo magico, spazio funebre per mostrarsi, per autoesibirsi' [All the short stories that precede, accompany and follow the Pirandellian theatre, not only supply the themes of his theatre, but they also show an immense expanse of cemeterial literature, a kind of Anthology of Spoon River with a narcissistic calling to the epitaph, 'Feeling incomplete in life and aspire to complete oneself on stage' means therefore to set oneself up on stage as a magic place, a funereal space to show off, to flaunt oneself] (Puppa, 'La scena e i suoi fantasmi', p. 84). My translation.

18. Borsellino, *Ritratto e immagini*, pp. 105–12. The villa, the setting of the play, resembles Pirandello's secluded ancestral home, as described in his late autobiographical fragments.

19. Pirandello, 'I pensionati della memoria', in *Novelle per un anno*, ed. by Mario Costanzo, 6 vols (Milan: Mondadori, 1987), II, 734–39 (p. 734).

20. Ernesto de Martino, *Morte e pianto rituale nel mondo antico* (Turin: Bollati Boringhieri, 2008), pp. 42–48.

21. De Martino, pp. 36–54. For a discussion of the funeral epiphanies in Pirandello see Puppa, 'La scena e i suoi fantasmi', which analyses the reach of de Martino's investigations.

22. Carlson, pp. 1–15.

23. Pietro Frassica, 'I giganti e la poetica dell'incompiuta', in *Le fonti di Pirandello*, ed. by Antonio Alessia and Giuliana Sanguinetti Katz (Palermo: Palumbo, 1996), 121–33 (p. 132).

24. *Questa sera si recita a soggetto*, ed. by Roberto Alonge (Milan: Mondadori, 1993), p. 12.

25. Pirandello, *Tonight We Improvise and 'Leonora, Addio!'*, ed. and trans. by J. Douglas Campbell and Leonard Sbrocchi (Ottawa: Biblioteca di Quaderni d'italianistica, 1987), p. 38.

26. 'Mi sento cader l'anima e il fiato, ogni luce si spegne nel mio cervello, e la mano mi casca sulla carta, inerte come una pietra. Ajutami, ajutami, per carità, Marta mia, non mi lasciare, non m'abbandonare, sono gli ultimi miei momenti', Paris, 10 February 1931, *Lettere*, p. 641 [I feel my soul and my breath falling apart; every light goes out in my brain, and my hand falls on the paper, motionless as a stone. Help me, help me. For God's sake, my Marta, don't leave me, don't abandon me, I am in my last moments] *Letters*, p. 173.

27. Macchia, *Pirandello, o La stanza della tortura*, p. 181.

28. Pirandello, 'I pensionati della memoria', p. 735.

29. Pirandello, *Trovarsi*, ed. by Marta Abba (Milan: Mursia, 1971), p. 152.

30. Pirandello, *Diana e la Tuda. Libero Andreotti e Pirandello* (Florence: Giunti, 1994), p. 40.

31. Pirandello, *Diana e la Tuda*, p. 126.

32. Through Cotrone, Pirandello had similarly criticized the snobbish intellectual approach of 'gente istruita' [Educated people] who 'laugh at the idea' at the centre of *TFC*: 'streghe della notte, streghe del vento, che il popolo chiama "Le Donne"' (p. 247) [wind-riding witches of the night that humble folk call *the Women*] (p. 175), who snatch and replace babies in their cradles.

33. Berlin, 22 April 1929, *Letters*, p. 72; *Lettere*, p. 142.

34. Castiglioncello, 7 July 1933, *Lettere*, p. 1099.

35. Rome, December 9, 1935, *Letters*, p. 304; *Lettere*, p. 1242.

36. *Lettere*, p. 1387.

37. Rome, 21 November 1936, *Letters*, pp. 335–36.

38. Pirandello, *Uno, nessuno e centomila*, *Tutti i romanzi*, ed. by Giovanni Macchia (Milan: Mondadori, 2010), pp. 901–02. Cf. also *Quaderni di Serafino Gubbio, operatore*, in the same volume, p. 614: 'Di questa vita, senza requie, che non conclude' [Of this life without rest, which never comes to an end], trans. in Pirandello, *Shoot! The Notebook of Serafino Gubbio, Cinematograph Operator*, trans. by C. K. Scott Moncrieff (New York: Dutton, 1926), p. 151.

39. Pirandello, *One, No One and One Hundred Thousand*, trans. by Samuel Putnam (New York: Dutton, 1933), pp. 264–65.

40. For information on the history of the representations of *MG*, cf. Stefania Giammarino, 'La messinscena come *restauro teatrale*: i *Giganti* di Pirandello', *Studi e problemi di critica testuale*, 93 (2016), 211–36.

CHAPTER 6

❖

The (Un)performability of Death and Violence on Stage

Dominic Glynn

Université d'Evry Paris-Saclay

Introduction

In Tom Stoppard's *Rosencrantz and Guildenstern are Dead* (1967), two characters on the lookout for their personal Godot bump into a troupe of travelling tragedians.[1] The company is from the 'blood, love and rhetoric school' that specializes in the performance of 'deaths and disclosures, universal and particular'.[2] In order to rouse, and no doubt arouse, the curiosity of the two passers-by, the company leader outlines the extent of his repertoire. It includes 'murderers', 'ghosts', 'battles from the skirmish level', and an uncensored version of the Rape of the Sabine Women in which the audience is invited to participate. As he wryly notes, the players 'do on stage the things that are supposed to happen off'.[3] The line fittingly describes the play, which rewrites William Shakespeare's *Hamlet* from the perspective of two minor characters.[4] It also provides an ironic commentary on Elizabethan and Jacobean revenge tragedy, a genre in which 'blood, love and rhetoric' take centre stage.

Death and violence have been star attractions in European theatre since the 'great homicidal classics'[5] of Aeschylus, Sophocles and Euripides. However, this has not necessarily meant performing all deaths in full view of an audience. Indeed, at different points in theatre history, attempts to show murder, suicide and corpses on stage provoked heated disputes among theorists, moralists and practitioners. For instance, in Sophocles' *Ajax* (Αἴας, 445 BCE), the title character runs onto his sword in order to commit suicide. However, scholars have argued for centuries about whether that death was originally performed on stage, while directors are unsure about whether to do so in modern productions today.[6]

From a practical perspective, a major issue is how to make a stage death credible. How might audiences be expected to believe the 'fake' deaths performed on stage, when they are exposed to 'real' deaths, either in the form of public executions in the Early Modern Period, or, more recently, in the news on TV and the Internet? From an ideological perspective, theorists have grappled with the question of whether it is 'right' to portray violent murders. Moralists have been concerned with the potential effects viewing violence and death might have on audience members. Some have feared that they could be incited to go on to replicate the violence they witness. Others, taking an opposing position, have argued that violence (and death) can act as a repellent, meaning that their performance may shock audiences into behaving well. Others still have suggested that the 'play's the thing wherein [to] catch the conscience'[7] of murderers in the audience, and that the viewing of violence might encourage them to disclose hitherto unknown crimes.

In short, there is both the issue of whether one 'does' portray violence and death, coupled with that of whether one 'should' do so. In order to comment on both the prevalence of on-stage deaths in drama and in the productions of theatre plays, as well as on the value of (not) performing death, my essay suggests that the conceptual notion of '(un)performability' may be used. I begin with a theoretical presentation of this concept, highlighting how it is relevant for comparative cross-cultural and cross-temporal analysis of theatre traditions, with the specific intention of gaging attitudes to the performance of death. I move on to reflect on how death is written into plays, such as *Hamlet*, and what this implies for their productions. I then provide critical discourse analysis of debates concerning both the practicalities and the morality of staging death. For the most part, examples are taken from the English and French theatre traditions, and primarily from the Early Modern stages, though references to other contexts will be provided where appropriate.

Performability

In engineering and computer science, performability refers to the relative feasibility of a given course of action while taking into account which resources are available.[8] Applied to the theatre, the term may describe how possible it is to produce a play in financial terms. Plays with frequent set changes or expensive props, for instance, may be 'unperformable' by small companies with limited budgets — it is not within every company's reach to put on a Broadway musical. Spectacular scenes resulting in on-stage deaths can be costly to stage. The barricade scenes and resulting deaths of Gavroche and the revolutionaries in the twentieth-century musical *Les Misérables*, for instance, requires considerable investment in sets and stage accessories (guns and smoke machines), as well as in actors. Death on stage was also an investment in the Early Modern era. The Elizabethan theatre manager Philip Henslowe recorded a number of items for the stage belonging to the Rose Theatre that were specifically relevant to the staging of violent endings in Christopher Marlowe's plays. These included a Hellmouth for the final scene of *Doctor Faustus* (1589), and a cauldron for Barabbas to fall into at the end of *The Jew of Malta* (1589).[9]

Material conditions, however, are only one part of the story when it comes to assessing performability. A play may be deemed 'unperformable' on moral or aesthetic grounds also. Theatre history is replete with instances where for political, moral, or religious reasons, performances were banned. In France, early versions of Molière's *Tartuffe ou l'imposteur* were forbidden between 1664 and 1667 because the play was ill received by Church leaders, who considered that their authority was under threat. In England, until its abolition in 1968, censorship by the Lord Chamberlain's office meant that certain scripts were deemed 'unperformable' on the British stages because they contravened the moral standards of the censors. One of the last plays to be refused a licence in the UK by the Lord Chamberlain's office was Barbara Wright's 1968 *The Car Cemetery*, a translation of *Le Cimetière des voitures* by Arrabal (1958). It was refused on the grounds that it mocked religion. Intriguingly, two deaths are mentioned in the censor's report: the killing (offstage) of a baby, and the crucifixion (on stage) of the lead character to a bicycle. While these are not the only reasons why the play was not granted a licence, they greatly contributed to the refusal. Specifically, the method of killing the lead character was objected to, as it invited the audience to consider him as a Christ-like figure — particularly given his name, 'Emanou'.[10]

The extent to which a text is deemed performable in this sense has less to do with its intrinsic qualities than how it is read by a particular culture. In this regard, discussions of the relative performability of a dramatic work, or part of a dramatic work, can usefully be linked to discussions of '(un)translatability' and 'non-translation'.[11] A work is not 'untranslatable' in absolute terms but rendered difficult or impossible to translate into a particular context. For instance, any material which is perceived to be 'anti-China' or 'obscene' will not be translated in the People's Republic of China.[12] Similarly, a play is not 'unperformable' in absolute terms. Such an understanding of the relativity of '(un)performability' helps allay Susan Bassnett's misgivings about 'performability'. Bassnett expresses concerns that '[a]ttempts to define the "performability" inherent in theatre translations never go further than generalized discussion about the need for fluent speech rhythms'.[13] At the same time, she contends that appreciating a text's performability plays a large part in its acceptance by theatre professionals, particularly in English-speaking contexts. This explains the relative lack of permeability of the contemporary English stage to works that do not fit the norms of British theatre writing.[14] The problem, for Bassnett, is that even if a set of criteria could be devised in order to assess the performability of a text, this set would be culture specific and subject to variation.

Cultures display considerable variations in performance traditions, and thus plays which are regularly performed in one context are not necessarily performed in another. This goes for cultures that are relatively 'distant', such as those of Africa and of Europe, but also for those that are relatively 'close', such as those of France and England. Regarding cultures that are relatively distant, Laura Bohannan provides an amusing account of her inability to tell the story of Shakespeare's *Hamlet* to the Tiv in Nigeria, owing to the fact that concepts such as the ghost of Hamlet's father, monogamous marriage and Hamlet's madness were unintelligible to the elders of the tribe.[15] Regarding cultures that are relatively close, Shakespeare may well be the most performed playwright on the twenty-first century French stages; however, this was not always the case. Victor Hugo's defence of Shakespeare's work in his preface to *Cromwell* (1827) is evidence enough of its lack of acceptability in France in the early part of the nineteenth century.[16] Another way of putting this is that Shakespeare's works were relatively unperformable on the French stage — though there had been notable adaptations by Jean-François Ducis.

Various factors make the work of a given author more or less performable. From a systemic perspective, certain cultures are more or less resistant to performance. A particular context might be labelled 'hostile' or 'hospitable' to performance depending on the levels of resistance to the performing arts in general or to theatre more specifically. In England, in the context of the Civil War, a parliamentary edict in 1642 effectively outlawed theatre performances until 1660, when it was repealed with the Restoration of the Monarchy. In this context, it was virtually impossible to stage any drama at all — irrespective of whether it contained any stage violence or deaths. It can be that a whole work is regarded as unperformable because it is completely at odds with the dominant poetics or ideology of a culture. In this case, it is highly unlikely that it will be staged. For instance, there is little to no tradition of Chinese traditional opera [戲曲, *xiqu*] in Europe, which means that *The Peony Pavilion* [牡丹亭, *Mudanting,* 1598] is relatively unperformable on contemporary European stages. It can also be that only part of a work is considered problematic and that steps are taken to either remove or adapt it. Scenes might be deleted or rewritten, and certain stage actions might be pushed into the wings. This is what regularly occurred during the Restoration period in England (1660–88) when French comedies were rewritten to suit the tastes of theatre patrons in London.[17] For instance, Thomas Shadwell adapted Molière's *L'Avare* (1668) as *The Miser* (1672) by adding eight new characters. Regarding the (un)performability of death, a notable rewriting of Shakespeare's *King Lear* by Nahum Tate (*The History of King Lear,* 1681) removed Cordelia's death from the play, an amendment that was much approved by Samuel Johnston, for one, who could not bear this event in the original.[18]

Analysis of the performability of a text requires analysis of discourse on performance practice in order to ascertain the norms in a set cultural and temporal context. Concerning the staging of death, clearly, in a very hostile environment to performance, it is unlikely that stage deaths will be authorized, since few or no performances are allowed at all.[19] However, even in comparatively hospitable environments it can be that certain acts are not permitted. Thinking through the (un)performability of death means reflecting on who is allowed to die, in what ways, and in which contexts. It involves considering how death is written into plays, how it is performed by actors and how it is discussed by theorists.

Poetic Norms

Elizabethan and Jacobean revenge tragedies were bloody affairs. To take *Hamlet*, arguably the most famous play in the English repertoire, and a leading example of the genre, much of the stage action revolves around death. A total of eight characters die in the play (Polonius, Ophelia, Rosencrantz and Guildenstern, Gertrude, Claudius, Laertes and Hamlet — in this order), while three deaths occur before the action begins (Yorick, Fortinbras Senior and King Hamlet — again, in this order). Those that happen during the course of the play are varied in nature, and occur as the result of stabbing, drowning, duelling and poisoning. Death from natural causes is conspicuously absent from the list. With the exception of

Ophelia, who dies offstage, and Polonius, who is killed in 'the arras', a liminal space somewhere between on and offstage, the deaths take place in full view of the audience. Additionally, there is a ghost (of King Hamlet) which roams the ramparts of Elsinore, Hamlet contemplates a skull (Yorick's), and jumps into an open grave (Ophelia's).[20] He also considers suicide in one of the most famous stage monologues of the English language ('to be or not to be').[21]

Hamlet is hardly exceptional in its portrayal of death and violence if one considers other tragedies from the same period (1558–1625) in which the lead protagonist sets out to avenge an affront. Indeed, these works display high levels of invention in the different deaths that they stage. *The Revenger's Tragedy* (1608), for instance, features a particularly unusual revenge killing.[22] The plot revolves around Vindice, who seeks to avenge his lover, murdered by a lecherous Duke for having refused his advances. In his opening soliloquy, Vindice contemplates the skull of his mistress in a manner not dissimilar to Hamlet's musings over Yorick:

> Thou sallow picture of my poison'd love,
> My study's ornament, thou shell of death,
> Once the bright face of my betrothed lady,
> When life and beauty naturally fill'd out
> These ragged imperfections
> When two heaven-pointed diamonds were set
> In those unsightly rings — then 'twas a face
> So far beyond the artificial shine
> Of any woman's bought complexion.[23]

It might be possible to interpret the above quotation as a reflection on the passage of time, were it not for the first line. The metaphors of decay are in keeping with poetry from the period, which featured melancholic musings on how all things must pass.[24] The 'sallow picture' has replaced the 'bright face' of Vindice's love, while 'unsightly rings' have displaced the 'two heaven-pointed diamonds'. As for the misogynistic remark about 'any woman's bought complexion', it could have been uttered by Hamlet ('I have heard of your paintings, well enough').[25] Like that of the Prince of Denmark, Vindice's melancholy is pathological, provoking murderous rage. His love was 'poison'd' by a jealous rival, and now this act of violence has infected his own memory to the extent that the object he holds functions solely as the catalyst for revenge. With the assistance of his brother Hyppolito, Vindice sets out to destroy the entire royal household. When it comes to the Duke, Vindice sets up a private meeting with what is supposed to be a bashful young country woman but is in fact the skull dressed up 'in tires' and covered in poison.[26] As the Duke leans over to kiss his mistress, his lips touch those of the anointed skull and he meets his fate while being taunted by the two brothers. Hyppolito stamps on the Duke as his 'teeth are eaten out' by the poison. Vindice then asks his brother to 'nail down' the Duke's tongue with his dagger before forcing him to watch his wife (The Duchess) and his illegitimate son (The Bastard) kiss and hatch a plan to get rid of him, unaware that he is in fact dying beside them.

Such creativity in staging violence is apparent in other plays of the period. *The Spanish Tragedy* (1587), *The Atheist's Tragedy* (1611), *Women Beware Women* (1621) all contain violent acts and deaths. Even within the Shakespearean canon, there is much blood spilt in *Macbeth* (1606), *King Lear* (1606) and *Titus Andronicus* (1594), with beheading, eye-gouging, rape, mutilation and murder on the menu. It is safe to assume that if these violent stage actions were performed on stage, as some undoubtedly were, there was sufficient appetite among the viewing public for such 'blood, love and rhetoric'. As Andrew Gurr puts it bluntly '[t]he playhouses were not places for art or culture, and their poetry was the very impure poetry of money'.[27] The violent acts in the dramaturgies of the plays imply that, at the very least, it was not unusual to die on stage, and it may even have been the norm. Indeed, there are over one hundred references to corpses in the stage directions of the period, suggesting that dead bodies were a common sight.[28] This is also apparent from the number of dumb shows that depicted murder. Hamlet makes use of the dumb show in the performance at court of the 'Murder of Gonzago', which he commissions to test Claudius in Act III, Scene 2. However, an even more imaginative use of this device occurs in John Webster's *The White Devil* (1612). The Duke Brachiano contrives to kill his wife, Isabella, as well as his brother-in-law, Camillo, who suspects that he has been unfaithful. The murders are pulled off with the assistance of Flamineo, his lover's brother. Since the Duke is not able to be present during the murders, he goes to see a conjurer who creates an impression of the scene. On stage, two murders are acted out then commented. In the first, Isabella dies through inhaling poisonous fumes from a picture of her husband. The conjurer then provides an explanation of what the character has seen:

> She's poisoned
> By the fumed picture. 'Twas her custom nightly,
> Before she went to bed, to go and visit
> Your picture, and to feed her eyes and lips
> On the dead shadow: Doctor Julio,
> Observing this, infects it with an oil,
> And other poison'd stuff, which presently
> Did suffocate her spirits.[29]

In the second mimed sequence, which takes place just a few moments after, another strange death occurs. Flamineo 'writhes' the neck of Camillo with the help of the neck of a vaulting horse and disguises the murder as an accident. Again, the conjurer describes what occurred right after:

> You saw them enter, charg'd with their deep healths
> To their boon voyage; and, to second that,
> Flamineo calls to have a vaulting horse
> Maintain their sport; the virtuous Marcello
> Is innocently plotted forth the room;
> Whilst your eye saw the rest, and can inform you
> The engine of all.[30]

The verbal description of what has occurred in stage action serves to clarify what may not have been pulled off effectively in performance. It also serves to reinforce the violence of the actions — particularly if they had been performed primarily for comic effect.

In other temporal and cultural contexts, the viewing of death on stage was not as common, or indeed, palatable. In tragedies with particularly bloody outcomes, such as those of Aeschylus, Sophocles and Euripides, deaths occurred as noises off, only to be commented by the characters on stage. As Amnon Kabatchnik puts it vividly:

> A messenger would arrive at a climactic moment and relate in stark, vivid images how Agamemnon was axed to bits by his wife, how Oedipus gouged out his own eyes, how Medea threw her sons from a rooftop, how Heracles was scorched to death by a poisonous robe, how the raging women of Thebes savagely lynched their king.[31]

Unlike their later Elizabethan counterparts, where the focus is on showing violence, here it is described. A famous example of such a description is in Euripides' *Iphigenia at Aulis* [Ἰφιγένεια ἡ ἐν Αὐλίδι], when a messenger comes on stage to relate the sacrifice of Iphigenia, stating that a heifer was substituted in her place at the last moment by the goddess Artemis. When Ariane Mnouchkine staged *Les Atrides* in 1992, *Iphigenia at Aulis* was followed by Aeschylus' *Agamemnon* [Ἀγαμέμνων] in which the Chorus, at the start of the play, give a different, more bloody account of the event. The inclusion of two contrasting narratives played doubt on the version provided by the messenger in the first place. In Mnouchkine's production, it was precisely because the action was related through two different accounts rather than seen by the audience that meant that doubt arose regarding the veracity of the first narrative.[32]

From a dramaturgical perspective, not performing death on stage provides dramatic affordance. The trade off, however, is a loss of spectacle. The extent to which violence and death are better as noises off is an issue that runs through discussions of performance in European theatre history. Indeed, dramatic theory, from Aristotle onwards, has grappled with whether it is better to shock by showing or to frighten by describing. For instance, Horace, in his *Ars Poetica*, argued that while the mind is stirred more by visual images than by descriptions, certain actions are best heard rather than seen: 'non tamen intus | digna geri promes in scaenam multaque tolles | ex oculis, quae mox narret facundia praesens' [But don't reveal | On stage what should be hidden, keep things from sight | That eloquence can soon relate to us directly].[33] Actions that are best described included, for Horace, violent actions and stage deaths. For later theorists, in early modern France, notably, there was much discussion about whether death or frightful actions should even be described. For instance, the dramatist and theorist Hippolyte-Jules Pilet de La Mesnardière argued that tragedy should be less interested in showing frightful actions than in getting audiences to pity the characters for their misfortunes.[34] In the nineteenth century, Victor Hugo's preface to *Cromwell* mocked Voltaire, quoting the latter's aversion to Greek drama that offered 'des spectacles non moins révoltants pour nous' [performances that are no less shocking to us] with blood running from the eyes of Oedipus, or Clytemnestra's cries for help as she is killed by her son.[35]

While the dramaturgies of seventeenth-century French tragedies do not soak the boards with blood, this does not mean that there are not any stage deaths at all. Among the deaths that do take place on stage is that of Phèdre in Racine's play of the same name. Phèdre falls hopelessly in love with her son in law (Hippolyte) and this consuming passion is the catalyst for the tragedy. At the end of the play, with the object of her affection dead, Phèdre exposes her illegitimate love to Thésée, her husband, and reveals she has taken poison. The inner turmoil of the character is manifested by this chosen mode of dying. From the text, it appears that she dies on stage. Panope exclaims: 'Elle expire, seigneur' [literally: She expires, my Lord]. Owing to the different values of the present simple in French, this line could be understood in several ways. It could potentially be rendered in English as 'she dies, my lord', 'she is dying, my lord', or 'she is dead, my lord'. It is possible that Phèdre dies immediately after having spoken her last line. Thus, Panope is like a doctor who pronounces her dead on the scene: 'she is dead, my lord'. With 'she dies', the situation becomes potentially more interesting, as it is his speech act that makes the Queen die. A third possibility is that Phèdre is dying but not yet dead when Panope speaks the lines. Phèdre could potentially agonize on stage for the remainder of the scene, since the last lines spoken by Thésée make no direct reference to her being either dead or alive. Conceivably, a director may decide to have Phèdre die alone after Thésée has left the stage in order to provide a physical manifestation of the inner turmoil that the character has experienced throughout the play.

During the seventeenth century, it was possible for Racine's Phèdre to die on stage because she had ingested poison and there was no blood spilt. Theoretical treatises from the period describe in detail what could be represented on stage and what was out of bounds. For instance, La Mesnardière, in setting out his rules of theatre practice, acknowledged that certain poets would find his maxims 'une contrainte insupportable' [an unbearable constraint], but at the same time argued that he was working for the judicious poets who were not content with just the 'vil applaudissement d'une populace ignorante' [the base clamour of an ignorant rabble].[36] A particular constraint that playwrights had to deal with in seventeenth-century France was how to imitate the Ancients. In their interpretative readings of Aristotle, theorists such as Abbé d'Aubignac and Georges de Scudéry evaluated the performability of death and violence on stage. Specifically, as Emmanuelle Hénin notes, the latter claimed that blood must not flow on stage by invoking 'cette règle qui défend d'ensanglanter la scène' [this rule that forbids the bloodying of the stage].[37] However, Hénin argues that there was 'un tabou implicite' [an implicit taboo] rather than a hard-and-fast rule in classical theory concerning blood on stage.[38] Corneille even tried to show that deaths occurred on stage in Ancient Greece, using the examples of Ajax's suicide in Sophocles's eponymous play and the murder of Clytemnestra in Electra [Ἠλέκτρα] by Sophocles and Euripides. In the 'Examen' of his own play Horace, he considers death in light of its credible representation and comes down firmly on the side of its lack of credibility.[39]

If Phèdre burns on the inside as the result of ingesting poison, there are other stage deaths that take burning more literally. Indeed, in Molière's Dom Juan, he is swallowed up as the Commander takes him down to hell. He exclaims: 'Ô Ciel, que sens-je? Un feu invisible me brûle, je n'en puis plus, et tout mon corps devient un brasier ardent, ah!' [Oh, Heaven! What is this feeling? I am being burned by an invisible fire. I can't take it. My whole body is a massive inferno. Ah!] (v. 6).[40] These lines are followed by the stage directions: '*Le tonnerre tombe avec un grand bruit et de grands éclairs sur Dom Juan, la terre s'ouvre et l'abîme, et il sort de grands feux de l'endroit où il est tombé*' [*Thunder and lightning fall on Don Juan; the earth opens and swallows him up. Large flames emerge from the place where he fell*].

The directions provide an indication of a literal fall. The earth opens and swallows him up. At what point exactly does Dom Juan die? It is precisely when he crosses through the stage. This is an example of a difficult moment to legislate, though the fact that the play was quickly taken off stage and not revived to any great extent until Louis Jouvet's version in the twentieth century says something about its relative (un)performability, of which this liminal death was a factor. It is also possible that the difficulty in pulling off this scene convincingly without considerable technical investment may account for its lack of performance history until the twentieth century.

Practical Concerns

Performing death raises a number of practical issues. These concern the props (swords, guns, bottles of poison, etc.) that are required to 'kill off' a character. However, they also concern how to make death on stage believable. While there are instances in history of particularly elaborate spectacular public executions, notably in Ancient Rome, deaths in drama are not, generally speaking, intended to be true.[41] The Player in *Rosencrantz and Guildenstern* gives an example of an actor who was sentenced to death and who chose to die on stage, but the result was unsatisfactory:

> I got permission to have him hanged in the middle of the play — had to change the plot a bit but I thought it would be effective, you know — and you wouldn't believe it, he just wasn't *convincing*! It was impossible to suspend one's disbelief — and what with the audience jeering and throwing peanuts, the whole thing was a *disaster*![42]

The reason for this disaster is that it was 'real' rather than 'fake' or performed. While death can be staged in multiple ways, the issue of its credibility remains: does the character look like they are dying? How is the actor going to best perform such and such an action in order for the audience to believe it? This interest in the veracity of stage action is evident in both dramatic theory and the reception of players' performances.

Even when considering the Ancients, there is scope for disagreement on whether death was appropriate or not on stage. Horace, for one, thought that stage deaths were not effective:

> Ne pueros coram populo Medea trucidet,
> aut humana palam coquat exta nefarius Atreus,
> aut in auem Procne uertatur, Cadmus in anguem.
> Quodcumque ostendis mihi sic, incredulus odi.

> [Folk shouldn't see Medea slaughter her children,
> Impious Atreus mustn't openly cook human flesh,
> Nor Procne turn into a bird, or Cadmus a snake.
> Any such scenes you show me, I disbelieve, and hate.][43]

Following in Horace's footstep, French neo-classical theory discussed 'vraisemblance' at great length, particularly in relation to the portrayal of death on stage. For instance, the death of Camille in Corneille's *Horace* is problematic. Corneille himself argues that this is due to the fact that the actress chose to die on stage, when, actually if she had died in a more realistic manner, she would have fled offstage. Corneille then pushes the death into the wings and into the liminal space (both on and off stage) that such a position implies.[44]

This is apparent in the 1641 edition, where Camille is 'blessée derrière le théâtre' [wounded backstage], according to the stage directions.[45] Running off stage to do the killing saves a badly choreographed stage death. It is a way to get around the impracticality of dying well on stage.

Moral Licence

In Western Europe, there have been moments in history when theatres have been shut or when what was authorized to be performed on stage was subject to vetting and caution. The moral caution about who may perform and how they might do so is one that actors and theatres have had to deal with for centuries. There is a history of strong resistance to theatre on moral grounds. Within the English theatre tradition, one of the most famous attacks on theatre is from William Prynne. Prynne attacked the stage in a famous diatribe against the performance of plays in *Histriomatix* (1632):

> [T]he penning of Playes for Play-houses, foments men in their sinnes & sinfull courses: It fostereth the spectators in their idlenesse, vanity, wantonesse, ribaldry, prodigality, lewdnesse, and the like; it drawes them on to many other sinnes, which else they might eschewe.[46]

Prynne's assault on the immorality of performance paved the way for the closing of the theatres a little under ten years later. However, he had not been the first to question the moral licence of presenting material on stage for public performance. There was a strong tradition of puritanical attacks on the stage, and it was to address an earlier onslaught of criticism that playwright Thomas Heywood replied in his *An Apology for Actors* (1612). More specifically concerning the representation of death, Heywood sets out explicitly the fact that an actor may be called upon to 'act out murder'. However, he frames the performance of murder on stage as a moral practice:

> If we present a Tragedy, we include the fatall and abortiue ends of such as commit notorious murders, which is aggrauated and acted with all the Art that may be, to terrifie men from the like abhorred practises.[47]

For Heywood, it is precisely by terrifying the audiences that the actors do a good deed. Indeed, by presenting such acts on stage, players 'terrifie' their audiences and prevent them from engaging in such activities in the future. Heywood's conception of the theatre as a moral service is even more developed. Indeed, in his understanding, the theatre can provide a type of conversion therapy not just for wannabee murderers but for a range of addictions. For instance, he explains that by acting as drunkards the players may make spectators hate this particular vice.[48] 'Art thou addicted to prodigallity, envy, cruelty, perjury, flattery, or rage?' he asks rhetorically.[49] The answer is to head to the stage where counter examples of good, temperate behaviour are provided. Likewise, for those looking to improve themselves, there are many examples of bad behaviour being ill recompensed. 'What can sooner imprint modesty in the souls of the wanton, then by discovering them unto the monstrousnesse of their sin'? In short, theatre is the remedy to all evil.

Heywood peppers his *Apology* with references to Horace and Aristotle in order to add authority to his argument. However, he is willing to go further than simply reaffirming the cathartic force of tragedy as he argues that the theatre can serve to uncover murder. He describes an episode that took place in Lin (King's Lynn) in Norfolk, in which a woman was moved by the presentation of a murder scene and the haunting of a ghost. She exclaimed, 'oh my husband', and thereby confessed to his murder.[50] Further examples of theatre's revelatory powers are provided, including that of another murderer being discovered through the performance of a play.[51] It is striking that the examples he uses resemble closely the events that occur in *Hamlet*, when the Prince seeks to establish Claudius's guilt by having the troop of players perform a murder.[52]

Heywood advocates that theatre can be a force for moral good and that performing death on stage, or murder specifically, can serve a useful public service. Yet, his treatise originated as a response to accusations about the theatre's lack of morality. Such quarrels on the morality of stage business and anti-theatrical thought have marked the English stage.

The attacks to which he was responding would eventually lead to the closure of performance venues during the Interregnum, rendering all death unperformable.

Conclusion

Dying is never easy, and particularly not on stage — even more so when the death in question is not 'true' or 'real' but needs to be considered as such by the audience. This essay has surveyed different practices of performing death on stage. It has shown that there have been different attitudes as to whether indeed death should feature on stage or whether it should happen out of sight. Theorists and practitioners have argued for diverging positions; however, it is possible to ascertain which aspects of death scenes posed greater or lesser problems to their realization. This essay has advocated performability, or rather (un)performability, as a conceptual tool through which to consider these discussions and to frame the acceptability of playing dead in front of a group of people. Such discussion seems particularly relevant at a time (2020–21) when many performance venues around the world have been closed on public health grounds.

Notes to Chapter 6

1. The research for this chapter was in part supported by the City University of Hong Kong [Grant Number 7200619], where I was formerly employed.

2. The first quotation is from Tom Stoppard, *Rosencrantz and Guildenstern are Dead* (London: Faber, 1967), p. 24. The second is from the same play, p. 17. Subsequent quotations, unless otherwise noted, are from p. 17.

3. Stoppard, *Rosencrantz and Guildenstern*, p. 21.

4. Under the generic title 'Hamlet' I am referring to the different versions of the play known as *The Tragicall Historie of Hamlet Prince of Denmarke*, or the first Quarto, published in 1603, the Second Quarto, published in 1604 under the same title, and *The Tragedie of Hamlet, Prince of Denmarke* in the First Folio edition (1623). The points made here are valid irrespective of the different versions. The same convention applies to other plays for which several versions exist, such as Christopher Marlowe's *Doctor Faustus*.

5. Stoppard, *Rosencrantz and Guildenstern*, p. 24.

6. See discussion in *Staging Ajax's Suicide*, ed. by Glenn W. Most and Leyla Ozbek (Pisa: Edizione della Normale, 2015).

7. William Shakespeare, *Hamlet*, MIT Shakespeare <http://shakespeare.mit.edu/hamlet/full.html> [accessed 9 November 2020], II. 2.

8. Discussion of '(un)performability' here follows the theoretical perspectives outlined in Dominic Glynn and James Hadley, 'Theorising (un)performability and (un)translatability', *Perspectives. Studies in Translation Theory and Practice*, 29.1 (2021), 20–32 <https://doi.org/10.1080/090767 6X.2020.1713827>.

9. See *Documents of the Rose Playhouse*, ed. by Carol Chillington Rutter (Manchester: Manchester University Press, 1984).

10. The reader's report by C. D. Heriot is available at the British Library in the Lord Chamberlain's collection: London, British Library, Lord Chamberlain's Collection, Licence Refused, LR 1968/3.

11. For a fuller discussion of 'non-translation', see Dominic Glynn, 'Towards a Theory of Non-Translation', *Across Languages and Cultures*, 22.1 (2021), 1–13 <https://doi.org/10.1556/084.2021. 00001>. Terms such as 'hospitable' and 'hostile', used in this chapter to describe performance cultures, are taken from this article.

12. See Tan Zaixi, 'Censorship in Translation: The Dynamics of Non-, Partial or Full Translations in the Chinese Context', *Meta*, 62.1 (2017), 45–68 (p. 49).

13. Susan Bassnett, 'Translating for the Theatre: The Case Against Performability', *TTR: Traduction, Terminologie, Rédaction*, 4.1 (1991), 99–111 (p. 102). Subsequent references are to the same page.

14. For more detailed analysis of the differences between French and British contemporary theatre practices, see Claire Finburgh, 'The Politics of Translating Contemporary French Theatre: How "Linguistic Translation" Becomes "Stage Translation"', in *Staging and Performing Translation*, ed. by Roger Baines, Christina Marinetti, and Manuella Perteghella (Basingstoke: Palgrave Macmillan, 2011), pp. 230–48.

15. Laura Bohannan, 'Shakespeare in the Bush', in *Investigating Culture*, ed. by C. Delaney with D. Kaspin (repr. New York: Wiley Blackwell, 2017), pp. 27–36.

16. Victor Hugo, *Cromwell-Préface* <https://fr.wikisource.org/wiki/Cromwell_-_Préface> [accessed 9 November 2020].

17. On translation as rewriting see André Lefevere, *Translation, Rewriting, and the Manipulation of Literary Fame* (London: Routledge, 1992).

18. See Samuel Johnson, 'From the Preface and Notes of his edition, 1765', in *King Lear: A Casebook*, ed. by Frank Kermode (London: Macmillan, 1969), p. 29.

19. France and the UK can be described as 'hostile' environments to performance in 2020 and 2021, since very few performances in front of live audiences have been permitted owing to social distancing rules implemented on public health grounds.

20. On spectral hauntings on stage, see contributions to this volume by Sarah Burdett and Julie Vatain-Corfdir.

21. *Hamlet*, III. 1.
22. There is some debate as to who wrote the play, though Cyril Tourneur and Thomas Middleton are likely candidates. I am using the 1744 edition, available online: <https://www.gutenberg.org/files/46412/46412.txt> [accessed 9 November 2020]. Different spellings for 'Vindice' are used, depending on the editions, but I am using the most commonly adopted version of his name.
23. *The Revenger's Tragedy*, I. 7.
24. See for instance, Eileen. M. Sperry, 'Decay, Intimacy, and the Lyric Metaphor in John Donne', *Studies in English Literature, 1500–1900*, 59.1 (2019), 45–66 <https://doi.org/10.1353/sel.2019.0002>.
25. *Hamlet*, III. 1.
26. *The Revenger's Tragedy*, III. 1. The following quotations are from the same scene.
27. Andrew Gurr, *The Shakespearean Stage, 1574–1642* (Cambridge: Cambridge University Press, 1970), p. 3.
28. N. M. Imbascio highlights how there are more than a hundred references to corpses in the stage directions of Elizabethan and Jacobean drama, in 'Corpses Revealed: The Staging of the Theatrical Corpse in Early Modern Drama' (unpublished doctoral dissertation, University of New Hampshire, 2010). Available at: <https://scholars.unh.edu/cgi/viewcontent.cgi?article=151 9&context=dissertation> [accessed 9 November 2020].
29. John Webster, *The White Devil* <https://www.gutenberg.org/files/12915/12915-8.txt> [accessed 9 November 2020], II. 2.
30. *The White Devil*, II. 2.
31. Ammon Kabatchnik, *Blood on the Stage, 1925–1950: Milestone Plays of Crime, Mystery, and Detection: An Annotated Repertoire* (Lanham, MD: Scarecrow Press, 2014), p. x.
32. See Dominic Glynn, *(Re)Telling Old Stories* (Brussels: Peter Lang, 2015), pp. 70–74.
33. Horace, *Ars Poetica* <https://www.thelatinlibrary.com/horace/arspoet.shtml> [accessed 9 November 2020].
34. Hippolyte-Jules Pilet de La Mesnardière, *La Poétique* (Paris: A. de Sommaville, 1639) <https://gallica.bnf.fr/ark:/12148/bpt6k50691s/f95.item>, p. 22 [accessed 9 November 2020]. All translations from French my own unless otherwise specified.
35. Hugo, 'Préface', in *Œuvres complètes: Cromwell-Hernani* (Paris: Librairie Ollendorff, 1912), XXIII, 7–51 <https://fr.wikisource.org/wiki/Cromwell_-_Préface> [accessed 9 November 2020].
36. La Mesnardière, *La Poétique* <https://gallica.bnf.fr/ark:/12148/bpt6k50691s/f95.item> [accessed 9 November 2020].
37. Emmanuelle Hénin, 'Faut-il ensanglanter la scène? Les Enjeux d'une controverse classique', *Littératures classiques*, 67.3 (2008), 13–32 (p. 13).
38. Hénin, 'Faut-il ensanglanter la scène?', p. 19.
39. Michael Hawcroft, 'Violence et bienséance dans l'Examen d'*Horace*: pour une critique de la notion de bienséances externes', *Dix-septième siècle*, 264.3 (2014), 549–70 (p. 565).
40. For the English translation, see Molière, *Dom Juan. The Feast of the Stone*, trans. by Daniel Smith <https://www.academia.edu/22112254/Translation_of_Don_Juan_by_Moliere> [accessed 9 November 2020].
41. See Chris Epplett, 'Spectacular Executions in the Roman World', in *A Companion to Sport and Spectacle in Greek and Roman Antiquity*, ed. by Paul Christesen and Donald G. Kyle (Oxford: John Wiley & Sons, 2013), pp. 520–32.
42. Stoppard, *Rosencrantz and Guildenstern*, p. 63.
43. For the English translation, see: Horace, *Ars Poetica*, trans. by A. S. Kilne, Poetry in Translation <https://www.poetryintranslation.com/PITBR/Latin/HoraceArsPoetica.php> [accessed 9 November 2020]. For the Latin text, see Horace, *Ars Poetica*, The Latin Library <https://www.thelatinlibrary.com/horace/arspoet.shtml> [accessed 9 November 2020].
44. See Pierre Corneille, 'Examen', in *Œuvres de Pierre Corneille*, ed. by C. Marty-Laveaux (Paris: Hachette, 1862), pp. 273–80 <https://fr.wikisource.org/wiki/Horace_(Corneille)/Édition_Marty-Laveaux> [accessed 5 May 2021].
45. Pierre Corneille, *Horace* (Paris: Augustin Courbé, 1641), p. 89 <https://fr.wikisource.org/wiki/Horace_(Corneille)/Édition_Courbé> [accessed 5 May 2021].

46. William Prynne, *Histriomatix* <https://quod.lib.umich.edu/e/eebo/A10187.0001.001/1:144.1?rgn=div2;view=fulltext > [accessed 20 November 2021] (p. 836).

47. Thomas Heywood, *An Apology for Actors* (London: Nicholas Oakes, 1612) <https://ota.bodleian.ox.ac.uk/repository/xmlui/bitstream/handle/20.500.12024/A03185/A03185.html?sequence=5&isAllowed=y> [accessed 5 May 2021].

48. Heywood, *Apology.*

49. Heywood, *Apology.*

50. Heywood, *Apology.*

51. Heywood, *Apology.*

52. On using theatre performance to force theatregoers to accept their culpability, see discussion in Sarah Burdett's contribution to this volume.

CHAPTER 7

❖

Rewriting Death on Stage:
Two Recent British Productions of
Lorca's Rural Tragedies

María Bastianes

University of Leeds

As a political martyr of the Spanish Civil War and as a supposed symbolic custodian of a Spanish *volksgeist*, the Granadan author Federico García Lorca has enjoyed an international profile and popularity afforded to no other author from Spain. Haunted by death (the subject was an obsession for the writer who, for instance, enjoyed posing as a corpse), he ironically came to this tragically premature end, which infiltrated the posthumous reception of his works. From the outset, what Barea termed 'his unceasing struggle with death' fascinated British readers, underpinned by romantic perceptions of Spanish/Andalusian culture (his association with flamenco and the popularity of his *Gypsy Ballads* (1928) contributed to this vision).[1] Unfortunately, this ostensibly 'very Spanish' and 'very un-English' taste for passion and death has also sabotaged aspects of performance, with critics (and actors) frequently complaining about the difficulties in understanding Lorca's characters' motivations and actions outside the local context.[2]

British audiences have, over the course of the decades, become more accustomed to Lorca, an author who nowadays unquestionably belongs to the hypercanon, to use Damrosch's term.[3] Paradoxically, Lorca's three so-called rural tragedies (*Blood Wedding, Yerma* and *The House of Bernarda Alba*) — the most popular elements of his theatre, albeit often considered the least avant-garde — are still largely read as merely the expression of a peculiarly Spanish culture. Trapped between a local 'realism' and a more universal interpretation, Lorca's particular model of tragedy (and the role and meaning of death within it) still constitutes a challenge for many British practitioners and sensibilities.[4] This essay explores this paradox from a comparative perspective, taking as a case study two recent English-language re-imaginings of Lorca's tragedies: Simon Stone's critically and commercially successful rewriting of *Yerma* (2017) and Marina Carr's adaptation of *Blood Wedding* (2019), directed by Yaël Farber. With the tragic denouements rewritten to (re)configure fate and mortality, these two recent commissions by the Young Vic provide a perfect opportunity to reflect on Lorca's tragic formula and its ability to inspire new dramaturgical practices in different time-space coordinates.

A Return to Tragedy: Federico García Lorca's *Blood Wedding* and *Yerma*

In a 1934 interview, Federico García Lorca proclaimed 'hay que volver a la tragedia' [we must return to tragedy].[5] By this time he had already staged with great success his first tragedy, *Blood Wedding*, and was working on a second, *Yerma*. His declaration was part of the renewed interest in Greek tragedy that sprouted in Europe and America at the beginning of the twentieth century (especially after the First World War). For evidence of this we need look no further than the many dramatic rewriting of plays and myth, such as Cocteau's *Antigone* (1922), O'Neill's *Mourning Becomes Electra* (1931), Giraudoux's *La Guerre de Troie n'aura pas lieu* (1935) and *Électre* (1937), Eliot's *The Family Reunion* (1939), Sartre's *Les Mouches* (1943), or Anouilh's *Antigone* (1944).[6] Spain, in fact, offered an early manifestation of this trend, namely Miguel de Unamuno's *Fedra* (1911), completed only one year after Gabrielle D'Annunzio's own version of the Greek myth (1909).

This movement was linked to the modernist rejection of naturalism and realism, but also to new trends in disciplines such as philosophy and the recently baptized psychoanalysis. Although in *The Cambridge Introduction to Tragedy* Wallace describes Lorca's tragedies as the result of a 'Freudian eroticized sense of fate', we can clearly distinguish a Nietzschean imprint behind the author's yearning for a return to tragedy.[7] And, in fact, the two plays this essay studies are frequently described as the closest to the Nietzschean model of tragedy, depicting the irruption of primitive/natural (Dionysian) forces that oppose the (Apollonian) principles of order, in an essentially unfair, chaotic, untameable, and destructive world. Embraced by the hero, these primitive forces replace the gods of Greek tragedy as the fatalistic drivers of the plot. As Wallace explains, 'fate for Nietzsche is a natural and irrational force [...] instead of the metaphysical dimension of the Greeks'.[8] And it is worthy of note that John Millington Synge's *Riders to the Sea*, probably an important source of inspiration for *Blood Wedding*, is also often said to have been written under the influence of Nietzsche.[9] To be more precise, Lorca's model of tragedy was the result of a combination of several dramatic trends of the period.

Another important influence was popular Spanish rural and social drama: after all, Lorca was an author who wanted to see his plays on stage and become a professional playwright.[10] Thus, the Granadan author peppered his rural tragedies with different elements and motifs frequently found in this dramatic tradition,[11] from issues related to the personal and familiar codes of honour or family feuds to socioeconomic differences or current affairs.[12] Considered a fit landscape to talk about passions and primitive forces, rural dramas were not just a Spanish fashion: this was the preferred setting for many playwrights of the period, such as Synge, Yeats, O'Neill, D'Annunzio and Tolstoy.[13] However, like the latter, Lorca left far behind the melodramatic and Manichean tradition of (late nineteenth-century and early twentieth-century) Spanish rural drama, adopting a new tragic formula:

introducing a chorus, giving natural fatality a major role in the plays, and infusing the idealized realism of rural drama with symbolic overtones that transformed everyday objects (like a knife) into the expression of telluric forces.[14] In doing so, he also surpassed the (false) localism of his predecessors — Spanish rural dramas were, after all, cultural products created by and for the city, offering a biased vision of countryside life for a bourgeois urban audience — examining instead the eternal and universal battle between instinctive and social drives.

Blood Wedding is based on a historical crime the poet discovered in the newspapers. In the play, erotic desire is the atavistic force that runs counter to the laws of marriage and conjugal love, and breaks the (unstable) peace between two rival families: The Bride (most human characters have schematic names in the play) is about to get married, but the occasion revives the old (inextinguishable) flames of a previous relationship with Leonardo (now the husband of her cousin). Dismissed by The Bride and her family in the past because of his lack of money and land — as Macintosh outlines 'in tragedy the past is never, strictly speaking, past'[15] — Leonardo also belongs to the family that killed the father and brother of The Groom. On the night of the wedding, Leonardo and The Bride elope and The Groom chases them. Both suitors find death at each other's hands and the play eventually closes with The Bride returning to the town to 'hand herself' to The Groom's mother. The latter is also a central character of the play: with her obsessive speeches about the violent deaths of her husband and first child, and her enquiries to a neighbour about The Bride's family and previous relationship with Leonardo, The Mother introduces fatality from the outset. Left with two small children and no husband at the end of the play, Leonardo's wife is set up to repeat, in a Nietzschean vein, The Mother's fate. The union of Leonardo and The Bride seems doomed to fail from the very start based on their names alone: the former is the only character referred to by his proper name, perhaps because he is the trigger of the dark 'asocial' forces of passion, whilst the latter is referred to merely by her social role, like the rest of the characters of the play. In the inner battle that Leonardo rouses in The Bride (superbly summarised in her complaints: '¡Ay, qué sin razón! No quiero | contigo cama ni cena | y no hay minuto del día | que estar contigo no quiera' [Oh, this is nonsense! I don't want to share my bed or table with you, and still, there is not a single moment I don't want to be with you]),[16] deadly sexual attraction will prevail.

In *Yerma*, Lorca simplifies the tragic structure and gives greater prominence to the chorus, while presenting a different and much more complex clash between social laws and desire. In an interview, Lorca describes the piece as lacking a plot.[17] Here, the conflict is completely internal to the main character: the play is focused on Yerma, whilst the rest of the characters around her seem to be there only to reveal the evolution and painful depth of her inner tragedy. Yerma wants to have a child, but she and her husband (Juan) are unable to conceive. With the passing of time and the fading of hopes, Yerma's desire grows ('cada vez tengo más deseos y menos esperanzas' [my desires increase progressively and in proportion to my descending hopes], she will say in Act II).[18] But, although several opportunities and temptations arise (among them the presence of the shepherd Victor) she remains stubbornly faithful to her husband. Yerma, in fact, has interiorized two social norms: the honour code that prevents a woman from cheating on her husband (or even looking as if she could),[19] but also the code that sees in motherhood the only available path for a woman's personal fulfilment, her only place and role in society. These interiorized social control devices also have external expressions: without the constraints of childcare, Yerma wanders outside the house more than she should, triggering the suspicions of her neighbours. Trapped in these social constrictions, the primitive forces of breeding that Yerma carries inside her will eventually discharge their power brutally: she will strangle her husband to death, simultaneously killing her only (morally) acceptable means of procreation.

Death in Lorca's Rural Tragedies

Death in Lorca's rural tragedies is the inevitable corollary of the unstoppable release of telluric forces put under pressure. It represents not only the feared solution to the battle between the Apollonian and Dionysian, but also the no man's land in which social codes lose their meaning. The artificial staged death is, paradoxically, a reminder that in the face of real death, social codes and conventions are equally artificial (and absurd). At the end of *Blood Wedding*, The Bride turns herself in to The Mother and asks to be punished with death — although not without proclaiming that, regardless of her flaws, she is still chaste. But, unexpectedly, her mother-in-law (not)-to-be's response is curt indifference: 'Pero ¿qué me importa a mí tu honradez? ¿Qué me importa tu muerte? ¿Qué me importa a mí nada de nada?' [What do I care about your honour, or about your death, or about anything at all?], a sentence that slams the door closed on the nineteenth-century vision of honour, which was an authentic obsession in previous rural dramas, as I have mentioned. In fact, it is possible to read the end of *Yerma* — where Juan is publicly murdered by his wife in the middle of the *romería,* a popular religious fertility festival — as a parodic inversion of the uxoricide motif of the Spanish honour drama tradition.[20] If in wife-murder plays the husband kills his spouse because the suspicion (or certainty) of infidelity prevents him from enjoying an honourable place in society, in *Yerma* the heroine's inability to produce a child has to some extent left her too without an 'honourable' social role to perform.

In her comparison of Attic tragedy and modern Irish drama, Fiona Macintosh explores how both traditions share a depiction of death as process.[21] A similar schema can be found in Lorca's tragedies. Prefiguration of death, the moment when the tragic character starts to die, is particularly prominent in *Blood Wedding*, for instance in the obsessive fears of the The Mother in the first act (see above). The third act breaks the apparent realism that has dominated the play up to that point; it is a break that puzzled critics in the first performances of Lorca, not only in Spain but also in the UK.[22] With the introduction of the figures of The Moon, the chorus of Woodcutters, the Beggar Woman and the Girls playing with a skein of yarn as the Fates, symbolism abruptly takes the stage, in a shift in style that points to the proximity of death, to the entrance into a ritual (liminal) new time and space.

Death itself in *Blood Wedding* happens offstage. As in Greek tragedy, we are informed about Leonardo and The Groom's violent ends: they kill each other at the same time, mixing their bloods in a second 'blood wedding'.[23] The messenger of death, in this case, is Death himself ('disguised' as a Beggar Woman) and the ellipsis of the moment of concrete departure from this world, together with the symbolic style used in the act, stands for the impossible representation of what cannot be expressed in everyday language.[24]

Macintosh also describes the several functions that the lament performs in Greek tragedy.[25] It is the medium by which mourners — and vicariously, also the spectator — can communicate with a world that transcends the empirical everyday. It also bestows a quasi-mythical status on a particular death (that through the lament becomes a representation of all deaths), ensuring a long-lasting (after-death) continuity of the deceased's name. In addition, it grants access to a shared inheritance, since lament is a collective response to death that dates from the Greeks. And last but not least, participation in this farewell ritual makes the survivors' 'prospect of a return to the world of the living a remote possibility, if not a definite reality'.[26]

However, Lorca's rural tragedies introduce an authorial touch into this final lament that closes the process of tragic dying. I will provisionally term Lorca's dramatic device here the interruption or suspension of the keening. In his rural tragedies, social expressions of grieving during the lament are invariably interrupted by the main survivors of the plays, those who have more reasons to cry and, thus, should be the chief mourners. Refusing to join the collective crying, and even ready to stop it, these characters remain suspended in an eternal grieving limbo, still alive, but divided forever from the world of the rest of the living. And of course, the suspension of this cathartic device (since the collective keen onstage calls for and facilitates a similar emotional discharge in the audience) also has an impact offstage. This is a distinctive feature that (to my knowledge, at least) has been disregarded by scholars, although I believe it to be the cause of the strong impression that the end of the play made on me when I saw *The House of Bernarda Alba* staged for the first time (in a school production).

The lament of The Mother in *Blood Wedding* soon after being informed of the death of her last son ('Ya todos están muertos. A medianoche dormiré, dormiré sin que ya me aterren la escopeta o el cuchillo. Otras madres se asomarán a las ventanas, azotadas por la lluvia, para ver el rostro de sus hijos. Yo, no' [They are all gone now. At midnight I will sleep peacefully, without trembling on the thought of a knife or a gun that could end my child's life. Lashed by the rain, other mothers will lean out their windows, looking for the faces of their sons. I won't]) has been often compared to Maurya's final surrender to her fate in *Riders to the Sea*: 'They're all gone now, and there isn't anything more the sea can do to me... I'll have no call now to be up crying and praying when the wind breaks from the south'.[27] This surrender, according to Macintosh, is only a symptom of the liminal situation of the mourner, of her/his alienation from reality.[28] However, whilst in Synge's play Maurya's lament in front of her son's body is accompanied by the crying of a chorus of female neighbours ('the women are keening softly and swaying themselves with a slow movement'),[29] *Blood Wedding* closes immediately before the corpses arrive — suppressing one more time the vision of death — and The Mother does not accept a role in the collective grieving. She stops the keening of The Neighbour and rejects The Bride's plea to be killed or allowed to weep with her. Her response is, once again, icy indifference ('Llora. Pero en la puerta' [Weep. But outside my door]).[30] It is interesting to note that *Señora Carrar's Rifles* — Brecht's 1937 (propaganda) rewriting of Synge's *Riders to the Sea*, relocated to the context of the Spanish Civil War — uses a similar suspension device. After hearing of her last son's death, Carrar dismisses the chorus of praying women (this time politely). But in Brecht's play of course this 'crying *interruptus*' (and the equally interrupted catharsis) turns into action: the character of the mother picks up a gun and joins the fight against the fascists.[31] In Lorca's play, conversely, The Bride, The Mother and Leonardo's Wife will eventually fuse in the final indistinct (Dionysian) choral lament that closes the play, the absence of a distinct transition in the character's evolution (from The Mother to a member of chorus) guaranteeing that some of the anguish previously generated in the audience remains in place.

As stated above, in *Yerma*, Lorca simplifies the dramatic structure while complicating the conflict. What is prefigured from the very name of the protagonist (and from the dreamy image of the child dressed in white that opens the play) is not the death of Yerma's husband Juan, but that of her potential child (an absent character with a great presence in the play). In fact, the impossible materialization of this child is what triggers Yerma's final lament, after she has strangled Juan to death. The lament introduces again the expression of apparent relief on the part of the chief mourner: like The Mother in *Blood Wedding* Yerma feels liberated after the complete extinction of hope ('Voy a descansar sin despertarme sobresaltada, para ver si la sangre me anuncia otra sangre nueva' [Now I will finally rest and I won't start up during the night wondering if there is new life in me]).[32] And when people start to gather around her husband's corpse, the protagonist once again severs herself from the collective response, both literally and in the focus of her mourning ('¿Qué queréis saber? ¡No os acerquéis, porque he matado a mi hijo, yo misma he matado a mi hijo!' [What do you want? Don't come near me! I have killed my son, I have killed my son with my own hands!]).[33] Instead of ending with the chorus of mourning women (as in *Blood Wedding*), *Yerma* closes with the distant (almost parodic) sound of the festive choral songs from the *romería*.

The House of Bernarda Alba introduces a new configuration of this suspended keening, which is perhaps the most effective on stage. After discovering Adela has taken her own life (she hangs herself, believing her lover has been killed by Bernarda, her mother), the sisters of the tragic heroine burst into tears. They cry for the loss of the youngest of their siblings, but also for their own fate: if at the beginning of the play the death of their father has thrown them into eight years of mourning under lock and key, this new departure forecasts decades of home imprisonment ('Nos hundiremos todas en un mar de luto' [We will drown ourselves in a sea of mourning], as their mother announces)[34], with spinsterhood their likely fate. But the sisters' tears are once again interrupted by the chief mourner, the rigorous and inflexible mother. Bernarda bans her daughters from any public or collective expression of grief: '¡Las lágrimas cuando estés sola!' [Don't cry until you are alone!], she says to one of the sisters.[35] The resounding 'Silence' that the mother raps out to her daughters at the very end of the play (an interruption of the keening that one can imagine repeating perpetually in Bernarda's house) leaves the audience in tense anguish. Probably written on the eve of a civil war that would take his life and prepare the ground for a global conflict, perhaps it is possible to glimpse in the absurdly cruel, unresolved mourning of *The House of Bernarda Alba* — paradoxically the most realistic of Lorca's rural tragedies (see below) — a hint of post-Second World War existential angst.

And yet, this interruption of the keening is absent in Simon Stone's *Yerma*, and Yaël Farber and Marina Carr's *Blood Wedding*, the two recent Young Vic productions that have inspired this chapter. I will devote the next two sections to explaining why and how, by taking two very different approaches, these new re-imaginings of Lorca's rural tragedies rewrite death on stage.

Dying for a Child: Simon Stone's Rewriting of *Yerma*

In 2016, the then-director of the Young Vic, David Lan, commissioned from Simon Stone a production of García Lorca's *Yerma*, with Billie Piper in the eponymous lead role. Known for his contemporary rewritings of classics, and his method of working with the actors to craft the text, the Swiss-born Australian director decided to set Lorca's play on infertility in present-day London: Stone's Yerma is a successful magazine editor, in a long-term relationship with a businessman who is continually travelling around the world. Michael Billington, a connoisseur of plays, appraised the experiment with these lukewarm words:

> Lorca's 1934 original is a rural tragedy about a socially imprisoned woman mocked by nature's fruitfulness; Stone's version is an urban drama about a privileged heroine who has access to every modern aid including IVF treatment. Given the purported radicalism of Piper's character, you also wonder why she subscribes to the notion that childbearing is the ultimate source of female fulfilment.[36]

It was a harsh statement about a production that, although polemical, has been praised by critics and practitioners alike: in 2017 the production won the Laurence Olivier Award for Best Revival, in 2018 it transferred to New York, and in 2021 a new German version was announced for the reopening of the Schaubühne. But, in my opinion, Billington's words were also the consequence of two revealing misunderstandings. The first has to do with Lorca's (and Stone's) model of tragedy, which is closer to the Nietzschean (more universal) conception, than to a more nineteenth-century model of conflict between the individual and his/her specific society (I will return to this later).[37] The second confusion is generational and maybe gendered. I don't have an answer to Billlington's question as to why this wealthy, cosmopolitan, and empowered contemporary Yerma feels so urgently the need to become a mother, but what I do know is that, as a childless woman in my late thirties, I have seen the behaviour of Stone's Yerma replicated in several of my own equally strong and independent friends and colleagues, from a range of socio-economic backgrounds and spread all around Europe and America.[38] I wouldn't be surprised if someone in the near future coined this phenomenon the Yerma complex. Moreover, it is useful to remember here that what escapes human rational understanding and control occupies a central role in tragedy (especially in the Attic model from which Lorca is drawing inspiration).

In any case, and irrespective of any personal views on the production, what is clear is that this reworking of Lorca's play about infertility and reproductive desire has been successful in two ways. First, by claiming that he was working with the 'Yerma myth'[39] (in the same way, for instance that Wadji Mouwad's works with the Sophoclean version of the Oedipus myth in *Incendies*), Stone was able to universalize a play that until then had been considered a hard nut to crack,[40] showing that *Yerma*'s inner battle is much more than the representation of the local problems of an outdated ultra-Catholic ultraconservative Spain — a discourse that, under the pretence of political correctness, is paternalistic and damaging for Lorca's legacy, and ultimately for the image of Spanish culture in the world. Second, in its transposition to our present, the rewriting was able to spot a contemporary conflict radically antithetical to the one that informs Lorca's *Yerma*, but similar in its tragic dynamics and consequences.

As in Lorca's *Yerma*, Stone's heroine has interiorized certain social impositions, such as being successful in her career (with the extra pressure, for a woman, of having to defy the 'angel of the house' Victorian stereotype). In the current competitive job market, the process of building a career has been extended (especially in highly qualified jobs) and it is delaying the age at which couples start to consider having a child. This delay, of course, is having an impact on fertility, which is also being affected by the two great evils of our times: stress and pollution. In these bleak times for procreation, the need to have a child — a need that many people experience as a biological one, as instinctive as the fear of death, thirst or hunger[41] — combined with trouble conceiving is the perfect recipe for tragic conflict, magnificently synthetized by Stone's career-wise successful Yerma: 'I was told I could have both. They fucking lied to me'.[42] As in the original play, in this longing for a child there is also room for some interiorized social impositions: if Lorca's Yerma explains her obsession to Juan by saying that while men work in the fields and socialize, the only social role of women is take care of the babies, at the end of Stone's version John suggests that his wife's obsession has to do as much with natural instinct as with ambition: 'you always loved projects and you'd always been such a high-achiever and God forbid you didn't achieve this too'.[43]

Stone's rewriting of *Yerma* shows a close reading of the original material from which he is drawing. It is still possible to recognize many of the original characters clearly (Yerma, Juan/John, Victor, María/Mary); however, the re-imagining strengthens the bonds between them and Yerma, and gives greater prominence and complexity to secondary characters: Victor is an ex (not a chaste fling), Mary is Yerma's sister (instead of her neighbour), and in the new characters of Yerma's mother (Helen) and young assistant (Des) we recognize features of the Second Girl and the Old Pagan Woman or Dolores respectively. Chorus and songs disappear from the modern version — the latter are relegated to the blackouts used in the transitions from one scene to another. In this sense, the style of this new production of *Yerma* is closer to realism, with the exception, perhaps of the scene of the *romería*, transformed in Stone's production into an equally Dionysian music festival: the audience sees distorted flashes of what is happening, almost as if we were placed in Yerma's (drugged) mind.

Sometimes we can hear echoes of the original play in motifs or small details. While in Lorca's *Yerma* the unruly Old Pagan Woman says she almost married a brother of Yerma's father, Enrique, in Stone's rewriting the equally sexually liberated Des mentions that she probably had sex with a guy called Henry after a party. With the same inversion of age, Yerma's mother's discovery of Deliveroo recalls the fact that the Second Girl, in her short appearance, is on her way to take food to her husband, working in the fields. In Lorca's *Yerma*, social context imposes silence and the concealment of feelings,[44] but blogs and Facebook's confessional discourse prove equally destructive and oppressing for Stone's heroine.

In the work of rewriting, of course, some elements must be sacrificed to keep a logical structure. And logical structure is an important feature in Stone's tragedy. Following the Aristotelian definition (a well-constructed plot in which events unfold logically up to an end that 'naturally follows [...] upon something else, but has nothing following it'),[45] Stone's version is, in fact, the result of a plot device strategy: 'I tried to invent a form, as if the end of *Yerma* were a newspaper article. So, the initial question was how on earth that happened, and then the rest of the play is just a series of glimpses that lead up to that final moment'.[46] One could argue that this is also what Lorca did in *Blood Wedding*, inspired, as mentioned above, by news from a crime column.

One of the more surprising changes made in Stone's version, in fact, is to be found precisely at the moment of death itself. In Lorca's play, Yerma ends up choking to death her drunken husband after he openly admits that he never cared about the only thing that preoccupies her, exhorting her to accept a childless marriage. Conversely, after a similar confession by John, Stone's Yerma threatens her husband with a kitchen knife before stabbing herself in the apartment they bought together (which, now, after deciding to leave her, John is selling). Some of the negative reviews that the production received had to do with this altered ending, considered less empowering for women (and perhaps more clichéd) than the original.[47]

I suspect that in this case the change is simply the result of Stone's Aristotelian plot device strategy. As we have mentioned, Yerma's tragedy is not so much that she kills her husband, but that with him dies her last chance of having a child; at least according to the moral impositions Yerma has interiorized. In our times, of course, those moral impositions don't quite rule anymore. Stone's Yerma, in fact, asks for help from Victor, threatens John that she will get a donor if he withdraws permission to use his sperm from the fertility clinic, and finally ends up sleeping with several men at a music festival. The only way for this contemporary Yerma to lose any hopes of (at this point almost miraculous) pregnancy is to kill herself: it is not by chance that in the production Yerma stabs her womb.[48] The production closes with the heroine's lament/last speech. These twenty-first-century final words are private; no one is there to hear them or to approach the dying body. But just before expiring, a final hope (a transcendental one) comforts Yerma: if her child is not possible in life, perhaps she could join the (unborn) baby in death ('Maybe | I'll be coming to you | I'll be coming | To you').[49] This final consolation is, paradoxically, completely denied to the original Yerma.

The Killing of a (Gypsy) Wolf: Factionalism and Conflict in Farber-Carr's *Blood Wedding*

In her introduction to *Dying Acts*, Fiona Macintosh studies how Greek tragedy played an important but complex role in the Irish Renaissance movement.[50] To quote Marianne McDonald: 'in many ways Ireland was and is constructing its identity through the representations offered by Greek tragedy'.[51] Although research remains to be done on the topic, this interest in classical tragedy and its role in the construction of an Irish cultural identity certainly had and still has an impact on the stage reception of Lorca's theatre, not only in Ireland, but also in the UK, especially during the first period of Lorca's reception on stage.[52] Set in a hybrid fictional landscape that Carr has described as 'Andalusia County Offaly', her 2019 adaptation of *Blood Wedding* bears testament to the contemporary resonance this association still has.[53]

The connection between Spain and Ireland in the production is based not only on a presumably common (oppressive) Catholic and rural background, but also (and especially) on their shared problematic colonial past. As Carr states:

> The repression of the individual by the long arms of Church and State is one obvious point of cohesion, but also both Spain and Ireland have endured the annihilation of identity and the psychic wound of colonization; Spain by the reconquest of the land from the Moors, Ireland by many invasions culminating with the English.[54]

Needless to say, this reductive and anachronistic 'one size fits all' dynamic of oppressors and oppressed is problematic.[55] As I stated in a review of the show, it relies upon external readings embedded into the play — just as the dust on neglected old paintings ends up being perceived as part of the canvas, to use Brecht's metaphor.[56] In this case, the dust is a quite sticky one, namely the old cliché of the gypsies (or rather, a distorted image of this community) as the bearers of some kind of more ancient, free and natural essence of Spain (and Ireland).

Although there are no references to gypsies in *Blood Wedding*, the popularity of Lorca's earlier *Gypsy Ballads* contaminated from the outset the reception of his first rural tragedy, an association that the Granadan author rejected.[57] Drawing on this misleading (although very popular) association (Farber, for instance, includes sung segments of poems from the *Gypsy Ballads* in the final production), Carr makes her Bride descend from a lineage of 'mischievous', 'unruly' gypsy women. The motif is not new in the work of Carr: she uses it too in plays such as *By the Bog of Cats* (a rewriting of the Medea myth) and *Portia Coughlan*. In these two titles, the rebellious protagonists (Hester and Portia, respectively) are each said to descend from a family of 'tinkers'. What it is more, this revindication of a figure that is perceived as a 'positive' 'otherness' inside Ireland's culture has its own literary tradition, based once again in the Irish Literary Renaissance. As Burke points out, Synge was 'at the heart of the Revival's valorisation of the tinker as an embodiment of exotic indigeneity'.[58]

But whilst in earlier plays the 'tinker' motif was just a touch of colour in the depiction of the main characters, in *Blood Wedding* the motif assumes a central place, linked to Carr's 'Gypsy' reading of the original text. It pervades the version so deeply that the central conflict of the play shifts: the Nietzschean model of the original (the release of atavistic desires that challenge social order as much as individual control) gives way to a more *fin-de-siècle* nineteenth-century model of tragedy, of the clash between an (alienated) individual and her/his particular society (the same heuristics for reading Lorca's plays that can be spotted in Billington's review of Stone's *Yerma*).[59] Thus, for Farber *Blood Wedding* is about 'sectarianism and factionalism', how a community learns 'to keep the wolves at bay', and 'within that, how we lose our personal freedoms'.[60] The individual versus society is a model that has two of its greatest exponents in Ibsen's and Strindberg's drama. It was also the model for much of the (far more Manichean and melodramatic) Spanish nineteenth-century tradition of social and rural drama.

For Nietzsche, this kind of theatre (the drama of his time) was the regrettable result of the 'Socratic optimism' that had pervaded European drama since Euripides. The philosopher from Röcken, in fact, rejected the 'rational' or moral explanation of the situations and motivations of the characters that could be found in the Greek playwright's pieces because it expelled 'the original and all-powerful Dionysian element from tragedy'.[61] Modern practitioners have apparently not shared Nietzsche's opinion, since in the twentieth and twenty-first centuries Euripides has been perhaps the most staged of the three Greek tragedians; at least, that's what some scholars claim in the Irish context (see for instance McDonald).[62] But taken with a pinch of salt, Nietzsche's 'excessive and highly idiosyncratic criticism of Euripides'[63] sheds light on Farber's production of Carr's *Blood Wedding* and the transformation of the original conflict into an individual/society model.

In the process of adapting the play Carr explores, explains, and foregrounds certain elements that in Lorca's play occupy a far less central (and much more subtle) role. Thus, the socioeconomic differences that prevented a wedding between The Bride and Leonardo, and the old feud between the Felix and The Groom's families (motifs all taken, as I have mentioned above, from the Spanish rural and social theatre tradition) become in the play the real motivations behind The Bride's and Leonardo's actions (replacing the irrational passion that drives their behaviour in Lorca's piece). As Carr states in the programme, '*Blood Wedding* asks the primal questions. The question of blood and blood lineage. Who was here first? What was taken? What is left?'[64]

While in Lorca's text the attraction that links the two lovers is represented as completely beyond their understanding, control or even wishes,[65] Carr's lovers elope together the day of the wedding for very different (and more rational) reasons. What Leonardo is after in this version is not getting The Bride but offending the Groom.[66] Conversely, The Bride's motivation is racialized: her thirst for (sexual and individual) freedom, inherited from her female gypsy ancestors (The Bride's grandmother is described as having had 'twenty children from twenty different men').[67] In fact, whilst in Lorca we find two main tragic figures — The Bride (left without husband or lover, and probably ostracized forever from the community) and The Mother (who loses her last son and the chance to continue her family line)[68] — Carr's version clearly zooms in on the former: the young and rebellious bride is the outsider that confronts an oppressive, asphyxiating and misogynistic social environment. This shift of motivations, protagonist and conflict is especially stressed in the way the process of dying and its staging is reworked.

Farber peppers the production with visual staging details that contribute to foreshadowing the deadly end. For instance, the show opens with a silent scene: The Mother cleaning in half-darkness a puddle of what it looks like blood (a detail that doesn't appear in Carr's published play-script). Instead of being restricted to the third act, The Moon and the chorus of Woodcutters, those symbolic heralds of death, appear onstage from the outset, in the transitions between one scene and the other. The songs that The Moon sings are also announcements of death, while the use of a different light for these transitions indicates they belong to a space and time out of this world. The version also fuses The Neighbour, The Beggar Woman and The Three Girls (Fates) into a single character (The Weaver). As a result, there is a clearer continuity between the first and the last acts. But, as in Stone's rewriting, it is the moment of death itself that is most radically reworked.

As well as exposing and amplifying elements that are only subtle details in Lorca's play, this modern version also openly reveals to the audience the simultaneous deaths of The Groom and Leonardo. This turns out to be problematic, at least in my experience as a spectator. It is very difficult to show how both men kill each other without falling into a comic register,[69] and, although the production frequently infuses the tragedy with acidic humour (another hallmark of the Irish drama tradition), I am not sure that in this case the sniggers I could hear during the performance were an intended effect. The messenger is once again The Beggar Woman (The Weaver in Carr's version), but the recipient and the content of her report have changed. After announcing to The Bride the death of her two suitors, The Weaver uses her thread to communicate (as a kind of medium) the words of those who inhabit death. Possessed by the spirit of The Bride's grandmother, The Weaver refers in first person to her tragic suicide (chased by the townspeople because of her behaviour with men, she has ridden off a cliff on her horse), before transmitting in a similar fashion other anonymous deaths. The ghosts that speak through her mouth (outsiders, children, women, and members of racial and religious minorities)[70] have also been the victims of violent and unfair societies: their voices are part of the 'endless ballad of blood and pain' that The Bride is about to join.[71]

The Bride's plea to be killed will, indeed, be heard in Carr's version. After The

Mother's lament (in this version a mixture of the words spoken by Lorca's characters and Synge's Maurya),[72] The Bride is surrounded by the rest of the characters of the play (including her own father) and stabbed to death by the community with the very same knives that Leonardo and The Groom have used to kill each other. In the last act (and especially in the last scene), fragments of Lorca's writings are embedded in the dialogue. The version closes, for instance, with a final intervention by The Moon.[73] Using the first person, the fragment mixes a reference to Lorca's own death in a poem from his collection *Poet in New York* (published posthumously in 1940) with an anecdote that Pablo Neruda included in a speech he gave in Paris in 1937, in the midst of the Spanish Civil War (and after Lorca's assassination). Lorca reportedly told the Chilean poet that one dawn, during a tour with La Barraca (the university student theatre group the Spanish writer directed for several years), he saw how six black pigs surrounded a lost little lamb and devoured it. Recalling the impression that the episode had on Lorca, Neruda describes it as a symbol, a vision of the Granadan author's own death.[74] The visual parallelism between this story, Lorca's execution, and the way The Bride is butchered is evident.

In another passage of this lecture — which is as much an elegy as a political exhortation — Neruda talks about his personal friend as 'the sounding guardian of Spain's heart', whose death symbolized the sufferings of a whole nation. In his words resound two facets of Lorca's myth: the martyr of the Spanish Civil War and the poet of the Spanish/Andalusian people. Together with the gypsy cliché (another component of the Lorca myth, as we have mentioned, was the image of the poet of the Gypsies or even the Gypsy poet), these discourses clearly had a decisive influence on Farber's and Carr's reading of *Blood Wedding* as a conflict between personal idea(l)s and social/national(ist) constraints.

Some Final Words

Usually employed as the expected closure of a sequence of events that unfolds as logically as it does inexorably, death is often a central (almost centripetal) force in tragedy: all the play converges upon it. This is certainly the case for *Blood Wedding* and *Yerma*, the two plays in which, under Nietzschean influence, Lorca first trials his innovative return to the model of Greek tragedy. This is done by taking ambience, situations and elements (some of them closer to real problems, others idealized literary constructions) from the Spanish tradition of popular rural and social drama. Against this backdrop of inherited motifs and discourses — sometimes even entangled with it (Yerma's longing for a child is as strong as her refusal to be unfaithful to her husband) — Lorca stages the eternal deadly battle between the Dionysian and the Apollonian.

As in the classical Greek model from which he is drawing, Lorca conceives death as a process. Yet this doesn't prevent the Granadan author from introducing his own creative touch to the schema: a suspension or interruption of the collective response to death. Lorca's tragedies therefore point to the future as much as to the past of theatre. If the revival of tragedy at the beginning of the twentieth century prepared the ground for the ritual-theatre trend that would be consolidated in the sixties, the suspension of the keening (a feature inextricably linked to Lorca's use of silence as a stage device)[75] and the effect it produces in the spectator anticipate the discomfort audiences experienced when confronted with the metaphysically alienated (and comfortless) characters that populated Occidental drama after the Second World War. With all the necessary disclaimers in place, adopting this perspective is a healthy way of evaluating how formally ground-breaking the ostensibly less 'experimental' entries in Lorca's dramatic *oeuvre* were.

Counterintuitively, when inscribing their recent versions of *Yerma* and *Blood Wedding* in a new spatiotemporal context, Stone, like Farber and Carr, dispenses with Lorca's innovative suspension of the collective keening. The change of the fatal end in these re-imaginings of Lorca's rural tragedies, nevertheless, is revealing in itself, since it shows two different (almost antithetical) approaches to understanding Lorca's relevance for our present. Following the Nietzschean model of tragedy that probably also inspired Lorca, Stone works with the *Yerma* myth, relocating the protagonist's Dionysian thirst for a child to present-day London. The rewriting of the bold original act of death (a woman who kills her husband with her own hands) responds to a logical evolution of the plot in the new context, and the result is ultimately the same: Juan's death in Lorca's *Yerma* and Yerma's death in Stone's re-imagining both stand for the death of the impossible child Yerma so desperately wants to have.

While Stone is interested in the *Yerma* myth, Farber's production of Carr's *Blood Wedding* draws heavily on Lorca's own myth(s). This version makes the play relevant to the present by establishing correspondences between Ireland's and Spain's oppressive histories and all their victims (among them Lorca himself). It does so by changing the nature of the conflict. Thus, death is reworked to make the tragedy of The Bride an additional example of the violent reaction of societies against individuals that don't fit into the community. While both creative procedures are of course valid for bringing Lorca's world into our present (there is no such thing as a faithful or correct way of staging or rewriting a play), the problem perhaps with the latter is that it is too ambitious. Making Lorca's work relevant for a contemporary audience by establishing parallels with his life and other individual/local injustices runs the danger of underplaying and trivializing the specificities underpinning instances of cultural or political oppression, and falling (like Farber's production of Carr's adaptation) into cliché.

Notes to Chapter 7

This work was supported by the projects 'EStages.UK. Teatro español en Reino Unido (1982–2019)' under Marie Skłodowska Curie Grant agreement number 797942; 'Performa2. Metamorfosis del espectador en el teatro español actual' under the Ministry of Science and Innovation of Spain Grant number PID2019–104402RB-100; and 'Cartografía digital, conservación y difusión del patrimonio teatral del Madrid contemporáneo' under Autonomous Community of Madrid grant number H2019/HUM-5722.

1. Arturo Barea, *Lorca: The Poet and his People* (New York: Cooper Square Publishers, 1973), p. 83.
2. María Bastianes, 'Negotiating Cultural Exchange: Lorca on the British Stage from the Spanish Civil War until the Mid-Fifties', *Studies in Theatre and Performance* (forthcoming 2022).

3. David Damrosch, 'World Literature in a Postcanonical, Hypercanonical Age', in *Comparative Literature in an Age of Globalization*, ed. by Haun Saussy (Baltimore, MD: Johns Hopkins University Press, 2006), pp. 43–53.

4. Although it would be unfair to blame practitioners when there are still scholars that describe Lorca's theatre as the result of 'the very backwardness' and oppression of 'his Spain' (Felicity Rosslyn, 'Lorca and Greek Tragedy', *The Cambridge Quarterly*, 29.3 (2000), 215–36 (p. 215) and 'reflejo de una España siempre inacabada; un país de muerte donde la muerte se celebra con el último rito dionisíaco, el de los toros' [a reflection of an unfinished Spanish nation, a country that celebrates death through the last surviving Dionysian ritual: bullfighting] (Miguel Medina Vicario, 'La tragedia en Lorca', *Acotaciones*, 1 (1998), 42–53 (p. 48). All translations are my own.

5. Federico García Lorca, *Obras completas*, ed. by Arturo del Hoyo, 2 vols (Madrid: Aguilar, 1974), II, 964.

6. For a list of twentieth-century plays using classical mythic themes see Susan Harris Smith, 'Twentieth-Century Plays Using Classical Mythic Themes: A Checklist', *Modern Drama*, 29.1 (1986), 110–34.

7. Jennifer Wallace, *The Cambridge Introduction to Tragedy* (Cambridge: Cambridge University Press, 2007), p. 142. There is no conclusive proof about Lorca's knowledge of Nietzsche's work, but several mentions (spread here and there in documents and interviews) testify that the poet was acquainted with the philosopher's ideas on tragedy. After all, the influence of Nietzsche in Spain was important (see Gonzalo Sobejano, *Nietzsche en España* (Madrid: Gredos, 2004)). For a detail exploration of this influence on García Lorca and his generation see also Encarna Alonso Valero, *La tragedia del nacimiento: el teatro de Federico García Lorca* (Granada: Atrio, 2008) and more recently, Sergio Santiago Romero, 'Nietzsche en el nacimiento de la tragedia española contemporánea' (unpublished doctoral thesis, Complutense University of Madrid, 2019), pp. 343–446.

8. Wallace, p. 141.

9. See, for instance, Wallace, p. 141.

10. See Felipe Pedraza, *El drama rural. Metamorfosis de un género: la perspectiva española y el contexto internacional* (Vigo: Academia del Hispanismo, 2011), p. 133.

11. The Spanish novelist and theatre critic Torrente Ballester describes the world of Lorca's rural tragedies as the same of Jacinto Benavente's *La Malquerida* or *Señora ama* (he refers specifically to *La casa de Bernarda Alba*). See Gonzalo Torrente Ballester, *Teatro español contemporáneo* (Madrid: Ediciones Guadarrama, 1968), p. 236.

12. For instance, Smith has studied Yerma against the backdrop of contemporary clinical discussions and discourses over maternity, that were the result of a 'progressive medicalization of pregnancy and childbirth in Spain (as elsewhere in Europe)'. See Julian Smith, *The Theatre of García Lorca* (Cambridge: Cambridge University Press, 1998), p. 19.

13. It is worth noting that rural ambience was also very much present in the post-romantic verismo opera movement, in pieces such as Mascagni's *Cavalleria Rusticana* (1890). Based on Giovanni Verga's tale, this opera was also quoted in connection with *Blood Wedding* in the reviews of Lorca's first productions in UK. See Bastianes, 'Negotiating Cultural Exchange'.

14. Pedraza, pp. 136–37.

15. Fiona Macintosh, *Dying Acts: Death in Ancient Greek and Modern Irish Tragic Drama* (Cork: Cork University Press, 1994), p. 56.

16. See Federico García Lorca, *Bodas de sangre*, ed. by Mario Fernández (Alianza: Madrid, 1998), p. 159.

17. García Lorca, *Obras completas* (1974), II, 997.

18. Federico García Lorca, *Yerma*, ed. by Antonio A. Gómez Yebra (Madrid: Castalia, 2004), p. 88

19. About Yerma Lorca said 'Yo soy cristiano. Mi protagonista tiene limitado su arbitrio, encadenada por el concepto, que va disuelto en su sangre, de la honra españolísima' [I am a Christian. A typically Spanish sense of honour limits my protagonist's will, it is in her blood]. See Federico García Lorca, *Obras completas*, ed. by Miguel García-Posada, 4 vols (Barcelona: Galaxia Gutenberg, 1997), III, 614.

20. Golden Age honour drama was a particular popular genre in Spain up to the end of the nineteenth century (see Sergio Adillo, 'Calderón en los escenarios españoles (1715–2015): canon,

construcción nacional y campo del teatro' (unpublished doctoral thesis, Complutense University of Madrid, 2018), p. 133). Nevertheless, and irrespective of the fascination that Golden Age honour drama produced in nineteenth-century audiences and playwrights, it would be a mistake to link directly both traditions of honour, as Pedraza (pp. 88–89) has stated.

21. Macintosh, *Dying Acts*. To learn more about Macintosh's study of the process of death see her enlightening analysis of Carr's *Woman and Scarecrow*, included in this book (see Chapter 10).

22. See Luis Fernández Cifuentes, *La norma y la diferencia* (Zaragoza: Universidad de Zaragoza, 1986), p. 141, and Bastianes, 'Negotiating Cultural Exchange'.

23. Miguel García Posada, 'Las tragedias lorquianas', in Federico García Lorca, *Teatro completo*, 4 vols (Madrid: Debolsillo, 2004), III, 9–16 (p. 11).

24. Or, as Petre has described, the 'moyen privilégié — le seul peut-être — pour dire le transcendant [...] l'instant terrible' that belongs 'au dieu autant sinon plus qu'aux hommes' [the preferred strategy, perhaps the only possible, to express what it is beyond life, the dreadful moment that belongs to gods as much as to (or even more than to) men]. Zoe Petre, 'La Représentation de la mort dans la tragédie grecque', *Studii clasice*, 23 (1985), 21–35 (p. 33).

25. Macintosh, *Dying Acts*, pp. 158–82.

26. Macintosh, *Dying Acts*, p. 175.

27. García Lorca, *Bodas de sangre*, p. 70; and John Millington Synge, *Riders to the Sea* (Boston, MA: John W. Luce and Company, 2011), p. 42. As Rosa Navarro observes, this kind of lament can also be traced inside a Spanish tradition, for instance, in Pleberio's *planto* in Fernando de Rojas's *La Celestina*. Rosa Navarro, 'Dos mujeres de tragedia en el teatro de Lorca', *El Ciervo. Revista Mensual de Pensamiento y Cultura*, 783 (2020), 32–33 (p. 33).

28. Macintosh, p. 176.

29. Synge, p. 41. On the role of keening in Synge's play see Yumiko Kataoka, 'Loss and Resolution in "Riders to the Sea": Reflecting on the Theory of Grief', *Journal of Irish Studies*, 32 (2017), 13–22.

30. García Lorca, *Bodas de sangre*, p. 173.

31. Bertolt Brecht, 'Señora Carrar's Rifles', in *Collected Plays* (London: Methuen, 1983), pp. 95–124 (pp. 123–24).

32. García Lorca, *Yerma*, p. 119.

33. García Lorca, *Yerma*, p. 119

34. Federico García Lorca, *La casa de Bernarda Alba*, ed. by Allen Josephs and Juan Caballero (Madrid: Cátedra, 2000), p. 205.

35. Lorca, *La casa de Bernarda Alba*, p. 205.

36. Michael Billington, 'Yerma review — Billie Piper gives a breathtakingly uninhibited performance', *The Guardian*, 5 August 2016 <https://www.theguardian.com/stage/2016/aug/05/yerma-review-billie-piper-young-vic-simon-stone-lorca> [accessed 16 April 2021].

37. Perhaps the critic is reading too literally *The House of Bernarda Alba*'s subtitle 'Drama de mujeres en los pueblos de España' [A Drama of Women in the Villages of Spain] (as if the conflict depicted in the play couldn't be transposed to other landscapes apart from an ultra-Catholic rural Spain). It is important to note that Lorca's third rural tragedy is the most realistic and thus the furthest from the Nietzschean classical model that inspired *Yerma* and *Blood Wedding* (it is not by chance that Lorca chose the word *drama* instead of *tragedy* to refer to it). As for *Yerma*, the reader should bear in mind that, as Fernández Cifuentes notes (pp. 164–66), Yerma's obsession was also perceived as unfamiliar in Lorca's own time, with critics failing to realize how the play was breaking with the horizon of expectations of traditional rural dramas and its idealized 'realistic' depiction of society in rural Spain.

38. I don't deny that perhaps this is a middle- and upper-class phenomenon, but it is important to note that in the original play Yerma and her husband are also among the wealthy people of the town. In fact, this is one of the reasons she decides to marry a man that she is not attracted to.

39. See live interview with Anne Bogart. Park Avenue Armory. Artist Talk, 'Yerma' <https://www.youtube.com/watch?v=QficpneoITo> [accessed 16 April 2021].

40. *Yerma* has been the least performed of Lorca's three rural tragedies in the UK.

41. Yerma's longing for a child (and The Bride's or Adela's sexual attraction to Leonardo and Pepe el Romano, respectively) are presented as physical needs, using the metaphor of thirst and water. See Maria Delgado, *Federico García Lorca* (New York: Routledge, 2008), p. 87.

42. Simon Stone, *Yerma* (London: Oberon, 2017), p. 60. It is interesting to note that without the external (and internalized) social demand to become a mother that oppressed the original Yerma, Stone's Yerma's fate seems, counterintuitively, more doomed. Having exhausted all her economic resources and all clinical possibilities available, the problems of this contemporary Yerma lack any moral or immoral solution. Reduced to the simple contradiction of an instinct that is biologically impossible to satisfy, her conflict feels more fatally tragic.

43. García Lorca, *Yerma*, p. 84; Stone, p. 86.

44. In the second act, Yerma says to Víctor: 'Hay cosas encerradas detrás de los muros que no pueden cambiar porque nadie las oye. [...] Pero que si salieran de pronto y gritaran, llenarían el mundo' [There are things that happen behind walls, under key and lock, those things cannot change because nobody ever hears about them [...] But if released, they will fill the world]. García Lorca, *Yerma*, p. 92.

45. Aristotle, *Poetics*, trans. by Anthony Kenny (Oxford: Oxford University Press, 2013), p. 26.

46. Live interview with Anne Bogart. Park Avenue Armory. Artist Talk, '*Yerma*', see above, n. 39.

47. In fact, Lorca's play generated great controversy when premiered. See Antonio Gómez Yebra, 'Introducción', in García Lorca, *Yerma*, pp. 15–38 (pp. 32–33). Negative responses to Stone's *Yerma* can be found also in academic works, such as the chapter that Meeuwis devotes to the production. On this occasion, the scholar's reading is, nevertheless, somehow weakened by the fact that his quotations from Lorca's *Yerma* often don't have even a remote equivalent in the original (I can only assume he has taken a free adaptation of the text as a translation of the original). Michael Meeuwis, *Property and Finance on the Post-Brexit London Stage: We Want What You Have* (London: Routledge, 2020).

48. Structural necessities are also behind the disappearance of another very audacious detail of Lorca's play: the frequent insinuations that Juan is the one to be blame for the fertility problems (the Pagan Woman refers to him as a man of 'simiente podrida' [rotten seed] (García Lorca, *Bodas de sangre*, p. 65). In Lorca's time of course this was a completely taboo subject, and society hasn't evolved much in this respect (see the recent documentary by Rhod Gilbert: *Stand up for infertility* (BBC 2, 2021)). Although, at the beginning of the play, Stone cleverly depicts John as reluctant to take a sperm test, when he finally does it, the test turns to be normal. Even if this solution is less bold than the original, it responds again to the logic of the plot: a modern Yerma could have found another donor or sexual partner.

49. Stone, p. 88.

50. Macintosh, pp. 1–18.

51. Marianne McDonald, 'The Irish and Greek Tragedy', in *Amid our Troubles: Irish Versions of Greek Tragedy*, ed. by Marianne McDonald and J. Michael Walton (London: Methuen, 2002), pp. 37–86 (p. 37).

52. Bastianes, 'Negotiating Cultural Exchange'.

53. See *Programme of 'Blood Wedding'*, dir. by Yaël Farber (Young Vic, 2019), p. 7. As Jordan points out, the influence of Greek tragedy became more pronounced in Carr's work when she started to write plays with Irish Midlands settings. Eamonn Jordan, 'Unmasking the Myths? Marina Carr's "By the Bog of Cats" and "On Raftery's Hill"', in *Amid our Troubles: Irish Versions of Greek Tragedy*, ed. by Marianne McDonald and J. Michael Walton (London: Methuen, 2002), pp. 243–62 (p. 244).

54. *Programme of 'Blood Wedding'*, p. 6.

55. Although it has been for a long time an important identity symbol for the conservatives and the right in Spain, the Reconquista (as its name shows) was just one of the several conquests and reconquests experienced by the Iberian Peninsula, at least since Roman times. As with other essentialist identities, the idea that Spain is 'essentially moor' (also confounding gypsy and Muslim heritages) is more a construction than a reality, a construction that, in addition, is based in a positive reversion of negative northern European visions of Spain. See Gayle Rogers, *Modernism and the New Spain: Britain, Cosmopolitan Europe, and Literary History* (New York: Oxford University Press, 2012), pp. 3–38.

56. María Bastianes, 'Blood Wedding Receives an Irish-Gypsy Makeover at the Young Vic', *European Stages*, 15 (2020) <https://europeanstages.org/2020/12/30/blood-wedding-receives-an-irish-gypsy-makeover-at-the-young-vic/> [accessed 16 April 2021]; Bertolt Brecht, *Brecht on*

Theatre: The Development of an Aesthetic, ed. and trans. by John Willet (London: Methuen, 1974), p. 272.

57. In a letter to Jorge Guillen from 1927 the Granadan poet stated: 'Me va molestando un poco mi mito de gitanería. Confunden mi vida y mi carácter. No quiero, de ninguna manera. Los gitanos son un tema. Y nada más. Yo podía ser lo mismo poeta de agujas de coser o de paisajes hidráulicos. Además el gitanismo me da un tono de incultura, de falta de educación y de poeta salvaje que tú sabes bien no soy. No quiero que me encasillen. Siento que me van echando cadenas' [This gypsy myth around myself is starting to upset me. They are mixing my life and my character. And I don't like it, no way. Gypsies are a theme, nothing more. I could just as well have been a poet of sewing needles or hydraulics landscapes. Besides, this Gypsyism gives me the uncultured, uneducated air of a savage poet, which you know I am not]. García Lorca, *Epistolario completo* (Madrid: Cátedra, 1997), p. 414. Although, as Charnon-Deutsch acknowledges, Lorca's vision of the Gypsies is far from simple and is also populated with nineteenth century romantic clichés. See Lou Charnon-Deutsch, *The Spanish Gypsy: The History of a European Obsession* (University Park: Pennsylvania State University Press, 2004), p. 207.

58. Mary Burke, *'Tinkers': Synge and the Cultural History of the Irish Traveller* (Oxford: Oxford University Press, 2009), p. 10.

59. See Northrop Frye, *Anatomy of Criticism* (Princeton, NJ: Princeton University Press, 1957), p. 285.

60. *Programme of 'Blood Wedding'*, p. 3.

61. Friedrich Nietzsche, *The Birth of Tragedy and Other Writings*, ed. by Raymond Geuss and Ronald Spiers, trans. by Ronald Spiers (Cambridge: Cambridge University Press, 1999), p. 59.

62. McDonald, p. 42.

63. In Albert Henrichs, 'The Last of the Detractors: Friedrich Nietzsche's Condemnation of Euripides', *Greek, Roman and Byzantine Studies*, 27.4 (1986), 369–97 (p. 397).

64. *Programme of 'Blood Wedding'*, p. 7.

65. This conception of love as out of individual control (as a force that chooses randomly its victims) is something that the Granadan author learnt from Shakespeare's *Romeo and Juliet*, but also, and especially, from *A Midsummer Night's Dream*. Rafael Martínez Nadal, a friend of the poet, recalls Lorca's personal remarks on the latter: 'Lo que Shakespeare nos está diciendo — fueron más o menos sus palabras — es que el amor no depende del individuo y que se impone con igual fuerza en todos los planos. [...] La clave de la obra es Titania enamorada del asno' [What Shakespeare is trying to express in the play — these were approximately his [Lorca's] words — is that love is out of individual control and pervades everything [...] The key aspect of the play is Titania falling in love with a donkey]. Rafael Martínez Nadal, *El público: amor y muerte en la obra de García Lorca* (Madrid: Comunidad de Madrid, 2019), pp. 109–10 <http://www.madrid.org/bvirtual/BVCM019761.pdf> [accessed 16 April 2021].

66. See Marina Carr, *Blood Wedding* (London: Faber and Faber, 2019), pp. 55–56, 61. In this respect, see also Delgado's review. Maria Delgado, 'Tribalism, Tragedy and Torment: Yaël Farber's "Blood Wedding" at the Young Vic', *The Theatre Times*, 10 October 2019 <https://thetheatretimes.com/tribalism-tragedy-and-torment-yael-farbers-blood-wedding-at-the-young-vic/> [accessed 16 April 2021].

67. Carr, p. 6. The image is almost an inversion of what Lorca's The Mother says of her father-in-law, who left a son in every corner. García Lorca, *Bodas de sangre*, p. 66.

68. See Luis González del Valle, '*Bodas de sangre* y sus elementos trágicos', *Archivum: Revista de la Facultad de Filosofía y Letras*, 21 (1971), 95–120 (p. 97).

69. In their reviews of the show, Wheeler and Delgado have both commented on this shift on the tone and the effect on the audience. Duncan Wheeler, 'Pain, passion, poetry and politics. A reworking of Federico García Lorca's rural tragedy', *TLS*, 4 October 2019 <https://www.the-tls.co.uk/articles/pain-passion-poetry-and-politics/> [accessed 16 April 2021]; (Delgado, 'Tribalism, Tragedy and Torment', 2019). On the unperformability of death due to the lack of credibility, see Dominic Glynn's chapter in this book (Chapter 6).

70. Maria Delgado has pointed out that many of them are references 'to Spain having usurped the Arabs, Jews and Romany whose legacy Lorca so admired' ('Tribalism, Tragedy and Torment', 2019).

71. Carr, p. 60.

72. For instance, the version includes Maurya's memory of the physical pain suffered during childbirth, a formulaic motif that Macintosh (pp. 160–62) spots in Greek and Irish tragic mother's laments, but that is absent in Lorca.

73. As Maria Delgado has acutely noted in her review of the production, The Moon wears a 'white suit that functions as a nod to the cream suit in which Lorca was often photographed in the grainy black and white images that remain of the writer assassinated on nationalist orders at the beginning of the Civil War' ('Tribalism, Tragedy and Torment', 2019).

74. Pablo Neruda, *Para nacer he nacido* (Barcelona: Seix Barral, 1978), p. 72.

75. See Dru Dougherty, 'El lenguaje del silencio en el teatro de García Lorca', *Anales de la literatura española contemporánea*, 11.1/2 (1986), 91–110.

CHAPTER 8

❖

Death of Tragedy: Modernist Drama and the Sense of a Non-Ending

Barry Murnane

St John's College, Oxford

In the final scene of *Frühlings Erwachen*, Frank Wedekind's landmark play about adolescent sexuality and social repression, one of the main protagonists, Melchior Gabor, climbs over the wall of a graveyard on a bright November night to experience his own personal encounter with death: 'Ringsum ist die Erde kahl ... Im Todtenreich!' [Nothing grows here ... in the land of the dead].[1] But death in this scene is not as final as one might expect, as Wedekind's extraordinary paratextual note makes clear when Melchior's deceased friend Moritz appears on stage: 'Moritz Stiefel *seinen Kopf unter dem Arm, kommt über die Gräber her*' (p. 316) [MORITZ STIEFEL, head under his arm, comes stumping across the graves (p. 75)]. Beginning with Wedekind's play, moving through Georg Kaiser's *Von morgens bis mitternachts*, and finishing with a consideration of Brecht's 'learning play' *Die Maßnahme*, this chapter will demonstrate how death both remains a central component in German modernist theatre but also is paradoxically shown to lose its finality. Whether in Naturalist plays that focus on the social forces that drive protagonists to their deaths, in Expressionist plays that celebrate a metaphysical rebirth heralded by the passing of the protagonist, or finally in epic theatre's criticism of capitalist, bourgeois individualism through the death of egotistical protagonists, the body count in modernist theatre is substantial. I will suggest, however, that death's inability to provide the closure required by traditional forms of drama, in general, and tragedy, in particular, becomes apparent over the roughly thirty-year period surveyed here. Death often emerges in these plays as preventable and hence not tragic in the established sense of sense of the word. These modernist works still offer reflections on death and hence help us 'to make sense of our lives', our place in time, and our relationship to 'the beginning and the end' — in the words of Frank Kermode[2] — but they do so in a manner which questions the possibility of tragedy and endings in quite fundamental ways. As the example chosen from Wedekind's *Frühlings Erwachen* suggests here, death doesn't even provide a finality of life, as Moritz haunts the stage to tell his story posthumously.

According to Kermode's seminal study *The Sense of an Ending*, one of literature's most important functions is to provide 'fictions of the End', meaning fictions in which 'we have imagined the ends of the world'.[3] Such — often apocalyptic — narratives function as 'the ways we try to make sense of our lives', but Kermode also acknowledges a more localized, personal component too: 'the End is a figure for [our] own deaths' (p. 7). For him, the function of fictions of the end is to 'project ourselves [...] past the End, so as to see the structure whole, a thing we cannot do from our spot of time in the middle' (p. 8). Alongside a historical account of apocalypse narratives, Kermode's study is fiercely preoccupied with the challenges to the finality of death and the formal closure of chronology and narration in the modern novel. Pointing towards Joyce, Sartre, Camus, and Robbe-Grillet, Kermode identifies the 'shrewd blow at paradigmatic expectations' (p. 19) of narration in the modern novel, with their warping of time, inversions, and disruptions to the chronology of simple 'clock-time' (pp. 19–23). Kermode summarizes: 'We cannot, of course, be denied an end; it is one of the great charms of books that they have to end. But unless we are extremely naïve [...] we do not ask that they progress towards that end precisely as we have been given to believe' (pp. 23–24). The book may indeed end, but it is an open end without 'End-feeling' (p. 25), a structural insecurity which mirrors the insecurities of our attempts at 'making sense of the world' (p. 29) in the modern era. Robbe-Grillet's *La Maison de Rendez-vous*, in which the same character is murdered four times over, is Kermode's prime example for modern narrative in that it simultaneously questions chronological ordering and narrative finality (formally) and the uniqueness and absolute finality of death (thematically). In this 'crisis' (p. 28) of constant transition, the certitude of an ending — both structurally, in terms of a teleology and plot closure, and thematically, in terms of the representation of death — seems to disappear.

Kermode's study is offered as a theory of fiction and the problems he identifies are a guide to reading modern prose writing, but his argument seems to be at the heart of modernist theatre's preoccupation with death too. The decreasing importance of Aristotelian principles of dramatic organization in theatre towards the end of the nineteenth century, leading to increased experimentation in naturalist, symbolist, and expressionist drama, has likewise been described a crisis.[4] As the dramatic form most clearly defined by death, suffering, and generating a sense of or through endings, the tragedy and its changing status around 1900 would seem to be the logical point of comparison with Kermode's 'studies in fiction'. Indeed, arguments about the incongruity of tragedy and modernity — whether in the sense of a macro-epoch since 1700 or the literary movement of modernism — are commonplace in debates around 1900 and contemporary criticism alike.[5] Péter Szondi's *Essay on the Tragic* and George Steiner's *Death of Tragedy*, referred to in the title of the present essay, are perhaps the most influential critical accounts of this tendency.[6]

In order to understand these arguments, it is necessary to dwell for a moment on the particular conceptualization of the tragedy as a dramatic form that informs these debates and informs my own argument. In the German context,[7] both the historical and contemporary discussions of the modern decline of tragedy are based on a (sometimes more, sometimes less) strict formal compliance with a (neo)-classicist understanding of tragedy developed by writers like Johann Christoph Gottsched, Gotthold Ephraim Lessing, Friedrich Schiller, Georg Wilhelm Hegel, and Friedrich Hebbel from the 1720s onwards.[8] In this tradition, we might identify tragedy with Mark Roche as the theatrical depiction of 'an action in which the hero's greatness leads inexorably to suffering',[9] whereby this path to suffering is determined by tragic necessity, whether caused by fate or character flaw. Greatness in this respect might mean social status (Gottsched), moral virtue (Lessing), feeling (also Lessing), or powers of reason and self-control (Schiller), and the tragic plot arises from insoluble aporias of opposing values around these factors which make action problematic and ultimately catastrophic. Of course, the idea that there is any one 'classicist' form of tragedy is a fallacy, as the well-known differences between Gottsched and Lessing on the definition of tragic greatness/*Fallhöhe* and even something so central as catharsis prove. In this respect, a minimal definition of tragedy would be the depiction of great suffering in a conflict structure with a generally negative conclusion,[10] whereby the Aristotelian idea that the conflict must be complete (i.e. composed of an introduction, a middle part and an ending) remains central. According to Roland Galle, enlightenment principles such as an optimistic anthropology, individual autonomy, reason, tolerance, and reconciliation call into question the general incompatibility of modern social life and tragic necessity.[11] Here it is worth remembering Rita Felski's description of how tragedy depicts 'the role of the incalculable and unforeseeable in human affairs, it forces us to recognize that individuals act against their own interests and that the consequences of their actions may deviate disastrously from what they expected and hoped for'.[12] If modernity defines itself in opposition to fatefulness through autonomy, progress and mankind's ability to determine its own course of life; if we identify democracy and compromise rather than absolutism as politically valuable; where scepticism with respect to tradition and established values dominates; and if the possibility of heroism is hollowed out by the psychological analysis of the subject — then the possibility of tragedy in modernism becomes a matter of some difficulty.

This questioning of tragedy also extends to the depiction of death in these plays — indeed Steiner's title *Death of Tragedy* is deliberately ambiguous and refers both to the tragic form and to the deaths depicted in ostensibly tragic plays.[13] When Moritz's death in Wedekind's play is undermined by his spectral afterlife, we are simultaneously offered a ghostly indication of a crisis of tragedy and its traditional modes of dramatic representations of death. In the presence of spectres, revenants, and tropes of regeneration, death is both rendered meaningless *and* continues to provide individuals' lives with a sense of meaning. It is to such accounts of death in three paradigmatic plays of German modernism that this chapter will now turn its attention.

Frank Wedekind, *Frühlings Erwachen*

Written and published in 1891 and first performed under the direction of Max Reinhardt and Hermann Bahr at the Kammerspiele of the Deutsches Theater in Berlin in 1906, *Frühlings Erwachen* neatly bookends a period which we might describe as 'early' modernism in Germany.[14] Both the play's content and Reinhardt's staging of it — albeit in a significantly shortened and censored version — prefigure many of Expressionism's central thematic and stylistic innovations and indicate an emerging modernist aesthetic distancing itself from established nineteenth-century modes of theatrical representation.[15] On the one hand, Wedekind uses the theme of youthful protagonists deformed by the repressive values of the parents' generation to criticize an increasingly calcified and authoritarian Wilhelmine social order. On the other hand, the use of grotesque caricature to represent this authority coupled with an economy of language and a largely discontinuous episodic structure provides a powerful illustration of the growing currency of a looser, 'open' dramatic form in modernism.[16] In *Frühlings Erwachen* Wedekind's social critique and the loosening of Aristotelian convention are intricately linked by means of a fixation with the mortality of the adolescents it presents.

Death and suffering are ubiquitous by the close of Wedekind's play, albeit not in an actual depiction of dying or death, but rather in the portrayal of their after-effects amongst the living. In Act II, Scene 7 we see Moritz Stiefel succumbing on the one hand to the weight of social pressure, and on the other to his inability to comprehend and control his awakening sexual urges, in his intention to commit suicide. As explicit as Wedekind's play is in its depiction of sexual acts, however, this is not replicated in the case of dying: we don't see Moritz's suicide itself, merely his final lines: 'Jetzt gehe ich nicht mehr nach Hause' (p. 296) [I'll never be at home again (p. 52)]. What we *do* actually see, however, in Act III, Scene 2, is the unwillingness to mourn his death. Set around Moritz's open grave in a 'Friedhof in strömendem Regen' (p. 301) [A graveyard in pouring rain (p. 59)], this scene has the parents and teachers both disown him: 'Der Junge war nicht von mir' (p. 302) [He was no son of mine (p. 59)], says Rentier Stiefel, and Professor Knochenbruch calls him '[v]erbummelt — versumpft — verhurt — verlumpt — und verludert!' (p. 302) [Dissipated — dissolute — debauched — destroyed — decaying! (p. 60)]. The adolescents, on the other hand, do mourn, and it is only from them that we find out how Moritz has died:

> ILSE.   Ich war schon über der Brücke drüben, da hört' ich den Knall. [...] Hier ist die Pistole.
> MARTHA.   Deshalb hat man sie nicht gefunden!
> ILSE.   Ich nahm sie ihm gleich aus der Hand, als ich am Morgen vorbeikam.
> MARTHA.   Schenke sie mir, Ilse! — Bitte, schenk sie mir!
> ILSE.   Nein, die behalt' ich zum Andenken.
> MARTHA.   Ist's wahr, Ilse, daß er ohne Kopf drinliegt?
> ILSE.   Er muß sie mit Wasser geladen haben! — Die Königskerzen waren über und über mit Blut besprengt. Sein Hirn hing in den Weiden umher.
>
> (p. 304)

[ILSE.   I'd just crossed the bridge when I heard the shot. [...] Here is the pistol.
MARTHA.   That's why no one found it.
ILSE.   It was in his hand. I took it when I went past this morning
MARTHA.   Let me have it, Ilse. Please give it to me.
ILSE.   No, I want to keep it for good luck.
MARTHA.   Is it true he's down there without his head?
ILSE.   He must have loaded the gun with water. The lupins were all sprayed with blood, and his brains were hanging round on the bulrushes. (pp. 62–63)]

As brutal and disturbing as this instance of death is, it is *narrated* to us, producing a paradoxical moment. On the one hand, this epic 'Botenbericht' returns to both teichoscopy and the death *récit* in (French) neoclassical drama; on the other hand, this formal referencing of a traditional technique breaks with those nineteenth-century representations of death in tragedy that were foremost in Wedekind's mind. It may seem like a minor point that we are not shown this death, we are told about it, but this prefigures the mistrust of established forms of dramatic closure that we have already seen in Moritz's postmortal presence at the end of the play.

The death of the leading female character, Wendla, in Act III, Scene 5 is at a similar chronological remove. Here we encounter Wendla for the last time lying pregnant with Melchior's child and drained of energy in her bed as she is attended to by her mother and her physician, completely unaware of her pregnant state. At the end of the scene her mother discloses her pregnancy to her, but not why she is ill, with the doctor and mother both simply saying she is suffering from anaemia ('Bleichsucht', p. 312). Dr. von Brausepulver is actually attending her because of a botched homemade abortion, the aftereffects of which Wendla depicts with a foreboding sense of premonition. Alongside the 'Herzbeklemmungen ... Kopfschmerz, das Frösteln, der Schwindel' and 'Erbrechen', Wendla says: 'Und dann kommt das Zahnweh, und ich meine, daß ich morgen am Tag sterben muß' (p. 311) [tightness round the heart — and the headaches and the cold shivering — faint feelings and vomiting ... and then the aching teeth and I think I'm going to die tomorrow (p. 71, translation amended)]. Once again, however, we don't actually see Wendla's death itself; the next time she 'appears' is underneath the gravestone that Melchior finds in the graveyard scene, Act III, Scene 7:

> Hier ruht in Gott
> WENDLA BERGMANN
> geboren am 5. Mai 1878
> gestorben an der Bleichsucht
> den 27. Oktober 1892.
> Selig sind sie, die reinen Herzens sind ... (p. 316)

> [Here rests in God
> Wendla Bergmann
> Born 5th May 1878
> died of anaemia
> 27th October 1892
> Blessed are the pure of heart. (p. 77)]

In *Frühlings Erwachen* death is not represented dramatically, then: it appears rather as a second-degree, or epic, order of representation — in this case through a gravestone as a mere sign that records and mourns Wendla's already occurred death.

Returning to the final scene of the play, we see Melchior Gabor, the father of Wendla's unborn child, climbing over the wall of the graveyard on a bright November night to experience his own personal encounter with death. This 'Totenreich' [realm of the dead] almost immediately becomes more than simply a pathetic fallacy of Gothic atmospherics ('An Busch und Bäumen raschelt das dürre Laub. — Zerissene Wolken jagen unter dem Mond hin' (p. 315) [Dry leaves rustle on bushes and trees. Torn clouds chase each other across the moon (p. 76)]) when Moritz, who by this stage has already committed suicide, appears on stage as a revenant: 'Moritz Stiefel *seinen Kopf unter dem Arm, stapft über die Gräber her*' (p. 316) [Moritz Stiefel, head under his arm, comes stumping across the graves (p. 77)]. In this 'Kindertragödie' [children's tragedy] death is not final, this scene suggests. Firstly, Moritz's revenant offers a continuing presence for a supposedly tragic hero who should by all rights no longer be present. Secondly, in the ensuing debate involving Moritz and an equally disturbing *Vermummten Herr* [masked man], Melchior gives up a plan to commit suicide himself ('kann ich aufatmen und mir sagen, wie weit ich bin' (p. 315) [I can breathe ... and think (p. 76)]) and returns with the stranger into the bosom of the same society that had previously rendered him an outsider. The *Vermummte Herr* offers Melchior an escape from his potentially tragic entrapment at the end of the play: 'Ich mache dir den Vorschlag, dich mir anzuvertrauen. Ich würde fürs erste für dein Fortkommen sorgen. [...] Ich führe dich unter Menschen. Ich gebe dir Gelegenheit, deinen Horizont in der fabelhaftesten Weise zu erweitern' (p. 319) [I'll make you a proposition. You trust me. The first thing we'll do is to get you out of this. ... I will take you among real people. Come with me and expand your horizon (pp. 80–81)]. Melchior ultimately accepts the offer and the Vermummte Herr 'legt seinen Arm in denjenigen Melchiors und entfernt sich mit ihm über die Gräber hin.' (p. 322) [lays his arm in Melchior's and they go over the graves (p. 83)]. Melchior's transformation from a broken young man on the verge of suicide into a newly empowered 'Mensch' [human] here (p. 321) offers an early vision of a Nietzschean vitalism that comes to dominate the dramas of Ernst Toller, Georg Kaiser, and others in Expressionism.[17]

The engagement with final questions — with dying, death, and postmortality — remains central in this final scene, raising questions over tragic inevitability and the finality of death that are no less innovative in terms of genre history than the sexually explicit content and use of adolescent characters in this titular 'Kindertragödie'.[18] With the openness of Moritz's and Melchior's present and future states, the play flouts the dramatic certitude of 'closed' Aristotelian tragic form and Melchior's story seems to begin anew. As Szondi discusses at length for the period around 1900,[19] theorists of drama and philosophers alike identified different reasons for this decline in tragedy, both with respect to purely formal considerations[20] and in philosophical, theological and sociological terms (with the dissipation of fate and necessity in the post-enlightenment, individualist worldview,[21] on the one hand, and the growth of a democratic, economic organization of society in modernity,[22] on the other). Rather than 'existing outside history' (p. 192), Szondi argues that traditional dramatic form 'came into being in seventeenth-century France and was perpetuated in the German classical period' (p. 193), exercising a normative power over nineteenth-century realism (p. 194). Starting from an observation that playwrights like Ibsen, Strindberg, Hauptmann and Maeterlinck show a decreasing belief in the ability of these tight rules and organization of the traditional dramatic form to represent a reality that clearly does not function in this way, Szondi sees the move towards formal experimentation and open endings as a sign of crisis and a concomitant need for innovation (pp. 197–98). With its thematic and formal dependence on death, tragedy becomes an important medium for dealing with such questions of ending and closure around 1900.

In *Frühlings Erwachen*, Wedekind's reasons for rejecting tragic closure seem clear: namely that Wendla's and Moritz's deaths are both avoidable, the unnecessary result of an intractable society. The body count in *Frühlings Erwachen* is still substantial, death is still an important component of the play and it enables a critical consideration of social life at the *fin de siècle*, but if death emerges as preventable by changing societal conditions, then it ceases to be tragic in the established, classicist conceptualization of tragedy. Traditional tragic models in German literature did not entirely exculpate individual characters from contributing to their downfall (the three most important German writers on tragedy in the eighteenth and early nineteenth centuries, Gottsched, Lessing, and Schiller, all stress the necessity of the tragic hero's 'mixed character' despite their differing levels of adherence to French neo-classicism), with the relationship between a character's fate and flaws remaining constant. Nevertheless, there is no sense of *hamartia*, the protagonists' tragic flaw here, unless we are prepared to accept socially induced ignorance about sexual and emotional matters in young people as such a failing. Perhaps the central difference is that we assume that the external, social conditions here can change whereas Oedipus simply *is* Laius' son, or Titus simply *is* a Roman emperor and thus unable to marry a foreign queen, but there may be more at stake. Rita Felski writes that 'tragedy undermines the sovereignty of selfhood and modern dreams of progress and perfectability, as exemplified in the belief that human beings can orchestrate their own happiness',[23] suggesting, like Christoph Menke, that modernity is defined by its 'Überwindung der Tragödie' [transcending tragedy], which may be seen as progressive (following Hegel) or as a decadent decline (following Nietzsche).[24] These factors coalesce in *Frühlings Erwachen*, and move the trajectory of the play closer towards the sphere of the comic, which Ralf Simon has defined on the basis of its ability to generate a distance from the tragic action in order to provide a metacommentary and thus the potential for relief and alternatives.[25] Perhaps this move towards the comic is why such a potentially powerful scene as Melchior's encounter with Moritz seems be dominated by bathos rather than tragic pathos, the headless chicken effect of Moritz-as-revenant appearing anything other than noble in his suffering. It is precisely this argument in favour of a flexibility and adaptability of societal norms and expectations that negates the potential for tragedy in this play.

This is not to suggest that there is no suffering in the stories of characters like Melchior, Wendla, or Moritz in *Frühlings Erwachen*. Nor do I suggest that we should ignore the fact that the polemical accounts of the 'death' of tragedy in modernity in Szondi and Steiner blend out many examples of playwrights attempting to 'rejuvenate' tragedy following Nietzsche.[26] Indeed, there is a sense of tragic suffering amongst the adolescents of *Frühlings Erwachen* in that their deaths are caused by familial, social, and educational conditions that they do not fully comprehend or control themselves. To what extent the contingencies of social life — which are by definition man-made and thus not necessary — or the positive surpassing of the limitations of bourgeois individualism in Expressionism conform to traditional (minimal) definitions of the tragedy as the depiction of great suffering in a conflict structure with a generally negative conclusion is, however, questionable.[27] These plays may indeed be part of the tragic discourse, they may even seek to represent a more general 'tragic' reality of modernity in their plots, but as socially critical dramas they have clearly moved beyond inherited, traditional models of the tragic genre. In demanding a change to the social conditions that caused the suffering in their fictions, these plays argue powerfully against passive acceptance of social norms and rules as inevitabilities, and hence against one of the basic traditional categories which has been used to define tragedy: fate, destiny, or necessity.

Georg Kaiser: *Von morgens bis mitternachts*

Georg Kaiser's *Von morgens bis mitternachts*, written in 1912, first published in 1916, and performed in Munich in 1917, tells the story of a bank clerk known simply by his function, 'Kassierer', who embezzles 60,000 marks one morning and then sets about trying to break out of the limitations of his petit-bourgeois life in search of a transcendental sense of value.[28] The play's title is an ironic reference to the Aristotelian unity of time, as the action of the play — which takes the cashier from Weimar to the Prussian metropolis in Berlin with its packed velodrome, its cabaret-styled speakeasies, and its Salvation Army halls — literally spans the course of one day as demanded by classicist poetics: 'von morgens bis mitternachts rase ich im Kreise' [From morning to midnight I chase round in a frenzied circle].[29] With its highly condensed form, its frequently truncated language, its grotesque and comic characterization, and its almost entirely discontinuous episodic structure, *Von morgens bis mitternachts* is both a powerful heir to *Frühlings Erwachen* and a paradigmatic example of Expressionism's wholesale rejection of nineteenth-century realism.

Perhaps less well known now than Kaiser's more programmatic dramas such as *Die Bürger von Calais*, this *Stationendrama* is a powerful illustration of the growing currency of open dramatic form, on the one hand, and Expressionism's dismay at the self-satisfied identities of the Wilhelmine bourgeoisie, on the other.[30] The term *Stationendrama* [station drama] describes the loose progression from one episode to the next which is typical of Expressionism and is even referred to in precisely these terms in Kaiser's play: 'Ich will euch mit den Stationen nicht aufhalten, an denen ich mich aufhielt' [I don't want to detain you with the stations where I stopped (my translation)] he says when summarizing his own story in the final scene at the Salvation Army Hall (p. 514). If there is any one coherent development that unites the play's episodes it is the Kassierer's growing realization that money cannot buy anything of any real value. In the final scene of Part I in the play, set in the snow-covered countryside outside Weimar following his attempt to purchase the erotic adventures of an Italian lady who had earlier visited his bank, the Kassierer comes to the conclusion that 'Wert und Gegenwert [nicht] in Einklang [zu] bringen [sind]' (p. 483) [value and value cannot be reconciled (p. 39, translation amended)] when economic criteria are predominant. But despite this moment of clarity, the Kassierer proceeds from one episode to the next in Berlin where he tries to do precisely this: to paradoxically purchase an absolute and transcendental experience. It is only when the soldiers of the Salvation Army begin fighting over his money that he ultimately realizes: 'Mit keinem Geld aus allen Bankkonten der Welt kann man etwas von Wert kaufen. [...] Das Geld verschlechtert den Wert' (p. 515) [Not all the money from all the banks in the world can buy anything of real value. [...] Money diminishes value (p. 71)].

Having reached this realization in Berlin, the Kassierer commits suicide at the play's conclusion:

> KASSIERER.   [...] Von morgens bis mitternachts rase ich im Kreise — nun zeigt sein fingerhergewinktes Zeichen den Ausweg ——— wohin?!! (*Er zerschießt die Antwort in seine Hemdbrust. Die Posaune stirbt mit dünner werdendem Ton an seinem Mund hin.*) [...] (*ist mit ausgebreiteten Armen gegen das aufgenähte Kreuz des Vorhangs gesunken. Sein Ächzen hüstelt wie eine Ecce — sein Hauchen surrt wie ein Homo.*) (p. 517)

> [CASHIER.   [...] From morning to midnight I chase around in a frenzied circle — his beckoning finger shows the way out — where to? (*He shoots the answer into his shirt-front. The trumpet dies out at his lips with a fading note.*) [...] (*has fallen back with outstretched arms against the cross sewn onto the curtain. His dying cough sounds like an 'Ecce' — his expiring breath like a whispered 'Homo'.*) (p. 73)]

At first this suicide seems to be born out of the frustration and disenchantment of running in circles while trying to escape the limitations of his petit-bourgeois, capitalist worldview. There is, however, a subtle subtext here that this final act of dying is the logical conclusion of the Kassierer having finally come to sense. Reflecting on the earlier snow scene, the Kassierer notes: 'Ein Fünkchen Erleuchtung hätte mir geholfen und mir die Strapazen erspart. Es gehört ja so lächerlich wenig Verstand dazu!' (p. 516) [A little spark of enlightenment would have helped me and spared me all that trouble. So ridiculously little intelligence is needed! (p. 73)]. There is a moment of awakening in this conclusion, a final act of self-realization and a movement beyond the capitalist, consumerist mind-set which the Kassierer had occupied up until this point. In the image of him in a Christ-like pose in front of the cross, we are encouraged to see this act of dying as an act of self-sacrifice: the Kassierer's death becomes a story of 'the End', offering, to borrow Kermode's term, 'the sense of an ending' from which he and — more importantly — the audience can make sense of his life and begin to change their lives accordingly. In short, this appears to be a tragic death.

At least it would appear to be a tragic death if the play finished with his whispered 'Ecce Homo'. But it doesn't. Instead, a policeman enters the Salvation Army Hall and says in the darkness after all the lights have exploded: 'Es ist ein Kurzschluss in der Leitung' (p. 517) [There must have been a short circuit (p. 73)].[31] As in *Frühlings Erwachen* the pathos of the Kassierer's final speech gives way to the bathos of a mundane short circuit. If the Kassierer's death was an act of self-sacrifice, this dull, everyday observation drags the play back into the world of the petty bourgeoisie from which he had sought to escape.[32] Even if one were to ignore this bathos, there is an additional problem insofar as the play's conclusion seems to offer up the Kassierer's death as an act of self-sacrifice in pursuit of a higher form of knowledge and living. The death of the Kassierer actually seems to be desirable rather than tragic, a necessary step on the path to becoming what Expressionists celebrated as the 'Neue Mensch', the 'New Man', and thus not strictly an ending either. In this respect *Von morgens bis mitternachts* can be classified as a *Wandlungsdrama*, a subgroup of Expressionist dramas in which the radical inner renewal or rebirth of an individual is used to transmit a utopian — and often pacifist — message.[33] The positive surpassing of the limitations of bourgeois individualism in such visions, and indeed at the close of *Von morgens bis mitternachts*, thus seems to vary rather than neatly conform to traditional definitions of the tragedy.

To what extent such a positive sense of martyrdom and the concomitant meaningfulness of death persists — however contradictory of tragic suffering in the traditional sense — is also debatable in the case of *Von morgens bis mitternachts*, however. It is here that the bathos surrounding the Kassierer's pose as a Christ-like redeemer is notable. This entire sequence of the play is presented to us as the repetition of an earlier instance of awakening and renewal in the play — namely the snow scene in Part I, which is now, at the end of the play, revealed to have been an empty promise. In the stage direction 'Die Lampe beleuchtet nun die hellen Drähte der Krone derart, daß sie ein menschliches Geripp zu bilden scheinen' [Single bulb lights up the bright wires in the crown of the chandelier in such a way that they seem to make a human skeleton] and in the Kassierer's monologue linking the 'Drahtgewirr des Kronleuchters' [wires of the chandelier] to the earlier 'schneelastenden Zweigen' [snow-laden branches] (pp. 516–17; p. 72) of the snow scene, the play's grand finale appears in the ironic mode of citation:

> Wo ist die Ware, die man mit dem vollen Einsatz kauft?! Ich muß bezahlen!! ——Ich habe das Geld bar!! ——[...] Ihr müßt mir doch liefern ——Ihr müßt mir Wert und Gegenwert in Einklang bringen!! [...] (*Sein Hut ist ihm entrissen. Der Orkan hat den Schnee von den Zweigen gepeitscht: Reste in der Krone haften und bauen ein menschliches Geripp mit grinsenden Kiefern auf. Eine Knochenhand hält den Hut.*) Bist du die erschöpfende Antwort auf meine nachdrückliche Befragung? Willst du mit einer einigermaßen reichlich durchlöcherten Existenz andeuten: das abschließende Ergebnis — deine Abgebranntheit? — Das ist etwas dürftig. Sehr dürftig. Nämlich nichts! [...] Ich habe noch einiges zu erledigen. [...] Rufen Sie mich gegen Mitternacht nochmals an. (pp. 483–84)

[I must pay! — I have the money in cash!! — Where are goods worth total investment?! ... You must deliver the goods — you must give a fair deal — value for value!! ... (*His hat is whipped off. The hurricane has lashed the snow from the branches. Remnants stick in the crown and form a human face with grinning jaws. A skeleton holds the hat.*) Are you the all-encompassing response to my emphatic interrogations? Do you wish to suggest with your well-perforated existence: the final solution — your immolation? — That is a bit meagre. Extremely meagre. In fact, nothing! [...] I still have things to do. [...] Call on me again at midnight. (pp. 38–39, translation amended)]

In this highly stylized setting, the landscape appears to become an allegorical moment of death and rebirth, a symbolic representation of the value of life and 'final questions'. Indeed, only a few moments later at the start of Part II, the Kassierer responds to his wife's questioning where he has come from with the words: 'Aus dem Grabe' (p. 486) [From the grave (p. 41)]. In the figurative, ideological dimension of the play, the Kassierer is already a dead man walking *even before* his final self-sacrifice.

As was the case with Moritz in the final scene of *Frühlings Erwachen*, the Kassierer of the second half of the play is painted as a revenant embarking on a seemingly fruitless process of renewal, or *Wandlung*, then. Similarly, just as Wendla's gravestone is a second-order representation of a death we don't actually see, the ironic citational gesture at the end of *Von morgens bis mitternachts* appears as the repetition of a death that was symbolic, bringing us back to the starting point of the Kassierer's journey of renewal: 'Ich melde dir meine Ankunft! (*Posaunenstöße*) Ich habe den Weg hinter mir' (p. 516) [(*Fanfares*) I announce my arrival to you. My path is behind me (p. 73)]. Depending on how one reads the Kassierer's death, it may — even in this citational mode — still appeal to the audience not to make the same mistakes as the Kassierer and to undertake a sense of renewal themselves, or may in its final bathos — in a defeatist gesture — question the audience's ability to derive any such meaning from the Kassierer's final monologue. In both cases, Kaiser's play presents an ending and a death which seem to repeat and return (*revenir*), which seem to pose more questions than provide meanings, and which, in either their positive or negated instances of sacrifice in the service of transcendence, cease to be tragic. Such an approach prefigures what Heiner Müller has called the 'spectral' citational nature of theatrical representation, noting that all performances of plays are exercises in 'Totenbeschwörung' [séance] and the 'Dialog mit den Toten' [dialogue with the dead].[34] In its multimedial and performative repetitions — each performance repeating and varying previous performances, which themselves portray repetition and haunting returns on the plot level — Kaiser's play suggests a 'hauntological' model of space and time in the theatre, which Jacques Derrida has identified at the heart of the spectre.[35]

Bertolt Brecht: *Die Maßnahme*

With its programmatic rejection of the conventions of both classical dramatic theatre and tragic form from the late-1920s onwards, the theatre of Bertolt Brecht is the apogee of the development this essay has been tracing thus far. In his 'Kleines Organon für das Theater', written in 1948, Brecht describes traditional dramatic representation deliberately as a 'business', suggesting that economic relations underlie theatre's focus on entertainment and 'fun' through 'living representations of reported or invented events involving human beings' that 'remain entirely superfluous'.[36] In earlier theoretical reflections such as 'Anmerkungen zur Oper *Aufstieg und Fall der Stadt Mahagonny*' Brecht developed a model of theatre radically opposed to the 'illusions' of reality offered in this business which he variously criticizes as 'culinary' and even 'intoxicating'/'narcotic' on the basis that they lull the spectator into the passive role of a consumer and hence stifle any political potential.[37] As he states with a polemical directness in his *Mahagonny-Notes*, Brecht's epic theatre derives from a belief in the ability of humans to change their minds and thereby to change the conditions of social organization, which in Brecht's burgeoning Marxist perspective means changing the structures of dependency and enforced passivity that he identifies in capitalist consumption in the late-Weimar years: 'Humankind [is] changeable and able to change things'.[38]

Within this project of politically inspired theatrical and dramatic reform, Brecht's most radical experiments included the *Lehrstücke*, the 'teaching and learning' plays of the period between 1929 and 1932 which he developed in cooperation with the musicians Kurt Weill, Paul Hindemith, and Hanns Eisler. These plays deploy many of the techniques of the epic theatre — such as distancing and self-reflexive alienation effects, anti-illusory staging methods, commentary functions etc. — but their guiding principle was to explore the possibilities of learning — about political and economic matters — through acting. Rather than presenting a lesson for the audience in the play's plot, the process of learning occurs through active engagement in the form of role-playing by adopting attitudes, postures, and intellectual positions in the course of the performance. As plays, the *Lehrstücke* are highly stylized and have a rigorous and formalized structure that enables processes of trial and reflection in the course of the performance. In *Die Maßnahme*, for example, Brecht's play of 1930/31 which rehearses a scenario in which a young communist activist in China assents to being murdered in order to further the cause of the revolution,[39] this idea of the performance as (in Benjamin's words) a 'political meeting'[40] is immediately clear. Its processual, performative structure demands a dialectical, interactional relationship between text, actor, and audience.

If 'humanity itself has become the fate of humanity', as Brecht writes in the later *Messingkauf* notes,[41] then there is little space for the necessity and intractability of the tragic form, of course: 'Nun ist es ganz richtig, daß die tragische Stimmung der Alten dadurch sehr gestört würde, daß die gesellschaftliche Grundlage des Schicksals eines Helden nicht mehr als etwas Dauerndes, von den Menschen nicht Abänderbares [...] dargestellt würde' [Now it is entirely correct that the tragic feeling of the Ancients has been most thoroughly destroyed by means of the fact that the fate of the hero [...] can no longer be represented [...] as something which is eternal, something not subject to change by humans].[42] Brecht sees himself 'almost' as a 'writer of comedies'[43] and criticizes the tragedy's structural reliance on presenting human suffering as necessary because it does not enable any real analysis of the social and political conditions responsible for this suffering: 'the tragedy more often portrays human suffering less seriously than the comedy'.[44] However Brecht is only 'almost' a writer of comedies — the real hallmark of his drama is a mixture of the comic and tragic in his presentation of often quite real instances of suffering: 'there is no longer any reason for the sharp division of genres — unless such a reason is found. The events take on a tragic or comic aspect as appropriate; their tragic or comic side is brought into the foreground'.[45]

The *Lehrstücke*, and *Die Maßnahme* in particular, offer a powerful illustration of this changed representation of death. *Die Maßnahme* is the third of Brecht's experiments with the form and the titular 'measure taken' refers to the acceptance by a young activist of the necessity for him to lose his life in order to further the aims of the Communist Party in China. However, the play follows an epic model of organization which complicates this simple plot. The actual action of the play is the return of four communist agitators to Moscow from China in order to report their execution of a young comrade who has repeatedly jeopardized the group's propaganda efforts with his overly empathic, spontaneous activism; the story of this figure — simply known as the Young Comrade — only appears in the retrospective performance of storytelling of his returning compatriots, and thus as a series of plays-within-a-play. The play opens with a 'Control Chorus' congratulating the activists on their successful agitation in China, but it is interrupted as the four agitators demand its judgment on their actions. The Chorus replies with a demand: 'Stellt dar, wie es geschah und warum, und ihr werdet hören unser Urteil' (p. 75) [Describe [Perform] how it happened and why, and you will hear our verdict (p. 9)], thus opening up a meta-dramatical replaying of the situations that led to the 'measure' of murder being taken. *Die Maßnahme* thus follows a spectral, haunting logic of epic re-presentation of the Young Comrade's death in its pursuit of instruction and learning: by the time the action of the play is being recounted, the Young Comrade is long since dead.

Many critics have identified a tragic nature in the Young Comrade's death as a result of the apparent conflict between the wider cause of revolution and his individual sense of empathic activism in his 'case';[46] Reinhold Grimm even describes the play as a 'klassische Tragödie des Kommunismus' [classic tragedy of communism].[47] All of these accounts may indeed be correct in locating *Die Maßnahme* within a broader engagement with tragedy in modernism, but they ignore one important fact: this is not a classical dramatic action culminating in the death of the Young Comrade but rather a group of activists recounting and walking the Control Chorus through a series of events, which may or may not have taken place (their reliability as 'narrators' is open to question, given their partiality):

DER ERSTE AGITATOR.   Wir wollen ihn fragen, ob er einverstanden ist, denn
er war ein mutiger Kämpfer. (Freilich das Gesicht, das unter der Maske
hervorkam, war ein anderes, als das wir mit der Maske verdeckt hatten, und

das Gesicht, das der Kalk verlöschen wird, anders, als das Gesicht, das uns
einst an der Grenze begrüßte.)

DER ZWEITE AGITATOR.   Aber auch wenn er nicht einverstanden ist, muß er
verschwinden, und zwar ganz.

DER ERSTE AGITATOR (*zum jungen Genossen*).   Wenn du gefaßt wirst, werden
sie dich erschießen, und da du erkannt wirst, ist unsere Arbeit verraten. Also
müssen wir dich erschießen und in die Kalkgrube werfen, damit der Kalk
dich verbrennt. Aber wir fragen dich: weißt du einen Ausweg.

DER JUNGE GENOSSE.   Nein.

DIE DREI AGITATOREN.   So fragen wir dich: bist du einverstanden? (*Pause*).

DER JUNGE GENOSSE.   Ja.

DIE DREI AGITATOREN.   Wohin sollen wir dich tun, fragten wir ihn.

DER JUNGE GENOSSE.   In die Kalkgrube, sagte er.

DIE DREI AGITATOREN.   Wir fragten ihn: Willst du es allein machen?

DER JUNGE GENOSSE.   Helft mir.

DIE DREI AGITATOREN.
    Lehne deinen Kopf an unsern arm
    Schließ die Augen.

DER JUNGE GENOSSE (*unsichtbar*).
    Er sagte noch: Im Interesse des Kommunismus
    Einverstanden mit dem Vormarsch der proletarischen Massen
    Aller Länder
    Ja sagend zur Revolutionierung der Welt.

DIE DREI AGITATOREN.
    Dann erschossen wir ihn und
    Warfen ihn hinab in die Kalkgrube.
    Und als der Kalk ihn verschlungen hatte
    Kehrten wir zurück zu unserer Arbeit. (pp. 96–98)

[THE FIRST AGITATOR.   We want to ask him whether he agrees with us,
because he was a courageous fighter. (That face, of course, which appeared
from under the mask, was not the same face which he had once hidden with
the mask; and that face, which the lime will extinguish, is different from the
face which once greeted us at the border.)

THE SECOND AGITATOR.   But even if he does not agree with us, he must
disappear, completely.

THE FIRST AGITATOR (*to the young comrade*).   If you are caught you will be shot;
and since you'll be recognized, our work will have been betrayed. Therefore
we must be the ones to shoot you and cast you into the lime-pit, so that the
lime will burn away all traces of you. And yet we ask you: Do you know any
way out?

THE YOUNG COMRADE.   No.

THE THREE AGITATORS.   And we ask you: Do you agree with us? (*Pause*).

THE YOUNG COMRADE.   Yes.

THE THREE AGITATORS.   We also ask you: What shall we do with your body?

THE YOUNG COMRADE.   You must cast me into the lime-pit, he said.

THE THREE AGITATORS.   We asked: Do you want to do it alone?

THE YOUNG COMRADE.   Help me.

THE THREE AGITATORS.
    Rest your head on our arm.
    Close your eyes.

THE YOUNG COMRADE (*unseen*).
    And he said: In the interests of Communism
    In agreement with the progress of the proletarian masses
    Of all lands
    Consenting to the revolutionizing of the world.
THE THREE AGITATORS.
    Then we shot him and
    Cast him down into the lime-pit
    And when the lime had swallowed him up
    We turned back to our work. (pp. 33–34)]

This scene is quoted at length for what it reveals about Brecht's alienation effects and epic methods. In the first passage spoken in chorus by the three agitators the self-reflexive reference to the masks highlights the performative situation itself; likewise in the switch in tense between 'fragen' and 'fragten' the agitators emphasize their own acts of narration. Strictly speaking this scene does not actually contain a death. Firstly, and naively, the death/murder itself is not actually visible in this scene; even if we are to suspend the epic, self-reflexive status of this performance as a re-telling of the story, we do not see the actual moment of dying, as the stage direction 'unsichtbar' makes clear. Secondly, and more importantly, the status of this scene as a representation within a representation means that once again this is a death which appears in a wholly citational mode; it is a second-order representation of dying in a play in which the dead figure takes on an entirely revenant status in the language and role play of the agitators. Thirdly, as indicated in the references to the masks, there is not even 'one' revenant Young Comrade who dies here: throughout the play, the role of the Young Comrade is constantly rotated and re-distributed among the four activists, a sense of confusion which is captured in this scene in the opaque distribution of speaking roles and the slippage of personal pronouns from 'ich' to 'er', most notably in the passage where the Young Comrade provides his acquiescence and praises the revolution. To view this death as a guarantor of tragic form is, as Reiner Steinweg points out, to misunderstand both the intentions and the formal structures of *Die Maßnahme* as a *Lehrstück*.[48]

Notwithstanding the formal complexities of this scene the question of acquiescence, of 'Einverständnis', also begins to negate the tragic nature of the Young Comrade's death here. Hans-Thies Lehmann notes: 'Dieses Einverstandensein ist ein Hauptelement von Brechts lebenslangem Versuch, in seinem Diskurs eine Verwandlung des Todes aus einer passiv hinzunehmenden in eine aktiv zu tuende Wirklichkeit zu bewirken' [This acquiescence is a main component of Brecht's lifelong attempt to metamorphose death from a passive into an active reality in his writing].[49] Brecht views death as a constitutive part of an active process, as an action amongst others rather than the end of all action or a borderline event. As Jost Hermand has discussed at length, this political aesthetics of death still borders on the idea of sacrifice, of course, and hence brings the death of the Young Comrade into the proximity of traditional tragic dramas of martyrdom.[50] There is something cold and calculating about the manner in which *Die Maßnahme* 'deploys' death almost as the decisive step towards necessary social change and progress in this respect and indeed Astrid Oesmann has argued that there is a form of cruelty in the 'investigation of the value of human life when ideological thought and revolutionary change are released into social interaction'.[51] From Brecht's perspective, however, this is a cruelty that is minimized by acknowledging that the individual is itself an economic and social construct rather than an existential constant. This is a lesson that emerges from the early experimentation with epic forms in *Mahagonny* where Brecht summarized his approach in the aphorism: 'Humankind [is] changeable and able to change things'.[52] Thus while Brecht calls his *Lehrstücke* in general a 'Sterbelehre' (an instruction in teaching/learning of death[53]), these are lessons based on the social, and hence changeable, implications of death, and not on intractable, existential necessities. More than that, death here is the basis for starting over again. Death as the dialectical precondition of the 'new' is precisely what *Die Maßnahme* depicts when it offers up the passing of the Young Comrade as the means by which revolution's progression is guaranteed. As the subject of active participation, then, the death of the Young Comrade is no longer figured as an absolute end-point of the action; in fact it is actually the play's starting point. This is a fact which is captured formally and structurally in his spectral, revenant status in the re-presentation of the supposed main action or event — the actively accepted death of the Young Comrade.

★   ★   ★   ★   ★

Death is still an important component of all the plays discussed here and it enables a critical consideration of social life in modernity. In *Die Maßnahme*, as in *Frühlings Erwachen* and even *Von morgens bis mitternachts*, death doesn't provide a finality, however. Both the Young Comrade and Moritz appear to haunt the stage to tell their stories posthumously in citational, epic structures, while the Kassierer's death appears to occur twice and is subject to a similar logic of beginning all over again that is visible in Brecht's *Lehrstück*. As suggested earlier, at issue here seems to be a rejection of the neo-classicist idea that the conflict depicted in the tragedy needs to be complete, that there needs to be a sense of closure. There is also a more fundamental point of criticism, however, as each of these dramatists apparently engages with tragic form and traditions in order to reject its fundamental reliance on tragic necessity. This is already apparent in Wedekind's suggestion that socially imposed — and thus changeable — ignorance rather than a fundamental character flaw is responsible for the death of the children in *Frühlings Erwachen*, but it remains central to Brecht's dialectical model of learning, whereby the transcendence of conflicting political motives is desirable. Kaiser, on the other hand, views the petit-bourgeois realities of the modern, capitalist employee as a matter worthy of bathos rather than pathos: any potential 'greatness' of the Kassierer is repeatedly undermined. Without wishing to flatten out the conceptual and formal differences between each of these plays, they are united by an approach to social criticism which renders death as either preventable (and hence not tragic in the established, traditional sense of sense of the word) or as desirable (and hence a therapeutic dose of optimism in the face of a potentially great suffering).

This questioning of tragedy also extends to the depiction of death in these plays. Notwithstanding the omnipresence of death in modernism, it appears as though death is actually up for debate. When Moritz's death in Wedekind's play is undermined by his spectral afterlife, when the Kassierer's death appears as a comic repetition in Kaiser's play, and where the Junge Genosse's death is no longer the end-point of the action and is indeed politically desirable in Brecht's play, modernism seems to distrust catharsis as a means of achieving social change. This is most explicitly the case in Brecht, whose 'Kleines Organon' — as we saw — engaged most directly with the passivity inducing, narcotic effects of traditional dramatic catharsis. Death is omnipresent in German modernism but it is far from final. In the presence of spectres, revenants, and tropes of regeneration, death is placed in the service of an innovative, socially critical, and politically active form of theatre that seeks to transcend the status quo. It is the sense of non-ending surrounding death that is important to Wedekind, Kaiser, and Brecht. Without fictions of finality, society and its catastrophes reveal themselves as contingent and thus subject to change — and that is the point of modernism's spectral performances.

Notes to Chapter 8

1. Frank Wedekind, *Frühlings Erwachen (1891)*, in *Werke. Kritische Studienausgabe*, ed. by Elke Austermühl, Rolf Kieser and Hartmut Vinçon, 15 vols (Darmstadt: Häusser, 1994–2013), II (2000), ed. by Mathias Baum and Rolf Kieser, pp. 259–322 (p. 315); *Spring Awakening*, trans. by Tom Osborne (London: John Calder, 1981), p. 76. All further references are to these editions and will appear as a simple page number in the main body of the text.
2. Frank Kermode, *The Sense of an Ending: Studies in the Theory of Fiction* (Oxford: Oxford University Press, 1979 [1966]), pp. 3 and 4.
3. Kermode, *The Sense of an Ending*, pp. 5 and 3. Further references in this paragraph are signalled by their page number.
4. Peter Szondi, *Theorie des modernen Dramas, 1880–1950* (Frankfurt am Main: Suhrkamp, 2004 [1956]). All subsequent quotations from Peter Szondi, 'Theory of the Modern Drama, Parts I–II', trans. by Michael Hays, *boundary 2*, 11.3 (1983), 191–230.
5. The list of writers who address the lack of tragedy around 1900 is remarkable and bring together multiple disciplines and cultural-political programmes: Friedrich Nietzsche, *Die Geburt der Tragödie aus dem Geiste der Musik* (1872); Georg Simmel, *Die Tragödie der Kultur* (1911); Walter Benjamin, *Ursprung des deutschen Trauerspiels* (1928).
6. Peter Szondi, *Versuch über das Tragische* (Frankfurt am Main: Suhrkamp, 1961); George Steiner, *The Death of Tragedy* (New York: Alfred A. Knopf, 1961).
7. Unlike the philosophers and critics mentioned above, the following essay makes no claim to a cross-cultural universality beyond German-language literature.
8. It is not my intention in the following essay to advocate for a particularly strict, neo-classical concept of tragedy; where I reference such models it is to enable a clearer picture of what the writers under discussion here, Wedekind, Kaiser, and Brecht, were distancing themselves from in the period I seek to reconstruct historically.
9. Mark W. Roche, 'The Tragicomic Absence of Tragedy', in *Signaturen der Gegenwartsliteratur. Festschrift für Walter Hinderer*, ed. by Dieter Borchmeyer (Würzburg: Königshausen & Neumann, 1999), pp. 265–76 (p. 266).
10. Daniel Fulda, 'Tragödie [Von Lessing bis zur Gegenwart]', in *Historisches Wörterbuch der Rhetorik*, 10 vols (Tübingen: Niemeyer, 1992–), IX (2009), ed. by Gert Ueding, pp. 762–67.
11. Roland Galle, 'Tragisch — Tragik', in *Ästhetische Grundbegriffe. Historisches Wörterbuch*, 7 vols (Stuttgart and Weimar: Metzler, 2000–05), VI: *Tanz — Zeitalter/Epoche* (2005), ed. by Karlheinz Barck et. al., pp. 117–70.

12. Rita Felski, 'Introduction', in *Rethinking Tragedy*, ed. by Rita Felski (Baltimore, MD: Johns Hopkins University Press, 2008), pp. 1–25 (p. 11).

13. Steiner, *The Death of Tragedy*.

14. On developments in German theatre around 1900 more generally, see for example Walter Hinck, *Das moderne Drama in Deutschland: Vom expressionistischen zum dokumentarischen Theater* (Göttingen: V&R, 1973). On Expressionism see Manfred Durzak, *Das expressionistische Drama* (Munich: Nymphenburger, 1978); Thomas Anz, *Literatur des Expressionismus* (Stuttgart, Weimar: Metzler, 2002). See also the relevant chapters on drama and theatre in *Hansers Sozialgeschichte der deutschen Literatur*, 12 vols, ed. by Rolf Grimminger (Munich: Hanser, 2000), VII: *Naturalismus, Fin de Siècle 1890–1918* (2000), ed. by York-Gothart Mix and Rolf Grimminger, and *Geschichte der deutschen Literatur von den Anfängen bis zur Gegenwart*, 12 vols, ed . by Helmut de Boor and Richard Newald (Munich: Beck, 1949–94), IX.1: *1870–1900: Von der Reichsgründung bis zur Jahrhundertwende* (1998), ed. by Peter Sprengel and IX.2: *1900–1918: Von der Jahrhundertwende bis zum Ende des Ersten Weltkriegs* (2004), ed. by Peter Sprengel.

15. On Wedekind's theatre more generally see Peter Skrine, *Hauptmann, Wedekind and Schnitzler* (Basingstoke: Macmillan, 1987); *Frank Wedekind*, ed. by Heinz Ludwig Arnold and Ruth Florack (Munich: Edition Text+Kritik, 1996); Ward B. Lewis, *The Ironic Dissident: Frank Wedekind in the View of his Critics* (Columbia, SC: Camden House, 1997).

16. Volker Klotz first introduced the distinction between 'open' and 'closed' dramatic form, pointing towards a spectrum of possibilities beyond reproducing the Aristotelian unities of time, place, and action and traditional distinctions between comedy and tragedy on the basis of their personnel, diction, and organization into acts. See Volker Klotz, *Geschlossene und offene Form im Drama* (Munich: Hanser, 1960).

17. See Hans Esselborn's excellent short article, 'Das Drama des Expressionismus', in *Die literarische Moderne in Europa*, 2 vols (Opladen: Westdeutscher Verlag, 1994), II: *Formation der literarischen Avantgarde*, ed. by Hans Joachim Piechotta, Ralph-Rainer Wuthenow, and Sabine Rothmann, pp. 271–82.

18. See for example Michael Patterson, *The Revolution in German Theatre* (Abingdon: Routledge, 2016 [1981]), pp. 44–45.

19. Peter Szondi, 'Versuch über das Tragische', in Peter Szondi: *Schriften I*, ed. by Jean Bollack and Henrietta Beese (Frankfurt am Main: Suhrkamp, 1978), pp. 149–260 (pp. 151–53). Further references in this paragraph are signalled by their page number.

20. See Hermann Bahr, *Dialog vom Tragischen* (Berlin: S. Fischer, 1904), pp. 19–20.

21. The most famous expression of this is Friedrich Nietzsche's *Die Geburt der Tragödie aus dem Geiste der Musik* (1872/1886).

22. See, for example, Georg Simmel, 'Der Begriff und die Tragödie der Kultur', in *Philosophische Kultur. Gesammelte Essays* (Berlin: Wagenbach, 1983 [1911]), pp. 183–207.

23. Felski, 'Introduction', p. 11.

24. Christoph Menke, 'Die Gegenwart der Tragödie. Eine ästhetische Aufklärung', *Neue Rundschau*, 111 (2000), 85–95 (p. 85), my translation. See also in more detail Christoph Menke, *Die Gegenwart der Tragödie. Versuch über Urteil und Spiel* (Frankfurt am Main: Suhrkamp, 2005). The most famous formulation of this incongruity of tragedy and modernity is of course Steiner's *Death of Tragedy*.

25. See Ralf Simon, 'Theorie der Komödie', in *Theorie der Komödie — Poetik der Komödie*, ed. by Ralf Simon (Bielefeld: Aisthesis, 2001), pp. 47–65.

26. For an excellent comparative account of this in German, French, and English-language literature see Werner Frick, *'Die mythische Methode'. Komparatistische Studien zur Transformation der griechischen Tragödie im Drama der klassischen Moderne* (Tübingen: Niemeyer, 1998).

27. Fulda, 'Tragödie [Von Lessing bis zur Gegenwart]', pp. 762–67.

28. For some introductory reading see Séan Allen, 'Kaiser: Von morgens bis mitternachts', in *Landmarks in German Drama*, ed. by Peter Hutchinson (Oxford: Peter Lang, 2002), pp. 159–217 and Frank Krause, *Georg Kaiser and Modernity* (Göttingen: V&R Unipress, 2005).

29. Georg Kaiser, *Von morgens bis mitternachts*, in *Werke*, ed. by Walther Huder, 6 vols (Frankfurt am Main: Propyläen, 1971), I: *Stücke 1895–1917* (1971), pp. 463–517 (p. 517); Georg Kaiser, *Five Plays*,

trans. by B. J. Kenworthy, Rex Last and J. M. Ritchie (London: Calder & Boyars, 1971), p. 73. All further references are to these editions and will appear as simple page numbers in the main body of the text.

30. See Ernst Schürer, 'Provocation and Proclamation, Vision and Imagery: Expressionist Drama between German Idealism and Modernity', in *A Companion to the Literature of Expressionism*, ed. by Neil H. Donahue (Rochester, NY: Camden House, 2005), pp. 231–54.

31. In Molière's *Dom Juan*, the eponymous hero is dragged down to hell in punishment for his libertinism, only for the play to end with the bathos of his valet, Sganarelle, asking who is going to pay him now. While Kaiser's play thus has precursors in the classical theatre from which it formally seeks to break, it is telling that this is a comedy and not a tragedy. Thanks to Jess Goodman for drawing my attention to this similarity.

32. On these contexts see Sabine Wilke, 'Ökonomie und Sexualität in Georg Kaisers *Von morgens bis mitternachts* und seiner Verfilmung durch Karl-Heinz Martin', *Orbis Litterarum*, 54 (1999), 203–19.

33. On this form see Horst Denkler, *Das Drama des Expressionismus Programm, Spieltext, Theater* (Munich: Fink, 1979), especially chapters 4 to 6 on 'Filmverwandte Wandlungsdramen', 'Opernahe Wandlungsdramen', and 'Einpolige Wandlungsdramen'.

34. Heiner Müller, *Gesammelte Irrtümer 2: Interviews und Gespräche*, ed. by Gregor Edelmann and Renate Ziemer (Frankfurt am Main: Verlag der Autoren, 1990), p. 64, my translation.

35. Jacques Derrida, *Specters of Marx: The State of the Debt, the Work of Mourning, and the New International*, trans. by Peggy Kamuff (New York and London: Routledge, 1994), p 10.

36. Bertolt Brecht, *Short Organon for the Theatre*, in *Brecht on Theatre*, ed. by Marc Silbermann, Steve Giles and Tom Kuhn (London: Bloomsbury, 2014), pp. 231–65 (p. 232).

37. Bertolt Brecht, 'Notes on the Opera *Rise and Fall of the City of Mahagonny*', in *Brecht on Theatre*, pp. 61–71, (pp. 63, 68, and 69).

38. *Brecht on Theatre*, p. 65.

39. For the purposes of this essay, I will refer to the first version of 1930. See Bertolt Brecht, *Die Maßnahme*, in *Werke. Große kommentierte Berliner und Frankfurter Ausgabe*, ed. by Werner Hecht et. al., 30 vols (Frankfurt am Main: Suhrkamp, 1988–2000), III: *Stücke* 3 (1988), pp. 73–98; *The Measure Taken*, trans. by Carl R. Müller, in *The Measure Taken and other Lehrstücke* (London: Methuen, 1977), pp. 7–34. All further references are to these editions and will appear as page numbers in the main body of the text.

40. My translation; see Walter Benjamin, 'Der Autor als Produzent: Ansprache im Institut zum Studium des Fascismus in Paris am 27. April 1934', in *Gesammelte Schriften*, ed. by Rolf Tiedemann and Hermann Schweppenhäuser, 17 vols (Frankfurt am Main: Suhrkamp, 1972–99), II.2 (1982), pp. 683–701 (p. 694).

41. Bertolt Brecht, *Messingkauf, or Buying Brass*, in *Brecht on Performance: Messingkauf and Modelbooks*, ed. by Tom Kuhn, Steve Giles, and Marc Silberman (London: Bloomsbury, 2014), pp. 1–141 (p. 35).

42. *Werke. Große kommentierte Berliner und Frankfurter Ausgabe*, XXII: *Schriften 2. Teil 1* (1993), pp. 399–400, my translation.

43. In a journal entry of 13 September 1953, Brecht writes: 'Wäre ich im ganzen ein Komödienschreiber, was ich beinahe bin, aber eben nur beinahe'. See *Werke. Große kommentierte Berliner und Frankfurter Ausgabe*, XXVII: *Journale 2* (1995), p. 348.

44. '[D]ie Tragödie [nimmt] die Leiden des Menschen häufiger auf die leichte Achsel als die Komödie' [the tragedy takes human suffering lightly more often than the comedy (my translation)]. Bertolt Brecht, 'Bemerkungen zu *Der aufhaltsame Aufstieg des Arturo Ui*', in *Werke. Große kommentierte Berliner und Frankfurter Ausgabe*, XXIV: *Schriften 4* (1991), pp. 315–18 (p. 318).

45. *Brecht on Theatre*, p. 285.

46. G. E. Nelson, 'The Birth of Tragedy out of Pedagogy: Brecht's 'Learning Play' *Die Maßnahme*', *The German Quarterly*, 46 (Nov. 1973), 566–80; Walter H. Sokel, 'Brecht's Split Characters and his Sense of the Tragic', in *Brecht*, ed. by Peter Demetz (Englewood Cliffs, NJ: Prentice-Hall, 1962), pp. 127–38; Jurgen Röhle, *Das gefesselte Theater* (Cologne and Berlin: Kiepenheuer & Witsch, 1957); Martin Esslin, *Das Paradox des politischen Dichters* (Frankfurt and Bonn: Athenäum, 1962); Benno von Wiese, *Zwischen Utopie und Wirklichkeit: Studien zur deutschen Literatur* (Düsseldorf: August Bagel, 1963).

47. Reinhold Grimm, 'Ideologische Tragödie und Tragödie der Ideologie: Versuch über ein Lehrstück von Brecht', in *Tragik und Tragödie*, ed. by Volkmar Sander (Darmstadt: Wissenschaftliche Buchgesellschaft, 1971), pp. 237–78, (p. 247) my translation.

48. Reiner Steinweg, 'Brechts *Die Maßnahme*. Übungstext, nicht Tragödie', *Alternative*, 14 (1971), 133–43.

49. Hans-Thies Lehmann, 'Den Tod sterben: Zu Brechts Dedramatisierung des Todes', in *The Brecht Yearbook 32: Brecht und der Tod*, ed. by Jürgen Hillesheim, Stephen Brockmann and Matthias Mayer (Madison: University of Wisconsin Press, 2007), pp. 176–87 (p. 179) my translation.

50. See Jost Hermand, '"Lieber nützlich leben als heroisch sterben": Brechts Märtyrerphobie', *The Brecht Yearbook*, 32 (2007), 210–22 (pp. 212–14)

51. Astrid Oesmann, 'Brecht's Economies of Death and the Gestus of Mourning', in *The Brecht Yearbook*, 32 (2007), pp. 188–97 (p. 192).

52. *Brecht on Theatre*, p. 65.

53. In his notes on the *Lehrstücke*, Brecht writes that 'Sterben lehren' is a central component of these plays. See the note in Reiner Steinweg, *Das Lehrstück: Brechts Theorie einer politisch-ästhetischen Erziehung* (Stuttgart: Metzler, 1976), p. 58.

CHAPTER 9

❖

'Much like at home':
The Quiet Eloquence of Death in
Our Town (Thornton Wilder) and
Eurydice (Sarah Ruhl)

Julie Vatain-Corfdir

Sorbonne Université, VALE

When I was fifteen the graveyard act of *Our Town* caused me to reconsider everything I knew about death in the theatre. Having grown up on a classical European diet of *Le Cid*, *The Oresteia* and *Hamlet*, I expected death to be eloquently built up to, mourning to be vocally lyrical, and ghosts to demand vengeance, in the (spectral) flesh or through the *bienséant* requirements of duty. Watching Thornton Wilder's play in an American classroom, I marvelled at a stage-full of dead people quietly discussing the weather, wondered whether Emily's euphemized passing was meant to be 'real', and was enduringly moved by the final image of George sinking down at the foot of his wife's invisible grave, not having uttered a word through the entire act. The silence of the living and the chatter of the dead proved strangely comforting yet utterly disturbing, presenting a tragic picture with intimate familiarity, and performing on my young mind what Peter Brook calls an 'acid test': 'When emotion and argument are harnessed to a wish from the audience to see more clearly into itself — then something in the mind burns'.[1] It was some years before I understood that Wilder's dramaturgy was anything but typical of American drama, and a few more before I witnessed a kindred dramatization of death in Sarah Ruhl's *Eurydice*, when a '*humming noise*'[2] briefly escapes her dead lips as she first tries to speak, once more gathering the poignancy of the separation into a quiet symbol. *Our Town* (1938) and *Eurydice* (2003) differ widely on various points of style, theme and context, and this essay does not mean to blot out their individuality, but rather to shed light on a common eloquence of restraint between two authors writing on the sidelines of American realism, in their dramatic handling of death as discreetly — and cruelly — ordinary.

'How should we enter death? Is this not the subject of all philosophy and all theatre, despite the protestations of all philosophy and all theatre that they are instruments for *living*?', asks Howard Barker.[3] Even beyond the seminal plays under scrutiny, both Wilder's theatre and Ruhl's fully enter into this discussion, routinely staging death, its approach and its aftermath in a range of tones and moods. We watch generations of one family die matter-of-factly in Wilder's *The Long Christmas Dinner*, as we watch generations re-stage the passion of Christ, across centuries and worldwide conflicts, in Ruhl's *Passion Play*. Other works range in theme from terminal disease (Ruhl's *The Clean House*) to war between father and son (Act III of Wilder's *The Skin of Our Teeth*), and from cynical comedy about the three Fates spinning and snipping the threads of life (Wilder's *The Drunken Sisters*) to gruesome humour about a dead organ trafficker whose phone will not stop ringing (Ruhl's *Dead Man's Cell Phone*). If, as Élisabeth Angel-Perez suggests, 'the mission of theatre has always been to let us hear the voices of the dead (prosopopoeia)',[4] the plays of Wilder and Ruhl, as classical (at times) in inspiration as they are decidedly unconventional in form, abundantly engage with that tradition of giving voice to what is lost, offering as they do so a reflection on irreversibility, and an exploration of the rituals of memory. As critics have often pointed out, this intense preoccupation with death can be traced, for both playwrights, to biographical roots: 'Wilder himself was born astride the grave; his twin brother, Theophilus, was stillborn', writes Lincoln Konkle,[5] borrowing a Beckettian phrase, while Ruhl has openly declared that, when deciding to write *Eurydice*, 'she was motivated by the possibility of having one more conversation with her deceased father'.[6]

As opposed to the staging of death as an emotional event in nineteenth-century melodramas — one thinks of the tearful passing of Little Eva in *Uncle Tom's Cabin*, or of Sarah Bernhardt brilliantly dying across the US in *La Dame aux camélias* — and in contrast to dying as climactic end to a tragic plot, as exemplified by the suicides and executions that conclude the canonical dramas of Arthur Miller; Ruhl and Wilder choose to answer Barker's question by 'entering' death as something close to a non-event. This allows *Eurydice* and *Our Town* to focus the spectators' attention on the state of *being dead*, rather than the fact or experience of dying. Thus theatre, a live art that speaks to the living, composedly embraces the visual and aural paradox of embodying the no-longer-alive, who are shown to converse in surprisingly natural fashion, side by side with the living whom they remember or forget. In order to unpack both the stage impact and the philosophical reach of these acts set among the dead, this essay means to explore the dramatic paradigms used by Wilder and Ruhl, in their distinct ways, to harness the impermanence of theatre to a meditation on the transience of human life, and to explore the greatest loneliness of all through a collective art form.

Euphemistic Death and Non-spectral Spectrality

Both Wilder's Emily and Ruhl's Eurydice die young and in love, at times in their lives which should be associated with an abundance of life rather than a philosophical acceptance of endings: Emily dies in childbirth, Eurydice on her wedding night. But instead of enhancing the inherent pathos of these plotlines through build-up or lament, the dramatic construction of the plays barely mentions their deaths as events. The third and final act of *Our Town* opens in the graveyard, where a number of characters, having apparently died in the interval between acts II and III, are found sitting on '*ordinary chairs*' in '*openly spaced rows*'.[7] When a funeral procession appears at the back of the stage hidden by umbrellas, the identity of the newcomer is revealed by the dead themselves:

> MRS SOAMES.   Who is it, Julia?
> MRS GIBBS (*Without raising her eyes*).   My daughter-in-law, Emily Webb.
> MRS SOAMES (*A little surprised, but no emotion*).   Well, I declare! The road up
> here must have been awfully muddy. What did she die of, Julia?
> MRS GIBBS.   In childbirth. (*Our Town*, III, p. 199)

The terse precision of Mrs. Gibbs's answers, along with the emphasis placed by the stage directions on curbing expressivity, defuse the situation's potential for sentimentality. The mention of the wet road, while transmuting the symbolism of falling water from the fertility of nuptials in Act II to sorrow in Act III, also creates an odd juxtaposition that puts death on a par with meteorological conditions. This immediately places individual tragedy in the larger perspective of the cosmos, the macrocosm, as Wilder explicitly did in a previous one-act play which considers the position of a train 'geographically, meteorologically, astronomically, theologically' at the time of a passenger's death.[8] As Robert Vork notes, the 'controlled'[9] nature of Emily's appearance among the dead is later belied by George's performance of traumatic grief as he '*falls full length at Emily's feet*'[10] and 'an excised, inadmissible cry of pain intrudes on the stage',[11] forcing the audience into a choice between heartrending empathy, voyeurism, or averting their eyes. But the trauma witnessed at this point is the survivor's rather than the victim's, whose death is prosaically announced by an indifferent family member, before being framed into a wider perspective by the running commentary of an omnipresent character, the Stage Manager, who breaks the Fourth Wall to arrange and situate scenes, folding the individual into the collective, and the past into the future.

In *Eurydice*, the central character's death also provides the transition from one Movement to the next, but this time we see it happen — or rather, we hear it happen:

> She runs, trips and pitches down the stairs, holding her letter.
> *She follows the letter down, down down...*
> *Blackout.*
> *A clatter. Strange sounds — xylophones, brass bands, sounds of falling, sounds of*
> *vertigo.*
> *Sounds of breathing.* (*Eurydice*, I, p. 356)

Ruhl's characteristic arrangement of stage directions as lines of verse outlines a distorted symmetry between a list of visible actions and a list of audible sounds, separated by a one-word, irrevocable break: '*Blackout*'. We see Eurydice start her fall, the steep verticality of which is emphasized by the ternary rhythms, but we do not see her land. Death is symbolically euphemized by the sudden absence of light, by depersonalized '*sounds of vertigo*', and paradoxical breath sounds. Besides a subdued and fittingly imaginative way of signifying death in the openly '*Alice in Wonderland*'[12] world of the play, Eurydice's fall also reads as a gesture of reclaiming her story from the Ancient myth in which, according to Megan Craig, 'Her voice was drowned out by the lyre, by Orpheus, by Ovid and Virgil and Rilke, all of them eager to describe her incomparable beauty and her mute death'.[13] In Ruhl's version, she is still '*breathing*' — the final word of the act — and will go on to make her more challenging choices in the two acts after her death. Here, as in *Our Town*, though in a different key, the potential for pathos is precluded by the unconcern of the neighbouring characters, in this case an almost grotesquely unsympathetic chorus of Stones who exclaim, as Eurydice enters the Underworld:

> LITTLE STONE.   Oh!
> LOUD STONE.   Oh!
> LITTLE STONE.   Oh!
>   We might say: 'Poor Eurydice' —
>   but stones don't feel bad for
>   dead people. (*Eurydice*, ii, p. 357)

What starts out as a triple lament echoing the rituals of tragic choruses swiftly turns into a deadpan rejection of empathy, ironically wrongfooting the audience's expectations. Befitting the initial stage direction according to which the Stones 'might be played as though they are nasty children at a birthday party',[14] this indecorous statement invites quirky performances, often accompanied in production by a range of outlandish outfits, from ghoulish Victorian garb (Berkeley Rep) to gaudy wigs, gaiters and lifejackets (Ashby Stage), or architectural stone-coloured garments (Los Angeles Opera).[15]

The eccentric presence of the Stones is also a way to ensure that the underworld eschews any clichéd images of an Ancient mythical Hades. Ruhl asks her actors to 'resist the temptation to be "classical"', and describes the set as containing objects appropriate to a basement rather than a legendary underworld ('some rusty exposed pipes', 'an old-fashioned glow-in-the-dark-globe'), alongside bizarre elements which reinvent the metaphorical journey of death into a ride down 'a raining elevator' and stylize Lethe into 'an abstracted River of Forgetfulness'.[16] There is no attempt at a realistic or conventional depiction of space, whether in the overworld or the underworld. Significantly, the opening of the Second Movement reads: '*The underworld.* | *There is no set change.* | *Strange watery noises.*'[17] The soundscape, dominated by music in the overworld (and around Orpheus) is gradually overtaken by a range of liquid sounds — rain, pipes, kettles or ponds — which echo and distort the sorrowful sound of tears or the flowing oblivion of the river; yet importantly, the set does not change. Nor do the voice and demeanour of the dead characters: Eurydice and her father talk, move, sing and dance without eeriness or solemnity. The burden of shifting the dramatic paradigm from life to death is left to the imagination of the spectators, who are advised by the Stones at the opening of the act to 'pretend for a moment that [they] understand the language of stones',[18] in order to follow conversations in the underworld. And when Orpheus reappears in the overworld, writing forlorn letters to his dead wife, he and she share the same stage space, with no perceptible division, making their invisibility to each other all the more afflicting — and all the harder to accept — for the audience who can see both side by side, within reach but unreachable. *Our Town* relies on a variation of the same paradigm: the living can't perceive the dead, but the dead characters sitting in their tombs can see the living, though they don't seem interested enough to turn their heads. Once again, for the viewer, the irrevocability of the divide between life and death relies on the anti-theatricality of its treatment. Wilder's dead '*sit in a quiet without stiffness*', facing the audience to whom they offer a disturbing mirror of deceased spectators, and when they speak, '*their tone is matter-of-fact, without sentimentality and, above all, without lugubriousness*'. Being dead does not require an important inflexion in acting style or scenery: Wilder's stage directions simply indicate that '*during the intermission, the audience has seen the stage hands arranging the stage*',[19] reorganizing the chairs used for pews at the wedding to stand for graves in the cemetery. Such metatheatrical rearranging of seats highlights a threatening continuity between celebration and mourning, and hints at a cyclic conception of time where, according to Anne Fletcher, the action of *Our Town* 'stretches across a lifetime set against eternity'.[20] The use of simple chairs for graves, on a stripped down stage which has had no elaborate scenery or props from the beginning, also anchors the presence of death in an ordinary context — though not one which is represented through naturalistic means — confirming the fact that, for Wilder, 'life's tragedies can best be seen in the drama of the everyday'.[21] For Ruhl too, in the theatre, 'the work emerges out of the ordinary',[22] on stages uncluttered with realistic furniture. Eurydice in the underworld '*plays hop-scotch without chalk*',[23] just as Emily strings beans and opens presents in mime. In the dramaturgies of *Our Town* and *Eurydice*, airy sets and invisible objects allow our attention to focus on the movement or stillness of the human body, as it travels through life and death in a de-dramatized journey.

Can the Dead Feel, Remember, or Learn?

As Jacques Derrida demonstrates, 'The spectrogenic process corresponds to a paradoxical incorporation'.[24] There can be no spectre, no dead character walking, without perceptible flesh, no dialogue among the dead without audible voices. The labile stage of the theatre offers a fit space to display these impossible bodies, which Wilder and Ruhl choose to write in a fairly unmarked way — excepting perhaps a hint of nostalgia in their attire, since Emily enters the graveyard with her hair '*down her back and tied by a white ribbon like a little girl*',[25] while Eurydice steps off the elevator '*in the kind of 1930s suit | that women wore when they eloped*'.[26] This nod to times gone by, whether past childhood or past decades, suggest a non-linear conception of time after death that allows characters to choose between looking back and looking forward. Looking forward to what, though? There is no notion of loss of function, decay or decomposition in either play: the dead body remains whole, retaining its capacity for sensory perception. *Our Town* alludes to this by persistently introducing remarks from the dead about the coolness of the air, foregrounding the sense of touch, while *Eurydice* widens the emphasis to further senses, such as smell or hearing:

> FATHER.   As for me, this is what it's like being dead: the atmosphere smells. And there are strange high-pitched noises — like a tea-kettle always boiling over. But it doesn't seem to bother anyone. And, for the most part, there is a pleasant atmosphere and you can work and socialize, much like at home. (*Eurydice*, II, p. 344)

This lingering capacity for sensory perception, however, appears directly contradictory to the dramatic progression of both texts, in which the protagonists openly bid farewell to the physical world in disarmingly sincere speeches. This might take the form of an anaphoric, sentimental review of realities left behind:

> EMILY.   Good-by, Good-by, world. Good-by, Grover's Corners... Mama and Papa. Good-by to clocks ticking... and Mama's sunflowers. And food and coffee. And new-ironed dresses and hot baths... and sleeping and waking up. (*Our Town*, III, p. 207)

Or it could entail the evocation of an impossible dissociation of body parts:

> EURYDICE.   Good-bye, head — I said —
> it inclined itself a little, as though to nod to me
> in a solemn kind of way.
> *She turns to the Stones.*
> How do you say good-bye to yourself? (*Eurydice*, II, p. 361)

The actor's head is visibly on her shoulders as she utters these words: we are given to see a body which looks intact, even as we are told that it is no longer whole. Eurydice's body becomes ambivalent, antithetic; concurrently denying physical existence and reasserting it; making its presence as impossible to process as the death of a loved one is impossible to accept. This calls to mind Peggy Phelan's analysis of the performance space as a space of paradox and in-betweenness rather than a place of clear separations: 'Part of what performance knows is the impossibility of maintaining the distinction between temporal tenses, between an absolutely singular beginning and ending, between living and dying'. Phelan further stresses 'the generative force of those "betweens"',[27] a force that perhaps, in the case of Ruhl's play, prompts the audience to confront its contrary human impulses both to dismiss the idea of death and to be fascinated by it.

The sarcastic gatekeepers to the underworld, the Stones, openly urge the spectators to identify with the situation:

> THE STONES.   Eurydice wants to speak to you.
> But she can't speak your language anymore. [...]
> LOUD STONE.   Listen to her the way you would listen
> to your own daughter
> if she died too young
> and tried to speak to you
> across long distances. (*Eurydice*, II, pp. 359–60)

Eurydice is able to speak normally as soon as the Stones have thus called for the audience's participation. The message is clear: facing a potential trauma of one's own is the only way to hear what the play has to say. The cathartic process is spelled out by the chorus, imploring us to grieve and pity, to listen and pay attention — not just to a dead girl but to the precariousness of words themselves, 'unmoor[ed] from their everyday anchorage and to be placed back at the mysterious advent of speech'.[28] The character's dead language is as paradoxical as her dead body: perceptibly functional, yet conceptually impossible. The embodied art of theatre, leaning on the mimetic power of sensory perception and the plasticity of words, invites us to inhabit a liminal, ambiguous space in which the physical world is simultaneously shown to linger and fade. This superposition of life and death raises the question — or hope — of reversibility, which is explored, then denied, by both plays.

The problematic normality of the dead body frames a discussion about the fatal loss of less corporeal functions, such as memory and emotional feeling. The impossible *dismembering* of Eurydice as she and her head say goodbye to each other mirrors her tragically *dis-remembering* her past after being dipped in the River of Forgetfulness. As infatuated with books as she is enamoured of Orpheus in the First Movement, she emerges in the Second, having forgotten both her husband's name and how to read. She also fails to recognize her father, or understand the meaning of filial relationships, once she meets him in the underworld where 'Fathers are not allowed'.[29] This echoes the more gradual process of oblivion in *Our Town*, where Emily, realizing she can 'go back there and relive those days all over again', is advised against it: 'When you've been here longer you'll see that our life here is to forget all that', warns her mother-in-law.[30] The provident Stage Manager, introducing the act, apologetically cautions the audience on this point: 'Some of the things [the dead]'re going to say maybe'll hurt your feelings — but that's the way it is: mother 'n daughter... husband 'n wife... enemy 'n enemy... money 'n miser... all those terribly important things kind of grow pale around here'.[31] His folksy New England speech and the humorously antithetic overlay of love, hate and avarice may temper the mercilessness of the fact, but the intimation is clear: here, as in Ancient Greece, dying means forgetting. Yet both Emily and Eurydice are given a chance to remember, and they seize it. In fact, not only does Eurydice remember, thanks to her father's patient re-education, but she also keeps on learning, as he teaches her the etymology of Greek words and regales her with anecdotes of her grandparents' youth. When Orpheus lowers a copy of Shakespeare's plays into the underworld, Eurydice and her father are found reading King Lear's 'We two alone will sing like birds in a cage' speech, a transparent parallel which highlights both the serene fruitfulness of their father–daughter exchanges, and the literal immortality of language, in all its fragile poetic beauty. Words emerge as the one connection between world and underworld: Eurydice receives correspondence from her dead father while alive, and from her living husband after death. These letters — viewed as illicit by the Stones — encapsulate memories and have the power to revive them across the divide. Through a device which is as much a driving force of the plot as it is a *mise en abyme* of theatre, the mechanism of remembrance, of re-animating thought and emotion, is rooted in the written word spoken out loud. Rather than Eurydice's initial death, or even her second one — when her 'decision'[32] to make Orpheus turn around sends her back to the underworld — the tragic climax of Ruhl's rewriting proves to be the renewed and ultimate loss of memory and language. Finding that her father has dipped himself in the River again, Eurydice does the same thing after drafting a final letter to Orpheus: father and daughter are curled up on the floor, asleep and oblivious, as Orpheus re-enters:

> He sees Eurydice.
> *He is happy.*
> *The elevator starts raining on Orpheus.*
> *He forgets.* [...]
> *He sees the letter on the ground.* [...]
> *He can't read it.* [...]
> *The sound of water.*
> *Then silence.*
> THE END (*Eurydice*, III, p. 411)

The illusion of reversibility, of remembering in death or snatching someone from the dead, shatters as characters ultimately forget, willingly or not, and the Third Movement ends in wordlessness. 'To mourn twice is excessive', 'To mourn three times is a sin',[33] warn the Stones, and yet the structure of the play encourages its audience to mourn more than once for each character, for lost children, parents and spouses, in an echoing cycle which, once again, offers a clear parallel to the ritual repetition and re-enactment that theatre relies on. After Orpheus forgets, we, the readers and spectators, are the ones left with visual and emotional memories of the action; and, as the palimpsestic allusion to Shakespeare implies, we are the ones entrusted with the words after the characters have lost them to silence.

The metatheatrical — almost Stanislavskian — idea of re-living and re-enacting is also at the core of *Our Town*'s third act. As the receding funeral procession leaves the stage in patient stillness, Emily '*sits up abruptly with an idea*'[34] and asks the Stage Manager, who has been arranging scenes by moving time forward and backward, to let her relive the day of her twelfth birthday. After some unheeded warnings, the Stage Manager duly announces the date and weather of that day, and characters from Emily's memory fill the stage as she watches, then participates, both playing her own part as a past twelve-year-old and commenting on it as a dead twenty-eight-year-old. Her reaction quickly switches from the wonder of re-discovery to despair at the way human beings fail to truly 'look at one another' or 'realize life while they live it', and she too makes a conscious choice to accept the irreversibility of death: 'Take me back — up the hill — to my grave'. Her final line challenges the audience to explore their own capacity for awareness and acceptance as she asks point-blank, about the living: 'They don't understand, do they?'[35] Wilder's script does not indicate any difference in staging between the memory and the rest of the play: Emily's mother meticulously mimes cooking breakfast in an invisible kitchen, just as she did in the first two acts. Eschewing the social realism and the political activism of other American plays of the 1930s, *Our Town* emulates both the metatheatrical tendencies Wilder admired in European playwrights like Pirandello or Obey, and other, non-dramatic American traditions, such as the Puritan jeremiad.

Konkle thus argues that *Our Town* 'can almost be read as a literal jeremiad in that its non-Aristotelian dramaturgy bears a close resemblance in form to a sermon with illustrative episodes'.[36] The constant austerity of the setting foregrounds this dynamic of the play, facilitating an easy flow between the Stage Manager's commentary and the individual scenes. Some recent productions have, however, chosen to accentuate the memory of Emily's twelfth birthday by handling it in a theatricalized way. David Cromer's highly successful production at the Barrow Street (2009) sharpened the opposition between past and present by contrasting a very immediate, bare, contemporary feel for most of the play with a curtain-framed period kitchen, complete with costumes, frosted windows and frying bacon for the memory scene. This unexpected foray into naturalistic style threw the *re-lived* episode into sharper relief than the *lived* ones, assailing the spectator's senses (not least through the smell of bacon) and neatly underscoring Emily's tragically ironic point: only in death do we truly notice what is and was around us. Conversely, Simon Mauclair's French production for the Collectif Zavtra (2016) went the opposite way by making the memory even more abstract: Emily stood alone on a darkened stage, listening to disembodied voices and answering them at a more and more frantic pace as a live electric guitar grew more deafening, underscoring her mounting anguish. These memorable reinterpretations of Wilder's third act attest to the breadth of his writing as they explore what it means to steep oneself in one's memories in visually and aurally affecting ways. Their striking choices could also be said, however, to point to more conventional conceptions of the contrast between life and death, whereas Wilder's unsettling originality lies in the simplicity of the way they mirror each other on stage, without specific effects: 'The climax of this play needs only five square feet of boarding and the passion to know what life means to us'.[37]

'We who are not dead but who will be dead'[38]

In a brief and caustic essay, Ruhl ponders the notion of literary death by wondering about the 'strange case' of Thornton Wilder as a dead playwright:

> How is it that e. e. cummings and Thornton Wilder, who radically challenged form, were transformed by intellectual opinion into treacly sentimentalists for the masses? Is it because they died? Is it because people liked them? When formal newness becomes populist by sheer dint of its ability to communicate broadly in its new form, why is it prosecuted (and found guilty) after death?[39]

The ironic concision of her style questions the life, death and resurrection of new form, and efficiently sums up an ongoing paradox in Wilder's reception, between appreciation of his experimental innovation and a certain condescendence for the perceived nostalgia of his world. As Vork argues in his study of *Our Town*'s handling of trauma and traumatic witnessing, the third act 'leaves the audience with a deeply disturbing expression of the human condition, one that hardly gratifies the expectations of theatrical comfort food which the play at first seems to promise [...]'.[40] The collective possessive of the title might initially be taken to bear limiting connotations, but the constant plurals and 'millions'[41] invoked by the Stage Manager prove it to be, instead, absolutely inclusive. '*Our*' points to the universals of human and theatrical experience, among which death and mourning are constants: 'unspeakable loss is indeed universal, for it envelopes the world each and every time a singular being is dissolved by eternal death'.[42] The enigmatic position of Wilder's theatre in the American canon — avant-garde yet old-fashioned, pivotal yet mistrusted for its popularity, intrinsically American yet more akin to the works of Anouilh or Giraudoux than to its US contemporaries — is a familiar question among critics. Frequent and imaginative productions nevertheless attest to the continued relevance of his theatre, as does his influence on other major playwrights, from Edward Albee to Paula Vogel, whose play *The Long Christmas Ride Home*, with its narrators and Bunraku puppets of the past, is an open tribute to Wilder's experimental one-acts. The non-Aristotelian, non-realist dramaturgy of Vogel's play in turn inspired her most famous student, Ruhl, thus translating Wilder's impact into a new generation of playwrights. If realism is to be viewed as the dominant tradition of the twentieth-century American stage — though it remains an ambivalent 'realism against itself',[43] in the words of Marc Robinson — it would not be amiss to see Wilder as the father of a *non-dominant* American playwriting tradition, less emphatic in its assertion, more quietly lyrical in its eloquence, and readily relying on international inspiration in order to investigate America, in a reflexive perspective reminiscent of Gertrude Stein's. This discreet filiation, I would argue, reaches all the way to the contemporary stage, constantly searching to re-affirm theatricality, and to explore and renegotiate a play's relationship to its audience.

'Instead of primal comfort, in a very good play, what we get is primal recognition', declares Ruhl, discussing her use of myth from the angle of impact: 'I'm interested in how the Greeks can refract in the gut'.[44] This directly echoes Wilder's views on the 'acquiescence' elicited by great theatre: 'The response we make when we "believe" a work of the imagination is that of saying: "This is the way things are. [...]" It is this form of knowledge which Plato called "recollection"'.[45] Both playwrights aim for the audience's instinctive acknowledgment of an essential truth at the heart of a play, stripped of the trappings and suits of realist production. And since the spectators cannot logically be expected to 'recognize' anything of death as an experience, it follows that any kernel of truth must have to do with living rather than dying. In his study of Renaissance tragedy, Michael Neill propounds that one of the cathartic merits of the genre was to allow the viewer to rehearse their own encounter with death: 'The psychological value of tragedy's displays of agony, despair, and ferocious self-assertion, one might argue, was that they provided audiences with a way of vicariously confronting the implications of their own mortality [...]'.[46] The diametrically opposed modalities of *Our Town* and *Eurydice*, without a hint of agony or ferocity, though with frequent touches of humour, suggest a slightly different focus. Engaging with one's own mortality is indisputably relevant to any play dealing with death — arguably, to any kind of ephemeral performance — but the plays under scrutiny seem to take a sharper look at the death of others. The characters of *Eurydice* are all tangled in reciprocal relationships of love and mourning, for which the River of Forgetfulness proves both poison and medicine. Eurydice's farewell letter to Orpheus materializes the letting go of loved ones, in an unforeseen — dare I say empowering? — reversal of the mourning relationship: 'I still love you, I think. Don't try to find me again. You would be lonely for music'.[47] The playful tenderness of the instructions she generously includes to her husband's next wife — 'Give him lots to eat. | He forgets to eat and then he gets cranky'[48] — corroborate Thomas Butler's analysis that, since her earliest work, Ruhl's drama 'has consistently explored mourning through a delicate balance of levity and incisiveness'.[49] The claim *Our Town* makes is perhaps even broader, as it investigates the very possibility and value of living, knowing that everything dies. 'Oh, earth, you're too wonderful for anybody to realize you'[50]: even as she is to be swallowed by it, Emily's direct address to earth is as disconsolate as it is admirative, the cadence of the sentence encouraging the actor to put a vocal stress on the central adjective. The verb 'realize', with its dual meaning denoting both awareness and full-fledged existence, underpins an urgent plea for attention that is anything but soothing. The tenuous loveliness and unique significance of each passing moment appears edged with the danger of disregard and death: '[Wilder's] bright visible world is backed by, flanked by, and built on a larger darkness, capable of swallowing the stage if he and we don't maintain the luminous power of our attention'.[51]

Mourning loved ones, mourning universal transience. As we have seen, the protagonists of both plays, though offered a chance to cling to life and memory, consciously choose the path of gradual or immediate oblivion, under the lucid gaze of a chorus, whether thoughtful (the Stage Manager) or ironic (the Stones). While this challenges the audience to sympathize with the characters' acceptance of death, it also mediates and qualifies the tone of the plays. The woeful elements of the dénouement find themselves overlaid with philosophical distance and a meditation on theatre as the art of impermanence: this prevents *Our Town* and *Eurydice* from conforming to Western conceptions of tragedy, blending them instead with Eastern influences. Richard Londraville indeed proposes an analysis of *Our Town*'s third act as an American Noh of the Ghosts where the Stage Manager, acting as the assistant, or *Waki*, whose role in traditional Japanese drama it is to guide the main character's soul away from corporeal attachments, gently leads Emily to 'an awakening about the nature of life'.[52] With a different angle, Anne Fletcher argues that Wilder's avowed aim 'to find a value above all price for the smallest events in our daily life'[53] echoes Buddhist concepts of enlightenment: 'With more surety than in the earlier plays, in *Our Town* Wilder's form and content parallel Buddhist thoughts on living, dying, and letting go'.[54] Ruhl similarly pleads for the embrace of ephemerality as a philosophical and dramatic stance when she writes that 'every night when a curtain comes down, a world dies, and one mourns the end by applauding', before extending her point through a Buddhist metaphor:

> Have you ever seen a Tibetan monk make a butter sculpture? The monks sculpt flowers and temples with colored butter, intricate and lovely, knowing they will melt, knowing that eventually they will feed the sculpture to the monkeys. [...]
> Many Western traditions pin the arts against mortality; we try to make something that will abide, something made of stone, not butter. And yet theatre

has at the core of its practice the repetition of transience. We take something intricate and lovely and feed it not to the monkeys, but to each other.[55]

The Ancient stones of the chorus are replaced by the short-lived butter of evanescent performance. Ruhl's collective 'we', echoing the Stage Manager's use of the pronoun to designate overlapping communities — the town, the theatre, humanity at large — re-emphasizes a familiar point: the significance of theatre as *shared* ritual. The ambivalent 'in-betweenness' of the dramatic space makes it the proper place where we can collectively visit and re-visit our dead, knowing they will disappear with the final curtain, and our celebration of theatre's artifice, our applause, will resonate as communal valediction.

★   ★   ★   ★   ★

In his analysis of Samuel Pepys's account of having publicly kissed the remains of Katherine of France in Westminster Abbey, Joseph Roach posits that performance 'discloses an urgent but often disguised passion: the desire to communicate physically with the past, a desire that roots itself in the ambivalent love of the dead'.[56] There is no kissing the dead in *Our Town* or *Eurydice* — though George does lies down on his wife's grave, and Orpheus warns Eurydice against kissing dead men because 'Their lips look red and tempting but put your tongue in their mouths and it tastes like oatmeal'[57] — but the desire to reach for them is amply thematized by both plays. The cathartic journey Ruhl and Wilder propose is not carried out through catastrophic emotion, violent event or flowing lament, but through the rehearsal of a mourning process whose quietly eloquent recurrence encourages us to face our dead and let them go. It is therefore no surprise that both plays, written half a century apart in distinct contexts, have easily found their intimate stories of grief endowed with echoes of national mourning. Among many others, *Our Town* received a Broadway production led by Paul Newman a few months after 9/11, and a charity reading organized by Scarlett Johansson after Hurricane Maria; while Ana Fernández-Caparrós places *Eurydice* 'among the most moving explorations of the theme of loss that American theatre has seen since the events of 11 September 2001'.[58] Neither play investigates the exemplary death of the hero; both immerse us in the universal ordinariness of dying, in a process that reasserts the power of the dramatic arts to rehearse for loss while affirming presence. In a similar gesture, relying on the 'live' to wrestle with its opposite, a recent moving performance by Young Jean Lee ended with a ten-minute song whose baseline was the following lyric: '*We're gonna die, we're gonna die someday | Then we'll be gone, and it'll be okay*'.[59] Lee first sang alone on a darkened stage, was then joined by her band supplying upbeat rock music and back-up vocals as the stage lit up, before all the performers finished the number a cappella, harmonizing, engaging in humorous group choreography, and ultimately leading the entire audience into singing along. *Our Town* and *Eurydice* are by no means so direct, but they are no less compelling in their intimation that, if death belongs in the everyday — 'much like at home' — then the theatre is a 'home' where we can visit it, and emerge with a heightened attention to life.

Notes to Chapter 9

1. Peter Brook, *The Empty Space* [1968], 3rd edn (London: Penguin Books, 1990), p. 152.
2. Sarah Ruhl, *Eurydice* [2003], in *The Clean House and Other Plays* (New York: TCG, 2006), pp. 325–411 (p. 359).
3. Howard Barker, *Death, the One and the Art of Theatre* (London and New York: Routledge, 2005), p. 18.
4. Élisabeth Angel-Perez, 'La Scène traumatique de Sarah Kane', *Sillages critiques*, 19 (2015), <http://journals.openedition.org/sillagescritiques/4328> [accessed 29 April 2020] (para. 10 of 28) (my translation).
5. Lincoln Konkle, *Thornton Wilder and the Puritan Narrative Tradition* (Columbia: University of Missouri Press, 2006), p. 135.
6. Ana Fernández-Caparrós, 'Death and the Community of Comic Romance: Sarah Ruhl's Poetics of Transformation in *Dead Man's Cell Phone*', *Contemporary Theatre Review*, 25.4 (2015), 488–501 (p. 489) <https://www.tandfonline.com/doi/full/10.1080/10486801.2015.1078324> [accessed 29 April 2020].
7. Thornton Wilder, *Our Town* [1938], in *Collected Plays & Writings on Theater*, ed. by J. D. McClatchy (New York: Library of America, 2007), pp. 145–209 (p. 195).
8. Thornton Wilder, *Pullman Car Hiawatha* [1931], in *Collected Plays*, ed. by McClatchy, pp. 93–108 (p. 99).
9. Robert Vork, 'Witnessing the Trauma of *Our Town*', *Comparative Drama*, 51.3 (2017), 338–63 (p. 341), <https://muse.jhu.edu/article/677376> [accessed 29 April 2020].
10. *Our Town*, III, p. 208.
11. Vork, p. 340.
12. *Eurydice*, author's note, p. 332.
13. Megan Craig, 'The Language of Stones', *Journal of Aesthetics and Phenomenology*, 5.2 (2018), 119–37 (p. 121), <https://doi.org/10.1080/20539320.2018.1516656> [accessed 29 April 2020].
14. *Eurydice*, author's note, p. 332.
15. Among many productions, *Eurydice* was directed by Les Waters at the Berkeley Rep. in 2004, and by Erika Chong Shuch at Ashby Stage in 2015. Matthew Aucoin's opera adaptation premiered at the LA Opera in 2020, directed by Mary Zimmerman.
16. *Eurydice*, author's note, pp. 332–33.
17. *Eurydice*, II, p. 357.
18. Ibid., p. 360.
19. *Our Town*, III, p. 195.
20. Anne Fletcher, 'No Time Like the Present: Wilder's Plays and Buddhist Thought and Time', in *Thornton Wilder: New Perspectives*, ed. by Jackson R. Bryer and Lincoln Konkle (Evanston, IL: Northwestern University Press, 2013), pp. 154–88 (p. 159).
21. Robert W. Corrigan, 'Thornton Wilder and the Tragic Sense of Life', in *Critical Essays on Thornton Wilder*, ed. by Martin Blank (New York: G. K. Hall & Co., 1996), pp. 77–83 (p. 79).
22. Paula Vogel and Sarah Ruhl, 'Sarah Ruhl by Paula Vogel', *BOMB*, 99 (2007), 54–59 (p. 59).
23. *Eurydice*, II, p. 367.
24. Jacques Derrida, *Specters of Marx: The State of the Debt, the Work of Mourning, and the New International*, trans. by Peggy Kamuf (New York: Routledge, 1994), p. 126.
25. *Our Town*, III, p. 200.
26. *Eurydice*, II, p. 359.
27. Peggy Phelan, 'Introduction', in *The Ends of Performance*, ed. by Peggy Phelan and Jill Lane (New York: New York University Press, 1998), pp. 1–19 (p. 8).
28. Craig, p. 121.
29. *Eurydice*, II, p. 382.
30. *Our Town*, III, p. 202.
31. Ibid., p. 197.
32. *Eurydice*, III, p. 396.
33. *Eurydice*, III, p. 406.

34. *Our Town*, III, p. 202.
35. Ibid., pp. 206–08.
36. Konkle, p. 131.
37. Thornton Wilder, 'Preface to Three Plays' [1957], in *Collected Plays*, ed. by McClatchy, pp. 682–88 (p. 686).
38. 'We who are not dead but who will be dead, inhabiting a world once filled with the now-dead, go to the place of death, which is not the mortuary [...] but the tragic theatre [...].' Barker, p. 70.
39. Sarah Ruhl, *100 Essays I Don't Have Time to Write* (New York: Farrar, Straus and Giroux, 2014), p. 130.
40. Vork, p. 340.
41. *Our Town*, II, p. 189.
42. Ibid., p. 362.
43. Marc Robinson, 'Realism against Itself' (chapter III), in *The American Play* (New Haven, CT, and London: Yale University Press, 2009), pp. 106–56.
44. Sarah Ruhl, 'Re-runs and Repetition', *Contemporary Theatre Review*, 16.3 (2009), 283–90 (pp. 286–87).
45. Wilder, 'Preface to Three Plays', p. 682.
46. Michael Neill, *Issues of Death: Mortality and Identity in English Renaissance Tragedy* (Oxford: Clarendon Press, 1997), p. 31.
47. *Eurydice*, III, p. 410.
48. Ibid.
49. Thomas Butler, 'Sarah Ruhl's *Dear Elizabeth* and the Mourning of Friends', *Journal of Dramatic Theory and Criticism*, 28.2 (2014), 67–84 (p. 79).
50. *Our Town*, II, p. 207.
51. Robinson, *The American Play*, p. 204.
52. Richard Londraville, '*Our Town*: An American Noh of the Ghosts', in *Thornton Wider: New Essays*, ed. by Martin Blank, Dalma Hunyadi and David Garrett Izzo (West Cornwall, CT: Locust Hill Press, 1999), pp. 365–78 (p. 369).
53. Wilder, 'Preface to Three Plays', p. 686.
54. Fletcher, p. 175.
55. Ruhl, *100 Essays*, pp. 145–46.
56. Joseph Roach, 'History, Memory, Necrophilia', in *The Ends of Performance*, ed. by Phelan & Lane, pp. 23–30 (p. 23).
57. *Eurydice*, II, p. 386.
58. Fernández-Caparrós, p. 489.
59. Young Jean Lee and her band Future Wife premiered *We're Gonna Die* in 2011. A recording of a later performance at Lincoln Center's LCT3 is available on the playwright's website: <https://youngjeanlee.org/work/were-gonna-die/> [accessed 5 June 2020].

CHAPTER 10

❖

'The whole point of living is preparing to die': Dying into Death in Tragic Drama

Fiona Macintosh

St Hilda's College, Oxford

In the Autumn of 2007, the actor Fiona Shaw starred at the Royal Court Theatre in London as the eponymous Woman in Marina Carr's *Woman and Scarecrow*, directed by Ramin Gray. The role involved dying in a large bed and left one dissenting reviewer, Fiona Mountford in *The Evening Standard*, with the urge 'to turf Shaw out of bed and settle down for a good snooze'.[1] For the most part, however, audiences were enthralled by this two-act, intensely witty and lyrical piece, in which the protagonist dies into death during the course of ninety minutes of playing time. This chapter seeks to bring to wider attention a play of great subtlety and verve that is especially resonant in its representation of death.

Woman and Scarecrow is very much in the Beckettian tradition and nods to the Theatre of the Absurd more generally (especially to Ionesco and Albee). The eponymous Woman has an alter ego in the form of Scarecrow (played brilliantly in the premiere by Brid Brenna), who (like all reliable Scarecrows) scares away, for as long as humanly/suprahumanly possible, the black-winged bird/crow-creature (Death). The bird/crow is locked in an onstage wardrobe and struggles at various points in the play to break out in order to devour its prey in striking reminiscence of the corpse in Eugène Ionesco's *Amedée ou comment d'en débarrasser* (1954), which breaks through the wall into the living room. Whilst motifs of the Absurd are strikingly evoked in this hilariously hyperreal, proto-posthuman world, *Woman and Scarecrow* participates very directly in a longstanding, and distinctly Irish, tradition of theatrical dying. Beckett's *Endgame, Rockaby* and *Not I* are all points of reference when the lights go down at the end of the play signalling some kind of exit from this world. And there are moments when the self-lament of Carr's dying Woman echoes those of the great chief mourners from the Abbey Theatre's early repertoire, notably Maurya's from J. M. Synge's *Riders to the Sea* (1904) and Juno's from Sean O'Casey's *Juno and the Paycock* (1924).

There are, however, other traditions at work in this play. Shakespeare is clearly sounded through Woman's admiration of Ophelia: 'she had a good death'.[2] And it is no doubt significant that shortly after *Woman and Scarecrow*, Carr went on to rework Shakespeare's *King Lear* in *The Cordelia Dream* (2008). Not surprisingly, opera with its own dying women has a role to play, notably with the nymph's aria from Dvořák's *Rusalka* sounding out from the cassette player and underscoring one of Woman's last speeches about self-alienation (p. 48). But it is the imprint of the ancient Greek tragic deaths that features most prominently here.

Some years ago,[3] I argued that the similarities between ancient Greek and modern Irish tragic drama were related to their shared sense of death as a process and their shared ritual practices surrounding death, because many Celtic practices had survived in Ireland, despite being overlaid by Catholic ritual, well into the twentieth century.[4] I also suggested that it was the relative absence of death from most western Protestant societies, where deaths are for the most part private and conceived of as happening in an instant, that had had some bearing on the relative eschewal of tragic drama in the period following the Second World War. However, the fact that tragedy — and especially Greek tragedy — has enjoyed a consistently vigorous afterlife on the stage from at least the 1960s onwards leads me to qualify my earlier position.[5] And a study of Carr's *Woman and Scarecrow* is instructive here, for Carr's tragi-comedy/comi-tragedy, like the reworkings of Greek tragedies that have become central to the international performance repertoire, shows that the tragic tradition of dying can survive in strikingly new forms. Indeed, it may well be that it is the hidden deaths of many modern western societies — in marked contrast to what Geoffrey Gorer called its 'pornography of death' available on film and in much news coverage[6] — that have refuelled this fascination with the tragic traditions of dying.

Greek and Irish Deaths

Carr regularly reworks material from Greek tragedy and from Euripides' plays, in particular.[7] The centrality of Woman and her exchanges with her alter ego/conscience, Scarecrow, in their eponymous play often recall the lyric exchanges between protagonist and chorus in Greek tragedies, especially those plays from early in the fifth century BCE. And readily detectable behind the entrances and exits of the minor characters (the curmudgeonly Him — the feckless husband who Woman continues to love despite his countless infidelities; and the cantankerous Auntie Ah, with her venomous barbs) are their prototypes who come to torture and to sympathize with the imprisoned Titan Prometheus in Aeschylus' *Prometheus Bound*. Indeed, Woman confined to her deathbed is strikingly reminiscent of Prometheus pinioned to the rock; and just as Prometheus learns that he is to have his liver devoured on a daily basis by the scavenging eagle, so Woman at the end of the play is tortured by the winged figure of Death and his minion, Scarecrow.

But it is, above all, those ancient tragedies that deal with female protagonists, whose presence is felt most acutely in *Woman and Scarecrow*. As in Euripides' tragi-comic/pro-satyric *Alcestis*, where Thanatos appears on stage in the prologue

(28–76),[8] the figure of Death in Carr's play also enjoys a prominent role, albeit one confined for the most part to the wardrobe in the bedroom. And Euripides' archetypal good wife, Alcestis, is heard in Woman's concerns about her children after her death: 'And keep her away from my children', she begs Him of one of his mistresses (p. 45) (compare the dying Alcestis' almost identical plea to Admetus: 'Allow [our children] to be the future master and mistress of my house and don't marry a step-mother over our children... [who] will spitefully raise her hand against these children, yours and mine [...] For a step-mother coming after is harsh to the children of a former marriage.')[9] Alcestis' morally ambiguous husband, Admetus, also lurks behind Carr's character Him as he makes his ludicrously selfish requests: '**you** have no right to leave me like this' (p. 41); 'Die if you're going to, or get up!' (p. 25). Like Admetus, Scarecrow says of Him: 'He's the high priest of remorse. He's jealous of your death. He's determined to wring the most he can from it. If you are not careful, he'll highjack your last breath' (p. 17). But Carr's treacherous Him has even more in common with Euripides' adulterous Jason (already the model for Carthage Kilbride in *By the Bog of Cats...*); and Carr can replace Medea's filicide with Woman's dying because bequeathing the responsibility for the children to the feckless husband/father is deemed a sufficiently effective act of revenge.

However, the references to the ancients that resound most clearly in *Woman and Scarecrow* are not related to mythical archetypes. It is the process of dying, the hallmark of Greek tragic deaths, that is represented in Carr's play; a process that mirrors the lengthy and elaborate ritual process of dying in ancient Greece and one that is equally present in conceptions of death in Ireland to this day.[10] In ancient Greece, this process extends over a considerable period of time: it begins when death is imminent, involves the laying out of the corpse followed by two days of lamentation culminating in a funeral on the third day, and a ritual meal over which the dead person was said to preside. The burial in no way marks the end of the process: thirty days later, the funeral rites were performed at the tomb with further lamentation and libations. The dead person is therefore not understood to be completely dead for a whole month after the death proper, but continues to live in a state of flux somewhere between the worlds of the living and the dead. This has, of course, significant implications not just for the dead but for the living too: it may well suggest that the dead are embarking on a long journey to a faraway place called Hades, but there is a sense too that the living are expected to participate in part of that journey. For this reason, the boundaries between the two worlds are equally porous for both living and dead, and separation between them is more often aspirational than actual. Death in ancient Greece, in this sense, is very much part of the processes of living.

Euripides' *Alcestis*, which, as I have argued, has much in common with Carr's play, is 'virtually unique in classical literature for its account of a normal death in the house'.[11] The emphasis here is more on the social processes of dying than the physicality of death itself. The process proper begins at the end of the prologue when Thanatos enters the house to perform the ritual act of cutting a lock of his victim's hair, thereby consecrating his victim to the gods of the underworld (74–76).

The process of Alcestis' dying continues with the arrival of the chorus who await news of her dying state, to be met by the servant who reports that the lady of the house is between life and death (141 ff.). Alcestis is understood to reside in this liminal state as she bids farewell to members of her household, and puts in place all the practical business of the house in preparation for her parting.

In the following episode, the audience witnesses a protracted series of last words uttered by Alcestis herself as she lies on a couch on stage. These last words are first delivered in elaborate lyrical form and then in the controlled, iambic trimeters of everyday speech. As Charles Segal comments: 'The moment of her departure is as uncertain to the spectators as it was to the chorus at the beginning of the play. For all we know, Alcestis might not die until, say, line 600 (instead of at line 392) [...] Death's consummation is beyond human prediction.'[12] This imprecision concerning the moment of 'Death's consummation' has nothing to do with artistic convention; instead, it relates to the conception of death as a process, during which any search for a precise 'point' of death proves vain.

Much time in the middle part of the play is given over to Alcestis' funeral rituals, not least because they take place alongside the discordant revels of Heracles. The final miraculous part of the play, the equivalent of the thirty-day rites over the tomb which normally marks the end of the death process proper, involves the miraculous restitution of Alcestis from the underworld undertaken by Heracles in honour of, and thanks to, his host, Admetus. Heracles, as ever in the Greco-Roman mythical tradition, may well be the creative-disrupter of normal processes here — but he is forced to work within the strict ritual framework of death in order to overcome it.

This elaborate process of dying in ancient Greece is in marked contrast to the traditional deaths of the modern western world, which are generally understood as events that occur in a medicalized instant, away from the public, and often even the familial, gaze.[13] If the ante-mortem stages of death have been largely banished from public view, the post-mortem stages in this modern schema have been reduced to a minimum, with professional agencies assuming responsibility for the corpse. The emphasis is now generally placed on the private and psychological dimension of grief and mourning, and state funerals and those of celebrities are the exceptions that prove the rule here.

However, death in Ireland, unlike in most modern western contexts, remains a public event even to this day and is still broadly understood to be durational rather than instantaneous. The phrase 'a good *death*' continues to be used (as opposed to the English consolatory, 'They had a good *life*'), and elderly Irish citizens routinely put aside their 'coffin suit'. Even with the marked shift since the 1990s from rural to urban living in the Irish Republic and in the North of Ireland, certain rituals concerning death have proved remarkably durable.[14]

In the late 1980s, belief in the messenger of death, the banshee (*bean sí*) was still strong;[15] and the banshee appears in Carr's play in the form of the black-winged bird/crow-creature that lurks menacingly in the wardrobe and half-emerges fleetingly, showing only a claw and a wing, at the end of Act 1. Just as Death and the dead encroach on the world of the living, so the living too can readily call on the dead both in times of need and when they are ritually compelled to do so during the Celtic festival of *Samhain*, held at the beginning of November, now better known elsewhere as the Christian festival of All Hallow's Eve (and, in turn, the secularized and commercialized jamboree, Halloween).[16]

The ancient Greek and Irish dramatic traditions share similar conceptions of death, which at root reflect ritual practices and beliefs in the two societies. But the theatricality inherent in the rituals in life is not merely incorporated into the plays; more importantly, it informs their shape as well. There have, of course, been religious, moral and practical prohibitions surrounding the representation of death on stage from Greco-Roman antiquity onwards, which Dominic Glynn ably explores in this volume.[17] In some ways, the practical reasons for excluding death from the Greek stage, with the limited number of actors, may well be the most convincing.[18] However, as we have seen in Euripides' *Alcestis*, the absence of the moment of death is considerably less significant when death is conceived as a process. Indeed in this context, it may only appear important when the death is brutal and bloody — when it is, in fact, a form of perverted sacrifice.[19]

The first stage in the theatrical process in the Greek tragedies is a form of dying into death, during which the protagonist's accession to tragic status is clearly signalled. The hallmark of the second stage is the protagonist's big speech before the exit for death proper, which (as we have seen) usually (but not always) occurs offstage.[20] The third stage concerns the reports of death from a messenger who has witnessed the offstage events; and the fourth and final stage involves the tragic lament with the chorus.[21] We find all these stages in Carr's play but some — notably the report and the lament — appear in slightly mutant form, not least because the climax of the action here is the death proper rather than what happens through the death. There is a sense that the events of *Woman and Scarecrow* may well be products of the protagonist's morphine-induced haze — perhaps her feckless husband never really shows up after all but is only there at the very end in her dreams; perhaps, too, Scarecrow is simply a quarrel with her other wiser, more cynical self. If so, then the process is even more elaborate in Carr's play because Woman occupies a permanent liminal state — a ritually, if not religiously, purgatorial space — in which the underlying pattern of Greek tragic deaths is very much present.

Indeed, Carr's funny, acerbic and deeply moving protagonist, poised on the threshold of death, is acutely aware of her theatrical forebears and her place within a tradition of the dying women of tragedy; and it is her alter ego Scarecrow, above all, who reminds her of this tradition. In this sense, Aeschylus, Sophocles, Euripides, Shakespeare, Synge, O'Casey and Beckett are all detectable in Carr's richly allusive lyrical tragi-comedy of dying into death. But it is equally important to stress that the mordant post-feminist wit, and the unique blend of myth and magical realism, are pure, and vintage, Carr.

Dying into Death

This first stage in the process of tragic deaths begins early. The tragic characters only begin to attain tragic status once they begin to die. This is the moment of decision in Sophoclean tragedies, when the protagonists begin to sever ties with reality. From this moment onwards — in Antigone's case, when she decides to bury her brother; in Oedipus' case, when he embarks on his quest to find out who murdered Laius — they have increasingly tenuous links with their environment and they enter a liminal/twilight realm. Both Antigone and her father in their respective name plays (for Oedipus, in both *Oedipus Tyrannus* and *Oedipus at Colonus*) become increasingly alienated from their immediate social and familial contexts in their apostrophes and turn increasingly to the natural and supranatural worlds.[22] 'The whole point of living is preparing to die', realizes Woman in Carr's play (p. 30); and this lyrical and often hilarious meditation on death seems to suggest that 'the whole point' of tragic drama is that it is a preparation for the death.

If the process of death in Irish culture traditionally begins with the cry of Banshee, the play opens with the process already underway as the crow (albeit hidden in the wardrobe) is already present. This female spirit, who attends certain families or neighbours, and less often appears to the dying person herself, heralds imminent death.[23] For Carr's tragic Woman, the process of dying into death is a painful one, and not only because of physical pain: here we watch her participate in a process that others have passed through before her, and yet she never quite sees herself living up to the theatrical, or her own actual, expectations of the role.

Woman is plagued by bitterness and a deep-rooted sense of inferiority, just as her own mother had been. Her one moment of self-belief, perhaps only a figment of her own imagination, occurred the day her dying mother led her to a mirror to admire herself in the red hat and the red coat, which were her mother's last gift: 'For one brief moment, a mirror glance, I was that thing she had yearned for and found' (p. 24). As Scarecrow says, 'Life withholds the epic. Until the end' (p. 18). 'Tell me', Woman implores Scarecrow, 'you know everything, tell me what it is about dying that is so sexy' (p. 18). But 'epic' remains elusive here because Woman's cynical alter ego, Scarecrow, is 'not in epic mood'. Instead, she brutally cuts Woman down to size: 'Too many things about you are small' (p. 18). Even Woman has to acknowledge that 'Epicness is for the brave, the beautiful' (p. 18). And whilst she might have had the requisite 'epicness' as a teenager, explains Scarecrow, she retreated from the 'battlefield' with her disastrous marriage. As a result, Woman's own death will be neither remotely 'sexy' nor 'epic'. She is not dying of madness, as did Shakespeare's Ophelia; nor is she without blemish, as was Euripides' Alcestis. Instead, she is overburdened with worries about packed lunches, school uniforms, homework and her husband's marital infidelities in a quotidian world that won't allow for epic flights. Here in Carr's *Woman and Scarecrow*, those 'intoxicating' deaths of the epic and theatrical traditions can only be broached with the aid of a glass of wine, a quaff of champagne.

Big Speeches

The tragic big speeches are generally cut off from the action proper in Greek tragedy, with time in these speeches being qualitatively different from the rest of the action proper. The *locus classicus* for this extratemporality in the big speech is Sophocles' *Antigone*, when Creon orders immediate dispatch of Antigone to her rocky vault at line 883 only for this order to be ignored from 891–928 (almost forty lines) and to be repeated again at line 931 (some fifty lines later).[24] There are in this passage some twenty disputed lines of text (904–20), but even without these there are nonetheless some twenty lines between the first and second of Creon's orders. What is going on here? It is not Creon's restraint, but artistic licence that makes this interlude analogous, temporally at least, to the choral odes, where the combination of gnomic utterances, reference to mythical otherworlds, and song and dance transport the spectators to different times and places beyond the world of Thebes and the House of Laius.

In many ways, this sense of extratemporality pervades *Woman and Scarecrow*, especially in the second act when both onstage characters and audience become increasingly aware of a suspension in the action. Woman decides to speed up the action and 'just go now' (p. 20), but Scarecrow is puzzled at Woman's defiance of artistic convention:

> SCARECROW.   Slip away mid-sentence is it?
> WOMAN.   Before we're interrupted again. They're all out there lining up for a gawk. I just heard an argument over brass handles, must be for my coffin. Can I just go?
> SCARECROW.   If that's what you really want.
> WOMAN.   I'll stop breathing so. (*Puts cover over her head.*) It'll be easier this way. Right. On the count of three.
> SCARECROW.   No final soliloquies.
> WOMAN (*Head from under covers.*)   What?
> SCARECROW.   No farewell speech.
> WOMAN.   None. (*Back under covers.*) Okay. One. Two. Three. Good-bye, Scarecrow.
> SCARECROW.   Yeah. (*Hold a minute. Scarecrow begins to suffer, doesn't fall this time. Enter Auntie Ah.*) (p. 20)

In a self-conscious, sideways glance at convention, the big speech is here teasingly denied to the audience. The linear logic of the plot with its climax in death is equally denied as the diversionary minor character, Auntie Ah enters to suspend the action further.

This sense of suspended action is continued by Auntie Ah's brutally harsh reprimand of her niece's dilatoriness in death and by her devastatingly blunt assessment of the realities of last moments:

> Your mother was the same. No finishing power. Anyone can get through the first half. You start a life. You finish it. You don't bail out at the crossroads because you don't like the scenery. It's weak. I despise it. And I'll tell you something else, my niece of a girl, there'll be no ecstasies at the finish. I've handed many of them back to their maker but not a [*sic*] one of them sang as the

curtain fell. They went confused, they went jabbering, they went silent, they went howling, but not one of them went with the beautifed light in the eye as if they's seen a vision of something pleasing. All I ever saw was the light draining from the basalt of the eyeball, the light draining. And the light gone. (p. 21)

The ancient Greek big speech enacts the dying characters' severing of self from their environment most acutely through a hyperconsciousness of self. Othello's last speech and his third-person self address was famously misread by T. S. Eliot in 1927 as an example of Othello's 'self-dramatisation' in order to cheer himself up.[25] But Eliot failed to notice that Othello here was merely conforming to a well-established artistic convention of the dying character on the threshold of death, and that this fissure between self and environment is the hallmark of the tragic big speech.[26] Even if Woman fails to reach 'epic' heights or even declaim any final big speech, she illustrates the split between mind and body well in her desire to look in the mirror. In response to Scarecrow's bewilderment as to why a dying woman should wish to look at herself in a mirror, Woman responds that she wants 'To watch myself die, I want to see how I am. I always look in mirrors to find out what's happening to me. Please bring me the mirror. I want to see if I'm still here' (p. 12).

Her hyperconsciousness of self is most keenly felt when she admires her decaying body, her bones protruding to produce a new 'graveyard chic' (p. 12). She enthuses to Scarecrow:

> Well, I always had good teeth and despite everything my hair is still magnificent. And now finally I have achieved bones. My dear, I have transformed myself into the ideal. Look at me, I am graveyard chic, angular, lupine, dangerous (*Raises an arm, turns it, lifts a leg, admires it*). Look at these arms, these legs, the contours of these limbs. I am slowly carving myself into a Greek statue. (p. 12)

Carr's Woman self-sculpts, as if she were a Sarah Bernhardt in the part of Medée or Phèdre, as she shapes her own premature death. As Ernst Bloch said of death in tragedy generally: 'death is merely the making visible of a shape which is already present anyway, in its essence; just as, for example, Michelangelo already saw the statue in the block and all his chisel had to do was remove the superfluous material around it.'[27]

By the end of the first act, Woman begins to learn how to commune not only with her environment but also with the dead, like other dying characters: 'I see tombs in shadow, mossy, weather-scarred tombs and all the dead squashed in and me with them wandering if there is starlight above' (p. 27). But Scarecrow cautions against alacrity and urges her instead to get it right: 'Shush for a while 'til we try and articulate it right' (p. 27). That this is merely a rehearsal for the final exit is made explicit in the stage directions, which read: '*A pause. The wardrobe door creaks open. Woman and Scarecrow turn to look, a wing appears from the wardrobe, then a clawed foot, then lights down.*'

Lament

There are clear parallels in Greek tragedy between the big speech and the lament:
the lament is also formally distinct from the rest of the action (it is sung rather than
spoken, like the odes, and culminates in formal patterns of movement — often a
funeral procession of chief mourners and the chorus). Like the dying character of
Greek tragedy, the chief mourner is abstracted from reality, shares similar formulaic
speech patterns and communes with the dead as they are understood to assume the
mantle of the dead person and to accompany them in part, at least, on their path to
death.[28] Both mourner and mourned are linked too in ritual terms with the dead —
they are barred from normal activity during the mourning process and their house
is understood to be unclean.[29]

Just as Carr's Woman acknowledges her place within a tradition of the dying
women of tragedy, the spectator is made equally aware of the survivors within that
tradition. As we have heard, there are moments when the dying Woman proffers her
own self-lament, which echoes those of the great chief mourners from the Abbey's
earlier repertoire, notably Synge's Maurya from *Riders to the Sea*. Maurya begins
her lament by referring to the irony of having survived the pangs of childbirth to
be rewarded with the far greater pains of being forced to outlive the life that she
herself engendered: 'six fine men, thought it was a hard birth I had with every one
of them and coming to the world — and some of them were found and some of
them were not found, but they're all gone now the lot of them...'.[30] The poignancy
of Woman's loss in Carr's play is greatly enhanced by these powerful resonances,
which align her with those earlier maternal archetypes: 'It was eight! Eight. Nine
if you count the one who didn't make it. My little half-moon baby with the shock
of blond hair. Where are you now, my half-cooked thing? Why couldn't you bear
me? Did something sift in the womb that appalled you? I should've had nine. There
should have been nine in the photograph...'...' (p. 8).

Woman and Scarecrow has a cast of five: the two characters of the title, Death in
the form of the bird-creature (not in the cast list) and two competing mourners
— the absconding Him and the ever-professional mourning Auntie Ah. But there
are other offstage mourners — the family members, whom the husband furiously
denounces for their excessive drinking and eating of the house's supplies. However
parasitical these family members are, they are important because they in turn know
something important that most have chosen to forget but is at the heart of Irish and
the Greek tragic deaths. As Woman reminds Him:

> Buy some more food and drink for my crowd. At least they know how to
> celebrate, ignorant old crones that they are. But they know this much. A
> person's passing is a sacred thing and merits some kind of overdose. So serve
> them well and let them drink and feast and sing me to my final place. Go! Look
> after them. You might learn something. (p. 26)

What they know, as Woman recognizes, is that this 'sacred thing' of transition is not
strictly the property of any one individual. On the one hand, they are experiencing
what Elias Canetti has observed of the link between survival and power, of the link
between loss and gain: 'The moment of survival is the moment of power. Horror at

the sight of death turns into satisfaction that it is someone else who is dead.'[31] But this is less about any selfish gene — rather it is, as René Girard points out, about permitting membership of a wider community:

> The death of the individual has something of the quality of a tribute levied for the continued existence of the collectivity. A human being dies, and the solidarity of the survivors is enhanced by his death.[32]

This sense of a wider community in matters relating to death is not peculiar, of course, to Ireland but is a noticeable feature in Irish funeral culture down to this day, where funerals are still public events that people attend very often out of general respect rather than because of any particular closeness to the deceased. And it is this sense of the general within the particular that Synge captures so powerfully in his account of a funeral on the Aran Islands at the beginning of the twentieth century:

> While the grave was being opened the women sat down among the flat tombstones [...] and began the wild keen, or crying for the dead. Each old woman, as she took her turn in leading the recitative, seemed possessed for the moment with a profound ecstasy of grief, swaying to and fro, and bending her forehead to the stone before her, while she called out to the dead with a perpetually recurring chant of sobs.
> All around the graveyard other wrinkled women, looking out from under the deep red petticoats that cloaked them, rocked themselves with the same rhythm, and intoned the inarticulate chant that is sustained by all as an accompaniment.
> [...]
> The grief of the keen is no personal lament for the death of one woman over eighty years, but seems to contain the whole passionate rage that lurks somewhere in every native of the island. In this cry of pain the inner consciousness of the people seems to lay itself bare for an instant, and to reveal the mood of beings who feel their isolation in the face of a universe that wars on them with winds and seas. They are usually silent, but in the presence of death all outward show of indifference or patience is forgotten, and they shriek with pitiable despair before the horror of the fate to which they are all doomed.[33]

The verbal parallels across these different theatrical traditions in the big speeches and in the laments make the spectators feel the particular and the general together, and in turn recognize the patterning afforded in the recognition and echoes across the millennia.

Conclusion

In the introduction to this volume, Jessica Goodman identifies a tension between ending and non-ending that is a recurrent feature of plays that figure death. Goodman continues:

> Human life, ephemeral like a performance, with an inevitable ending that is simultaneously enormously significant (for the individual/that night's audience) and totally insignificant (in the broader scheme of humanity/a long-running

production); but which also forms a part of a greater whole, giving its individual components meaning, and perhaps therefore providing them with consolation.[34]

This provides a fitting commentary on the protracted 'performance' of Woman in Carr's play, where the tragic tradition, albeit now played out in tragic-comic mode, still 'forms a part of a greater whole, giving its [...] components meaning'.

In 1966 T. R. Henn noted how the decline in the rituals surrounding death had had a deleterious effect on modern tragic drama;[35] and he is surely correct to identify a correlation between tragic drama and attitudes to death. However, it is now possible to realize that tragedy is very far from 'dead', in any Steinerian sense, as commentators had confidently predicted from the end of the Second World War onwards.[36] Even leading theatre theorist Hans-Thies Lehmann identifies elements of the tragic in, for example, the use of gesture in what he designates 'post-dramatic' theatre.[37] And the huge resurgence of interest in Greek tragedy since at least the 1960s is clear testament to the fact that despite, or even because of, this perceptible decline in ritualized death in western societies, there is hunger for theatre which reminds audiences, adopting the words of Carr's Woman to Auntie Ah, that *'The whole point of living is preparing to die'*.

Notes to Chapter 10

1. Fiona Mountford, 'Death Stalks Sesame Street', *Evening Standard*, 22 June 2006, <https://www.standard.co.uk/culture/theatre/death-stalks-sesame-street-7387447.html> [accessed 20 April 2021]. A 2018 revival at Irish Repertory Theater in New York played for laughs instead of capturing the 'blistering beauty of a play that rages with regret and black-pitch humour'. See Laura Collins-Hughes, *New York Times*, 22 May 2018, <https://www.nytimes.com/2018/05/22/theater/woman-and-scarecrow-marina-carr-irish-rep.html> [accessed 21 April 2021].

2. Marina Carr, *Woman and Scarecrow*, actors' edn (New York: Dramatists Play Service, 2010), p. 9. All quotations are taken from this edition kindly shared with me by the author. Subsequent page references appear in parentheses in the text.

3. Fiona Macintosh, *Dying Acts: Death in Ancient Greek and Modern Irish Drama* (Cork: Cork University Press, 1994; New York: St Martin's Press, 1995).

4. This is not to deny the evident parallels between other traditions, notably between ancient and modern Greece, on which see the classic study of Margaret Alexiou, *The Ritual Lament in Greek Tradition* (Cambridge: Cambridge University Press).

5. On the resurgence of interest in Greek tragedy since the 1960s, see Edith Hall, Fiona Macintosh and Amanda Wrigley (eds), *Dionysus Since 69: Greek Tragedy at the Dawn of the Third Millennium* (Oxford: Oxford University Press, 2004).

6. Geoffrey Gorer, 'The Pornography of Death', *Encounter*, 5 (1955), 49–52 [repr. in Geoffrey Gorer, *Death, Grief, and Mourning in Contemporary Britain* (London: Cresset Press, 1965), pp. 169–75].

7. Euripides' *Medea* in *By the Bog of Cats...* (Cian's Gaff, 1998); *Iphigenia in Aulis* (as well as Aeschylus' *Oresteia*) in *Ariel* (Abbey Theatre, 2002); both *Hecuba* and *Trojan Women* in her *Hecuba* (RSC, 2015); *Electra*, *Iphigenia in Aulis*, and possibly *Orestes* (along with the Aeschylus' *Oresteia* and Sophocles' *Electra*), in *Girl on an Altar* (2021, in a live-streamed, rehearsed reading for Kiln Theatre, London). And she has reworked Euripides' *Phoenician Women*, together with Sophocles' *Antigone*, *Oedipus Tyrannus* and *Oedipus at Colonus*, in *The Boy* (originally scheduled to open at Dublin's Abbey Theatre late in 2020 but postponed owing to the Covid-19 pandemic). For Carr's reworking of other 'classic' plays, see the chapter by María Bastianes in this volume on Lorca's *Blood Wedding* (Young Vic, 2019).

8. Euripides' *Alcestis* (438 BCE) was performed as the fourth play at the Festival of Dionysus, the

usual position of a satyr play, which followed three tragedies by the same playwright. *Alcestis* is usually referred to as 'pro-satyric' because it was the fourth play in a group of plays entered by Euripides for the festival of Dionysus in Athens and took the place traditionally reserved for the satyr play proper. It also includes many features that resemble the satyric rather than tragic genre: both the interlude with the drunken Heracles in the middle of Alcestis' funerary rites and especially Heracles' descent to the underworld to bring back the 'dead' Alcestis.

9. Euripides' *Alcestis*, 300–10, edited with translation and commentary by D. J. Conacher (Warminster: Aris and Phillips, 1988).

10. For theatrical representations of death in both these traditions, see Macintosh, *Dying Acts*, pp. 32–66. For an account of the ritual process of death in ancient Greece, see Robert Garland, *The Greek Way of Death* (London: Duckworth, 1985).

11. Charles Segal, 'Euripides' *Alcestis*: How to Die a Normal Death in Greek Tragedy', in *Death and Representation*, ed. by Sarah Webster Goodwin and Elisabeth Bronfen (Baltimore, MD, and London: Johns Hopkins University Press, 1993), pp. 213–41 (p. 214).

12. Segal, 'Euripides' *Alcestis*', p. 227.

13. The *locus classicus* is Phillipe Ariès, *Western Attitudes towards Death* (Baltimore, MD: Johns Hopkins University Press, 1974). The hospice movement has been strongly resisting the practices associated with this modern, sanitized death since at least the 1960s but has not yet managed to eclipse them.

14. Nina Witoszek and Patrick F. Sheeran, *Talking to the Dead: A Study of Irish Funerary Traditions* (Amsterdam and Atlanta, GA: Rodopi, 1998).

15. Patricia Lysaght, *The Banshee: The Irish Supernatural Death-Messenger* (Dublin: O'Brien Press, 1986).

16. Patricia Lysaght, '*Convivium Mortis*: Feast and Death in Irish Literature and Oral Tradition', in *The Life Cycle: SIEF's Third Congress April 8–12, 1987, Zürich Switzerland* (Stockholm: International Society for Ethnology and Folklore, 1987), pp. 1–10. For the Greek equivalent of *Samhain*, the third day of the *Anthesteria* (*Chutroi*, 'the day of pots'), see Robert Parker, *Miasma: Pollution and Purification in Early Greek Religion* (Oxford: Oxford University Press), p. 39.

17. Dominic Glynn, 'The (Un)performability of Death and Violence on Stage', in this volume.

18. The chief exponent of this theory is Peter Arnott, *Greek Scenic Conventions in the Fifth Century BC* (Oxford: Clarendon Press, 1962).

19. Macintosh, *Dying Acts*, pp. 126–47.

20. The exceptions to this rule in Greek tragedy are: Alcestis' onstage death in her eponymous Euripidean play; the death of Hippolytus at the end of Euripides' *Hippolytus*; and (possibly, but not without considerable debate) the suicide of Ajax in Sophocles' *Ajax*.

21. Macintosh, *Dying Acts*, chapters 4–7.

22. For the classic discussion of the Sophoclean tragic figure's alienation from their immediate environment, see Bernard M. W. Knox, *The Heroic Temper: Studies in Sophoclean Tragedy* (Berkeley: University of California Press, 1983).

23. Lysaght, *The Banshee*.

24. For detailed description, see Macintosh, *Dying Acts*, pp. 94–95.

25. T. S. Eliot, 'Shakespeare and the Stoicism of Seneca', in *Selected Essays*, 3rd edn (London: Faber, 1951), pp. 126–50.

26. Cf. Ajax's death speech in Soph. *Ajax*, 859–65, especially.

27. Ernst Bloch, 'Death as the Chisel in Tragedy', in *The Principle of Hope*, trans. by Neville Plaice, Stephen Plaice and Paul Knight, 3 vols (Oxford: Blackwell, 1986), III, 1169 [= 'Der Tod als Meißel in der Tragödie', in *Das Princip Hoffnung*, 3 vols (Frankfurt am Main: Suhrkamp, 1959), II, 1357]. Bloch is commenting on Lukács' views on death in tragedy.

28. See Macintosh, *Dying Acts*, pp. 158–82.

29. On pollution and the mourners, see Parker, *Miasma*, pp. 35–41, pp. 55–65.

30. J. M. Synge, *Collected Works*, vol. III: *Plays Book I*, ed. by Ann Saddlemyer (Oxford: Oxford University Press, 1968; repr. Gerrards Cross: Colin Smythe Ltd., 1982), p. 21.

31. Elias Canetti, *Crowds and Power* (New York: Seabury Press, 1978), p. 277 [= *Masse und Macht* (Hamburg: Claassen, 1960)].

32. René Girard, *Violence and the Sacred*, trans. by Patrick Gregory (Baltimore, MD: Johns Hopkins University Press, 1977), p. 255 [= *La Violence et le sacré* (Paris: Éditions Bernard Grasset, 1972)].

33. J. M. Synge, *The Aran Islands* (1907) [= J. M. Synge, *Collected Works*, vol. II: *Prose I*, ed. by Alan Price (Oxford: Oxford University Press, 1966; repr. Gerrards Cross: Colin Smythe Ltd, 1982)], p. 75.

34. Jessica Goodman, 'Introduction: Death on Stage: A Never-Ending Ending', in this volume.

35. Thomas Rice Henn, *The Harvest of Tragedy*, 2nd edn (London: Methuen, 1966), pp. 257–69.

36. George Steiner, *The Death of Tragedy* (London: Faber and Faber, 1961).

37. Hans-Thies Lehmann, *Tragedy and Dramatic Theatre* (London: Routledge, 2016).

BIBLIOGRAPHY

❖

ADILLO, SERGIO, 'Calderón en los escenarios españoles (1715–2015): canon, construcción nacional y campo del teatro' (unpublished doctoral thesis, Complutense University of Madrid, 2018)

ALEXIOU, MARGARET, *The Ritual Lament in Greek Tradition* (Cambridge: Cambridge University Press)

ALLEN, SÉAN, 'Kaiser: Von morgens bis mitternachts', in *Landmarks in German Drama*, ed. by Peter Hutchinson (Oxford: Peter Lang, 2002), pp. 159–217

ALVARO, CORRADO, *Scritti dispersi, 1921–1956* (Milan: Bompiani, 1995)

ANGEL-PEREZ, ÉLISABETH, 'La Scène traumatique de Sarah Kane', *Sillages critiques*, 19 (2015), <http://journals.openedition.org/sillagescritiques/4328> [accessed 29 April 2020]

ANON., *A Ballad on the death of Louis the unfortunate [...] and A description of the appearance of Marie Antoinette's ghost* (Bristol: John Rose, 1793)

ANON., *L'Office du Mort, ou Le Mariage du Bas Clergé de France, comédie en trois actes & en prose dans le genre du Théâtre espagnol* ([n.p.]: [n.pub.], May 1790)

ANZ, THOMAS, *Literatur des Expressionismus* (Stuttgart, Weimar: Metzler, 2002)

ARIÈS, PHILIPPE, *L'Homme devant la mort* (Paris: Seuil, 1977)

—— *The Hour of Our Death*, trans. by Helen Weaver (New York: Knopf, 1981)

—— *Western Attitudes towards Death* (Baltimore, MD: Johns Hopkins University Press, 1974)

ARISTOTLE, *Poetics* (Oxford: Oxford University Press, 2013)

ARNOLD, HEINZ LUDWIG and RUTH FLORACK (eds), *Frank Wedekind* (Munich: Edition Text+Kritik, 1996)

ARNOTT, PETER, *Greek Scenic Conventions in the Fifth Century BC* (Oxford: Clarendon Press, 1962)

Arrest de la Court de Parlement contre Gaspart de Colligny, qui fut admiral de France [13 sept. 1569] (Lyon: M. Iove, 1569)

BAECQUE, ANTOINE DE, *La Gloire et l'Effroi: sept morts sous la Terreur* (Paris: Grasset, 1997)

BAHR, HERMANN, *Dialog vom Tragischen* (Berlin: S. Fischer, 1904)

BARBAGLI, MARZIO, *Farewell to the World: A History of Suicide*, trans. by Lucinda Byatt (Cambridge and Malden, MA: Polity Press, 2015)

BAREA, ARTURO, *Lorca: The Poet and his People* (New York: Cooper Square Publishers, 1973)

BARKER, HOWARD, *Death, The One and the Art of Theatre* (London and New York: Routledge, 2005)

BARRELL, JOHN, '"An Entire Change of Performances?" The Politicisation of Theatre and the Theatricalisation of Politics in the mid 1790s', *Lumen*, 17 (1998), 11–50

—— *Imagining the King's Death: Figurative Treason, Fantasies of Regicide, 1793–1796* (Oxford: Oxford University Press, 2000)

BARSELLA, SUSANNA, 'Il silenzio dei *Giganti*: arte e parola nell'ultima opera di Pirandello', *Italian Quarterly*, 38 (2001), 37–51

BARTHOLOMEW, JOHN, *The Fall of the French Monarchy; or, Louis XVI. An historical tragedy. In five acts* (London: E. Harlow and W. Richardson, 1794)

BASSNETT, SUSAN, 'Translating for the Theatre: The Case Against Performability', *TTR: Traduction, Terminologie, Rédaction*, 4.1 (1991), 99–111

BASTIANES, MARÍA, 'Blood Wedding Receives an Irish-Gypsy Makeover at the Young Vic', *European Stages*, 15 (2020), <https://europeanstages.org/2020/12/30/blood-wedding-receives-an-irish-gypsy-makeover-at-the-young-vic/> [accessed 16 April 2021]

——'Negotiating Cultural Exchange: Lorca on the British Stage from the Spanish Civil War until the Mid-Fifties', *Studies in Theatre and Performance* (forthcoming 2022)

BATAILLE, GEORGES, *The Accursed Share: An Essay on General Economy* [1949], trans. by Robert Hurley, 3 vols (New York: Zone Books, 1988)

BATAILLON, MICHEL, *Un Défi en province: Chéreau, Planchon et leurs invités, 1972–1986: chronique d'une aventure théâtrale* (Paris: Marval, 2005)

BATE, JONATHAN, *Shakespeare and the English Romantic Imagination* (Oxford: Clarendon Press, 1986)

——*Shakespearean Constitutions: Politics, Theatre, Criticism, 1730–1830* (Oxford: Clarendon Press, 1989)

BEECHER HOGAN, CHARLES, *Shakespeare in the Theatre, 1701–1800* (Oxford: Clarendon Press, 1957)

BENJAMIN, WALTER, 'Der Autor als Produzent. Ansprache im Institut zum Studium des Fascismus in Paris am 27. April 1934', in *Gesammelte Schriften*, ed. by Rolf Tiedemann and Hermann Schweppenhäuser, 17 vols (Frankfurt am Main: Suhrkamp, 1972–99), II.2 (1982), pp. 683–701

BÉRARD, SUZANNE J., *Le Théâtre révolutionnaire de 1789 à 1794: la déchristianisation sur les planches* (Nanterre: Presses Universitaires de Paris Ouest, 2009)

BERNARDIN DE SAINT-PIERRE, 'Les Harmonies de la Nature', 3 vols, in *Œuvres complètes de Jacques-Henri Bernardin de Saint-Pierre*, 12 vols, mises en ordre et précédées de la vie de l'auteur par Louis-Aimé Martin (Paris: Méquignon-Marvis, 1818), VIII–X

BIET, CHRISTIAN, and MARIE-MADELEINE FRAGONARD (eds), *Le Théâtre, la violence et les arts en Europe (XVIe–XVIIe s.)* (Paris: Champion, 2010)

BILLINGTON, MICHAEL, 'Yerma review — Billie Piper gives a breathtakingly uninhibited performance', *The Guardian*, 5 August 2016 <https://www.theguardian.com/stage/2016/aug/05/yerma-review-billie-piper-young-vic-simon-stone-lorca>

BINHAMMER, KATHERINE, 'Marie Antoinette was "One of Us": British Accounts of the Martyred Wicked Queen', *Eighteenth Century: Theory and Interpretation*, 44 (2003), 233–56

BLAKEMORE, STEVEN, *Crisis in Representation: Thomas Paine, Mary Wollstonecraft, Helen Maria Williams, and the Rewriting of the French Revolution* (London: Associated University Press, 1997)

BLAU, HERBERT, 'Universals of Performance or Amortalizing Play', *Substance*, 11.4 (1983), 140–61

BLOCH, ERNST, 'Death as the Chisel in Tragedy', in *The Principle of Hope*, trans. by N. Plaice, S. Plaice and P. Knight, 3 vols (Oxford 1986), III, p. 1169 [= 'Der Tod als Meißel in der Tragödie', *Das Princip Hoffnung*, 3 vols (Frankfurt am Main 1959), II, p. 1357]

BOADEN, JAMES, *Fontainville Forest: A Play, in five acts* (London: Hookham and Carpenter, 1794)

——*Memoirs of Mrs Siddons: Interspersed with anecdotes of Authors and Actors*, 2 vols (London: H. C. Carey & I. Lea, 1827)

——*Memoirs of the Life of John Philip Kemble, Esq.*, 2 vols (London: Longman, Hurst, Rees, Orme, Brown and Green, 1825)

BOHANNAN, LAURA, 'Shakespeare in the Bush', in *Investigating Culture*, ed. by C. Delaney with D. Kaspin (New York: Wiley Blackwell, repr. 2017), pp. 27–36

BOOR, HELMUT DE, and RICHARD NEWALD (eds), *Geschichte der deutschen Literatur von den Anfängen bis zur Gegenwart*, 12 vols (Munich: Beck, 1949–94)

BORSELLINO, NINO, *Ritratto e immagini di Pirandello* (Bari: Laterza, 1991)

BOURGEON, JEAN-LOUIS, *L'Assassinat de Coligny* (Geneva: Droz, 1992)

BOURQUIN, LAURENT (ed.), *Mémoires de Claude Haton (1553–1582)*, 4 vols (Paris: Editions du Comité des travaux historiques et scientifiques, 2005)

BOYLE, NICHOLAS, 'Goethe's Theory of Tragedy', *MLR*, 105.4 (2010), 1072–86

BRECHT, BERTOLT, 'Notes on the Opera *Rise and Fall of the City of Mahagonny*', in *Brecht on Theatre*, pp. 61–71

—— 'Señora Carrar's Rifles', in *Collected Plays* (London: Methuen, 1983), pp. 95–124

—— *Brecht on Theatre: The Development of an Aesthetic*, ed. and trans. by John Willet (London: Methuen, 1974)

—— *Die Maßnahme*, in *Werke. Große kommentierte Berliner und Frankfurter Ausgabe*, ed. by Werner Hecht et al., 30 vols (Frankfurt am Main: Suhrkamp, 1988–2000), III: *Stücke 3* (1988), pp. 73–98

—— *Messingkauf, or Buying Brass*, in *Brecht on Performance. Messingkauf and Modelbooks*, ed. by Tom Kuhn, Steve Giles and Marc Silberman (London: Bloomsbury, 2014), pp. 1–141

—— *Short Organon for the Theatre*, in *Brecht on Theatre*, ed. by Marc Silbermann, Steve Giles and Tom Kuhn (London: Bloomsbury, 2014), pp. 231–65

—— *The Measure Taken*, trans. by Carl R. Müller, in *The Measure Taken and other Lehrstücke* (London: Methuen, 1977), pp. 7–34

—— *Werke. Große kommentierte Berliner und Frankfurter Ausgabe*, ed. by Werner Hecht et al., 30 vols (Frankfurt am Main: Suhrkamp, 1988–2000)

BRIGGS, JULIA, 'Marlowe's *Massacre at Paris*: A Reconsideration', *The Review of English Studies*, 34 (1983), 257–78

BROOK, PETER, *The Empty Space* [1968], 3rd edn (London: Penguin Books, 1990)

—— 'The Opening of the Depths', in *The French Revolution, 1789–1989: Two Hundred Years of Rethinking*, ed. by Sandy Petrey (Lubbock: Texas Tech University Press, 1989)

BRUYN, FRANS DE, 'Shakespeare and the French Revolution', in *Shakespeare in the Eighteenth Century*, ed. by Fiona Ritchie and Peter Sabor (Cambridge: Cambridge University Press, 2012), pp. 297–313

BUCKLEY, MATHEW, *Tragedy Walks the Streets: The French Revolution in the Making of Modern Drama* (Baltimore, MD: Johns Hopkins University Press, 2006)

BURKE, EDMUND, *Reflections of Revolution in France* (London: J. Dodsely, 1790)

BURKE, MARY, *'Tinkers': Synge and the Cultural History of the Irish Traveller* (Oxford: Oxford University Press, 2009)

BURWICK, FREDERICK, 'The Ideal Shatters: Sarah Siddons, Madness, and the Dynamics of Gesture', in *Notorious Muse: The Actress in British Art and Culture, 1776–1812*, ed. by Robyn Asleson (New Haven, CT: Yale University Press, 2003), pp. 129–50

BUTLER, THOMAS, 'Sarah Ruhl's *Dear Elizabeth* and the Mourning of Friends', *Journal of Dramatic Theory and Criticism*, 28.2 (2014), 67–84

CAMERON, KEITH, *La Tragédie de feu Gaspard de Colligny* (Exeter: University of Exeter, 1971)

CANETTI, ELIAS, *Crowds and Power* (New York: Seabury Press, 1978) [=*Masse und Macht* (Hamburg: Claasen, 1960)]

CAPEFIGUE, J.-B. H. R., *Histoire de la réforme, de la ligue, et du règne de Henri IV*, 8 vols (Paris: Duféy, 1834)

CARLSON, MARVIN, *The Haunted Stage: The Theatre as Memory Machine* (Ann Arbor: University of Michigan Press, 2003)

CARR, MARINA, *Blood Wedding* (London: Faber and Faber, 2019)

—— *Woman and Scarecrow*, actors' edn (New York: Dramatists Play Service, 2010)

CARROLL, STUART, *Martyrs and Murderers: The Guise Family and the Making of Europe* (Oxford: Oxford University Press, 2009)

CARSON, NEIL, *A Companion to Henslowe's Diary* (Cambridge: Cambridge University Press, 1988)

CARTER HAILEY, R., 'The Publication Date of Marlowe's *Massacre at Paris*, With a Note on The Collier Leaf', *Marlowe Studies: An Annual*, 1 (2011), 25–40

CAVE, KATHRYN (ed.), *The Diary of Joseph Farington*, 16 vols (New Haven, CT: Yale University Press, 1983), XI: *January 1811–June 1812*

CHARNON-DEUTSCHE, LOU, *The Spanish Gypsy: The History of an European Obsession* (University Park: Penn State Press, 2004)

CIFUENTES, LUIS FERNÁNDEZ, *La norma y la diferencia* (Zaragoza: Universidad de Zaragoza, 1986)

CIXOUS, HÉLÈNE, 'Enter the Theatre (in between)', *Modern Drama*, 42.3 (1999), 301–14

COLLINS-HUGHES, LAURA, *New York Times*, 22 May 2018, <https://www.nytimes.com/2018/05/22/theater/woman-and-scarecrow-marina-carr-irish-rep.html>

CONNORS, LOGAN, *The Emergence of a Theatrical Science of Man in France, 1660–1740* (Liverpool: Liverpool University Press, 2020)

CORNEILLE, PIERRE, 'Examen', in *Œuvres de Pierre Corneille*, ed. by C. Marty-Laveaux (Paris: Hachette, 1862), pp. 273–80 <https://fr.wikisource.org/wiki/Horace_(Corneille)/Édition_Marty-Laveaux> [accessed 5 May 2021]

——*Discours du poème dramatique*, in *Œuvres complètes*, ed. by Georges Couton, 3 vols (Paris: Gallimard [Pléiade], 1980–98), III, 115–90

——*Horace* (Paris: Augustin Courbé, 1641) <https://fr.wikisource.org/wiki/Horace_(Corneille)/Édition_Courbé> [accessed 5 May 2021]

——*Œuvres complètes*, ed. by Georges Couton, 3 vols (Paris: Gallimard [Pléiade], 1980–98)

CORRIGAN, ROBERT W., 'Thornton Wilder and the Tragic Sense of Life', in *Critical Essays on Thornton Wilder*, ed. by Martin Blank (New York: G. K. Hall & Co, 1996), pp. 77–83

CRACIUN, ADRIANA, *Fatal Women of Romanticism* (Cambridge: Cambridge University Press, 2003)

CRAIG, MEGAN, 'The Language of Stones', *Journal of Aesthetics and Phenomenology*, 5.2 (2018), 119–37, <https://doi.org/10.1080/20539320.2018.1516656> [accessed 29 April 2020]

CROUZET, DENIS, *La Nuit de la Saint-Barthélemy: un rêve perdu de la Renaissance* (Paris: Fayard, 1994)

CURTIN, ADRIAN, *Death in Modern Theatre: Stages of Mortality* (Manchester: Manchester University Press, 2019)

CURULLA, ANNELLE, *Gender and Religious Life in French Revolutionary Drama* (Oxford: Oxford University Studies in The Enlightenment, 2019)

DAMROSCH, DAVID, 'World Literature in a Postcanonical, Hypercanonical Age', in *Comparative Literature in an Age of Globalization*, ed. by Haun Saussy (Baltimore, MD: Johns Hopkins University Press, 2006), pp. 43–53

DARLOW, MARK, *Staging the French Revolution: Cultural Politics and the Paris Opera, 1789–1794* (New York and Oxford: Oxford University Press, 2012)

DAVIES, THOMAS, *Dramatic Miscellanies: consisting of critical observations on several plays by Shakespeare*, 3 vols (Dublin: S. Price et al., 1784)

DELGADO, MARIA, 'Tribalism, Tragedy and Torment: Yaël Farber's "Blood Wedding" at the Young Vic', *The Theatre Times*, 10 October 2019, <https://thetheatretimes.com/tribalism-tragedy-and-torment-yael-farbers-blood-wedding-at-the-young-vic/> [accessed 16 April 2021]

——*Federico García Lorca* (New York: Routledge, 2008)

DENKLER, HORST, *Das Drama des Expressionismus Programm, Spieltext, Theater* (Munich: Fink, 1979)

DENTON, MARGARET FIELDS, 'Death in French Arcady: Nicolas Poussin's *The Arcadian Shepherds* and Burial Reform in France c. 1800', *Eighteenth-Century Studies*, 36.2 (2003), 195–216

DERRIDA, JACQUES, *Specters of Marx: The State of the Debt, the Work of Mourning, and the New International*, trans. by Peggy Kamuff (New York and London: Routledge, 1994)

DESAN, SUZANNE, *The Family on Trial in Revolutionary France* (Berkeley: University of California Press, 2006)

DIEFENDORF, BARBARA, 'Simon Vigor: A Radical Preacher in Sixteenth-Century Paris', *Sixteenth-Century Journal*, 18 (1987), 399–410

——, *The St. Bartholomew's Day Massacre: A Brief History with Documents* (Bedford: St. Martin's Press, 2008)

DOUGHERTY, DRU, 'El lenguaje del silencio en el teatro de García Lorca', *Anales de la literatura española contemporánea*, 11.1/2 (1986), 91–110

DRAKAKIS, JOHN, and DALE TOWNSHEND, 'Unsexing Macbeth: 1623–1800', in *Macbeth: A Critical Reader*, ed. by Dale Townshend (London: Bloomsbury, 2013), pp. 172–204

DUBOS, JEAN-BAPTISTE, *Réflexions critiques sur la poésie et sur la peinture* (Paris: Mariette, 1739)

——*Réflexions critiques sur la poésie et sur la peinture*, 3 vols (Paris: Pissot, 1770 [1719])

DUMOULIÉ, CAMILLE, 'L'entre-deux-morts: Jacques Lacan entre philosophie, littérature et psychanalyse', *Princípios*, 10.13 (2003), 191–206

DURZAK, MANFRED, *Das expressionistische Drama* (Munich: Nymphenburger 1978)

ELIOT, T. S., 'Shakespeare and the Stoicism of Seneca', in *Selected Essays*, 3rd edn (London: Faber and Faber, 1951), pp. 126–50

ENGEL, LAURA, 'The Personating of Queens: Lady Macbeth, Sarah Siddons and the Creation of Female Celebrity in the Late Eighteenth Century', in *Macbeth: New Critical Essays*, ed. by Nick Moschovakis (London: Routledge, 2007), pp. 251–52

EPPLETT, CHRIS, 'Spectacular Executions in the Roman World', in *A Companion to Sport and Spectacle in Greek and Roman Antiquity*, ed. by Paul Christesen and Donald G. Kyle (Oxford: John Wiley & Sons, 2013), pp. 520–32

ESCHE, EDWARD (ed.), 'Introduction' to *The Massacre at Paris*, in *The Complete Works of Christopher Marlowe*, 5 vols (Oxford: Oxford University Press, 1998), V, 309–16

ESSELBORN, HANS, 'Das Drama des Expressionismus', in *Die literarische Moderne in Europa*, 2 vols (Opladen: Westdeutscher Verlag, 1994), II: *Formation der literarischen Avantgarde*, ed. by Hans Joachim Piechotta, Ralph-Rainer Wuthenow, Sabine Rothmann, pp. 271–82

ESSLIN, MARTIN, *Das Paradox des politischen Dichters* (Frankfurt and Bonn: Athenäum, 1962)

ETLIN, RICHARD, *The Architecture of Death: The Transformation of the Cemetery in 18th-Century Paris*, (Cambridge, MA: MIT Press, 1984)

EURIPIDES, *Alcestis*, 300–10, edited with translation and commentary by D. J. Conacher (Warminster: Aris and Phillips, 1988)

FEILLA, CECILIA, *The Sentimental Theater of the French Revolution* (Aldershot: Ashgate, 2013; Abingdon: Routledge, 2016)

FELSKI, RITA, 'Introduction', in *Rethinking Tragedy*, ed. by Rita Felski (Baltimore, MD: Johns Hopkins University Press, 2008), pp. 1–25

FERNÁNDEZ-CAPARRÓS, ANA, 'Death and the Community of Comic Romance: Sarah Ruhl's Poetics of Transformation in *Dead Man's Cell Phone*', *Contemporary Theatre Review*, 25.4 (2015), 488–501, <https://www.tandfonline.com/doi/full/10.1080/10486801.2015.1078324> [accessed 29 April 2020]

FINBURGH, CLAIRE, 'The Politics of Translating Contemporary French Theatre: How 'Linguistic Translation' Becomes 'Stage Translation', in *Staging and Performing Translation*, ed. by Roger Baines, Christina Marinetti, and Manuella Perteghella (Basingstoke: Palgrave Macmillan, 2011), pp. 230–48

FLEEMING JENKIN, H. C., 'Mrs Siddons as Lady Macbeth and as Queen Katherine' (1878), in *Papers on Acting*, ed. by Brander Matthews (New York: Hill & Wang, 1958), pp. 65–114

FLETCHER, ANNE, 'No Time Like the Present: Wilder's Plays and Buddhist Thought and Time', in *Thornton Wilder: New Perspectives*, ed. by Jackson R. Bryer and Lincoln Konkle (Evanston, IL: Northwestern University Press, 2013), pp. 154–88

FONTENELLE, *Œuvres complètes*, 7 vols (Paris: Fayard, 1991–2001)

FRASSICA, PIETRO, 'I giganti e la poetica dell'incompiuta', in *Le fonti di Pirandello*, ed. by Antonio Alessia and Giuliana Sanguinetti Katz (Palermo: Palumbo, 1996), pp. 121–33

FRICK, WERNER, *'Die mythische Methode': Komparatistische Studien zur Transformation der griechischen Tragödie im Drama der klassischen Moderne* (Tübingen: Niemeyer, 1998)

FRIEDLAND, PAUL, *Political Actors: Representative Bodies and Theatricality in the Age of the French Revolution* (London: Cornell University Press, 2002)

FRYE, NORTHROP, *Anatomy of Criticism* (Princeton, NJ: Princeton University Press, 1957)

FULDA, DANIEL, 'Tragödie [Von Lessing bis zur Gegenwart]', in *Historisches Wörterbuch der Rhetorik*, 10 vols (Tübingen: Niemeyer, 1992–), IX (2009), ed. by Gert Ueding, pp. 762–67

FURET, FRANÇOIS, and MONA OZOUF (eds), *A Critical Dictionary of the French Revolution*, trans. by Arthur Goldhammer (Cambridge, MA: Harvard University Press, 1989), pp. 694–703

GALLE, ROLAND, 'Tragisch — Tragik', in *Ästhetische Grundbegriffe: Historisches Wörterbuch*, 7 vols (Stuttgart, Weimar: Metzler, 2000–05), VI: *Tanz — Zeitalter/Epoche* (2005), ed. by Karlheinz Barck et al., pp. 117–70

GAMER, MICHAEL, *Romanticism and the Gothic: Genre, Reception and Canon Formation* (Cambridge: Cambridge University Press, 2000)

GARCÍA LORCA, FEDERICO, *Bodas de sangre*, ed. by Mario Fernández (Alianza: Madrid, 1998)

—— *Epistolario completo* (Madrid: Cátedra, 1997)

—— *La casa de Bernarda Alba*, ed. by Allen Josephs and Juan Caballero (Madrid: Cátedra, 2000)

—— *Obras completas*, ed. by Arturo del Hoyo, 2 vols (Madrid: Aguilar, 1974)

—— *Obras completas*, ed. by Miguel García Posada, 4 vols (Barcelona: Galaxia Gutenberg, 1997)

—— *Yerma*, ed. by Antonio A. Gómez Yebra (Castalia: Madrid, 2004)

GARLAND, ROBERT, *The Greek Way of Death* (London: Duckworth, 1985)

GARNAI, AMY, ' "One Victim from the Last Despair": Mary Robinson's Marie Antoinette', *Women's Writing*, 12.3 (2005), 388–94

GIAMMARINO, STEFANIA, 'La messinscena come *restauro teatrale*: i *Giganti* di Pirandello', *Studi e problemi di critica testuale*, 93 (2016), 211–36

GILBERT, JANE, *Living Death in Medieval French and English Literature* (New York and Cambridge: Cambridge University Press, 2017)

GIRARD, RENÉ, *La Violence et le sacré* (Paris: Éditions Bernard Grasset, 1972)

—— *Violence and the Sacred*, trans. by Patrick Gregory (Baltimore, MD: Johns Hopkins University Press, 1977)

GLYNN, DOMINIC, 'Towards a Theory of Non-Translation', *Across Languages and Cultures*, 22.1 (2021), 1–13 <https://doi.org/10.1556/084.2021.00001>

—— *(Re)Telling Old Stories* (Brussels: Peter Lang, 2015)

——, and JAMES HADLEY, 'Theorising (un)performability and (un)translatability', *Perspectives. Studies in Translation Theory and Practice*, 29.1 (2021), 20–32 <https://doi.org/10.1080/0907676X.2020.1713827>

GONZÁLEZ DEL VALLE, LUIS, '*Bodas de sangre* y sus elementos trágicos', *Archivum: Revista de la Facultad de Filosofía y Letras*, 21 (1971), 95–120

GOODMAN, JESSICA (ed.), *Commemorating Mirabeau: 'Mirabeau aux Champs-Elysées' and other texts* (Cambridge: MHRA, 2017)

GORDON, AVERY F., *Ghostly Matters: Haunting and the Sociological Imagination* (Minneapolis: University of Minnesota Press, 2008)

GORER, GEOFFREY, 'The Pornography of Death', *Encounter*, 5 (1955), 49–52 [repr. in Geoffrey Gorer, *Death, Grief, and Mourning in Contemporary Britain* (London: Cresset Press, 1965), pp. 169–75]

GOULART, SIMON, *Memoires de l'Estat de France, sous Charles Neufiesme*, 3 vols (Geneva: H. Wolf, 1578)

GRIMM, REINHOLD, 'Ideologische Tragödie und Tragödie der Ideologie: Versuch über ein Lehrstück von Brecht', in *Tragik und Tragödie*, ed. by Volkmar Sander (Darmstadt: Wissenschaftliche Buchgesellschaft, 1971), pp. 237–78

GRIMMINGER, ROLF (ed.), *Hansers Sozialgeschichte der deutschen Literatur*, 12 vols (Munich: Hanser, 2000)

GUEST, HARRIET, *Unbounded Attachment: Sentiment and Politics in the Age of the French Revolution* (Oxford: Oxford University Press, 2013)

GURR, ANDREW, *The Shakespearean Stage, 1574–1642* (Cambridge: Cambridge University Press, 1970)

HALL, EDITH, FIONA MACINTOSH and AMANDA WRIGLEY (eds), *Dionysus Since 69: Greek Tragedy at the Dawn of the Third Millennium* (Oxford: Oxford University Press, 2004)

HALLIWELL, STEPHEN, *Aristotle's Poetics* (London: Bloomsbury, 1986)

—— *The Aesthetics of Mimesis: Ancient Texts and Modern Problems* (Princeton, NJ: Princeton University Press, 2002)

HAMILTON, WILLIAM, *Marie-Antoinette conduite à son exécution, 16 Octobre 1793* (1794)

HARRIS SMITH, SUSAN, 'Twentieth-Century Plays Using Classical Mythic Themes: A Checklist', *Modern Drama*, 29.1 (1986), 10–134

HARRIS, JOSEPH, 'Dying of the Fifth Act: Corneille's (Un)natural Deaths', in *French Studies*, 69.2 (July 2015), 289–304

—— *Inventing the Spectator: Subjectivity and the Theatrical Experience in Early Modern France* (Oxford: Oxford University Press, 2014)

HAWCROFT, MICHAEL, 'Violence et bienséance dans l'Examen d'*Horace*: pour une critique de la notion de bienséances externes', *Dix-septième siècle*, 264.3 (2014), 549–70

HAZLITT, WILLIAM, *A View of the English Stage, or, A Series of Dramatic Criticisms, by William Hazlitt*, ed. by W. Spencer Jackson (London: George Bell and Sons, 1906)

HEGEL, *Aesthetics: Lectures on Fine Art*, trans. by T. M. Knox (Oxford: Clarendon, 1975)

HÉNIN, EMMANUELLE, 'Faut-il ensanglanter la scène? Les Enjeux d'une controverse classique', *Littératures classiques*, 67.3 (2008), 13–32

—— 'Le Plaisir des larmes, ou l'invention d'une catharsis galante', *Littératures classiques*, 62 (2007), 223–44

HENN, THOMAS RICE, *The Harvest of Tragedy*, 2nd edn (London: Methuen, 1966)

HENRICHS, ALBERT, 'The Last of the Detractors: Friedrich Nietzsche's Condemnation of Euripides', *Greek, Roman and Byzantine Studies*, 27.4 (1986), 369–97

HERIOT, C. D., Reader's report, Licence Refused, London, British Library, Lord Chamberlain's Collection, LR 1968/3

HERMAND, JOST, '"Lieber nützlich leben als heroisch sterben": Brechts Märtyrerphobie', *The Brecht Yearbook*, 32 (2007), 210–22

HEYWOOD, THOMAS, *An Apology for Actors* (London: Nicholas Oakes, 1612) <https://ota.bodleian.ox.ac.uk/repository/xmlui/bitstream/handle/20.500.12024/A03185/A03185.html?sequence=5&isAllowed=y> [accessed 5 May 2021]

HILLMAN, RICHARD, 'The Admiral, Upside-Down, or Apocalypse Now and Then: Marlowe's *The Massacre at Paris* and François de Chantelouve's *La Tragédie de Feu Gaspard de Colligny* (1575)', in *Les Huguenots dans les îles britanniques de la Renaissance aux Lumières:*

écrits religieux et représentations, ed. by Anne Dunan-Page and Marie-Christine Munoz-Teulié (Paris: Champion, 2008), pp. 61–85

—— *Shakespeare, Marlowe and the Politics of France* (Basingstoke: Palgrave Macmillan, 2002)

—— *The Tragedy of the Late Gaspard de Coligny / François de Chantelouve; And, The Guisiade / Pierre Matthieu* (Ottawa: Dovehouse, 2005)

HINCK, WALTER, *Das moderne Drama in Deutschland: Vom expressionistischen zum dokumentarischen Theater* (Göttingen: V&R, 1973)

HOLLAND, EDWARD, *A Poetical Miscellany* (Cork: J. Connor, 1794)

HORACE, *Ars Poetica* <https://www.thelatinlibrary.com/horace/arspoet.shtml> [accessed 9 November 2020]

—— *Ars Poetica*, trans. by A. S. Kilne, Poetry in Translation <https://www.poetryintranslation.com/PITBR/Latin/HoraceArsPoetica.php> [accessed 9 November 2020]

HOTMAN, FRANÇOIS, *De furoribus Gallicis* (1573)

—— *Vita Colinii* (1575)

HUET, MARIE-HÉLÈNE, *Mourning Glory: The Will of the French Revolution* (Philadelphia: University of Pennsylvania Press, 1997)

HUGO, VICTOR, 'Préface', in *Œuvres complètes: Cromwell-Hernani* (Paris: Librairie Ollendorff, 1912), pp. 7–51 <https://fr.wikisource.org/wiki/Cromwell_-_Préface> [accessed 9 November 2020]

—— *Cromwell-Préface* <https://fr.wikisource.org/wiki/Cromwell_-_Préface> [accessed 9 November 2020]

HUNT, LYNN, 'The Many Bodies of Marie Antoinette: Political Pornography and the Problem of the Feminine in the French Revolution', in *Marie Antoinette: Writings on the Body of the Queen*, ed. by Dena Goodman (New York: Routledge, 2003), pp. 117–36

HUTCHEON, LINDA, and MICHAEL HUTCHEON, *Opera: The Art of Dying* (Cambridge, MA: Harvard University Press, 2004)

IMBASCIO, N. M., 'Corpses Revealed: The Staging of the Theatrical Corpse in Early Modern Drama' (unpublished doctoral dissertation, University of New Hampshire, 2010) <https://scholars.unh.edu/cgi/viewcontent.cgi?article=1519&context=dissertation> [accessed 9 November 2020]

IRIGARAY, LUCE, *Être Deux* (Paris: Grasset, 1997)

JACOBUS, MARY, ' "That Great Stage. Where Senators Perform": *Macbeth* and the Politics of Romantic Theatre', *Studies in Romanticism*, 22.3 (1983), 353–87

JOHNSON, SAMUEL, 'From the Preface and Notes of his edition, 1765', in *King Lear: A Casebook*, ed. by Frank Kermode (London: Macmillan, 1969), p. 29

JONES, FRANK, 'Scenes from the Life of Antigone', *Yale French Studies*, 6 (1950), 91–100

JORDAN, EAMONN, 'Unmasking the Myths? Marinna Carr's "By the Bog of Cats" and "On Raftery's Hill" ', in *Amid our Troubles: Irish Versions of Greek Tragedy*, ed. by Marianne McDonald and J. Michael Walton (London: Methuen, 2002), pp. 243–62

JOUANNA, ARLETTE, *The Saint Bartholomew's Day Massacre: The Mysteries of a Crime of State (24 August 1572)*, trans. by Joseph Bergin (Manchester: Manchester University Press, 2015)

KABATCHNIK, AMMON, *Blood on the Stage, 1925–1950: Milestone Plays of Crime, Mystery, and Detection: An Annotated Repertoire* (Lanham, MD: Scarecrow Press, 2014)

KAISER, GEORG, *Five Plays*, trans. by B. J. Kenworthy, Rex Last, J. M. Ritchie (London: Calder & Boyars, 1971)

—— *Von morgens bis mitternachts*, in *Werke*, ed. by Walther Huder, 6 vols (Frankfurt am Main: Propyläen, 1971), I: *Stücke, 1895–1917* (1971), pp. 463–517

KATAOKA, YUMIKO, 'Loss and Resolution in "Riders to the Sea": Reflecting on the Theory of Grief', *Journal of Irish Studies*, 32 (2017), 13–22

KEMBLE, JOHN PHILIP / WILLIAM SHAKESPEARE, *Macbeth: written by Shakespeare. As Represented by Their Majesties Servants on Opening the Theatre Royal Drury Lane* (London: C. Lowndes, 1794)

KERMODE, FRANK, *The Sense of an Ending: Studies in the Theory of Fiction with a New Epilogue* (New York: Oxford University Press, 2000)

——*The Sense of an Ending: Studies in the Theory of Fiction* (Oxford: Oxford University Press, 1979 [1966])

KLATTKE, CORNEILA, 'Il teatro onirico di Pirandello alla luce della sua ricezione di Nietzsche: *I giganti della montagna*, in *La Germania di Pirandello tra sogno e realtà*, ed. by Cornelia Klettke (Berlin: Frank & Timme, 2019), pp. 169–94

KLOTZ, VOLKER, *Geschlossene und offene Form im Drama* (Munich: Hanser, 1960)

KNOX, BERNARD M. W., *The Heroic Temper: Studies in Sophoclean Tragedy* (Berkeley: University of California Press, 1983)

KOCHER, PAUL, 'Contemporary Pamphlet Backgrounds for Marlowe's *The Massacre at Paris*', *Modern Language Quarterly*, 8.2 (1947), 151–73

——'François Hotman and Marlowe's *The Massacre at Paris*', *PMLA*, 56.2 (1941), 349–68

KONJIN, ELLY A., 'Spotlight on spectators: Emotions in the Theater', *Discourse Processes*, 28 (1999), <https://doi.org/10.1080/01638539909545079>

KONKLE, LINCOLN, *Thornton Wilder and the Puritan Narrative Tradition* (Columbia: University of Missouri Press, 2006)

KRAUSE, FRANK, *Georg Kaiser and Modernity* (Göttingen: V&R Unipress, 2005)

LA MESNARDIÈRE, HIPPOLYTE-JULES DE, *La Poétique*, ed. by Jean-Marc Civardi (Paris: Champion, 2015)

LA MESNARDIÈRE, HIPPOLYTE-JULES PILET DE, *La Poétique* (Paris: A. de Sommaville, 1639) <https://gallica.bnf.fr/ark:/12148/bpt6k50691s/f95.item> [accessed 9 November 2020]

LACAN, JACQUES, *The Ethics of Psychoanalysis, 1959–1960: The Seminar of Jacques Lacan: Book VII*, ed. by Jacques-Alain Miller, trans. by Dennis Porter (New York: Routledge, 1992)

LAZARD, MADELEINE, *Le Théâtre en France au XVIe siècle* (Paris: Presses universitaires de France, 1980)

LECERCLE, FRANÇOIS (ed.), *Réécritures du crime: l'acte sanglant sur la scène (XVIe–XVIIIe s.)* (Paris: Champion, 2009)

LEFEVERE, ANDRÉ, *Translation, Rewriting, and the Manipulation of Literary Fame* (London: Routledge, 1992)

LEHMANN, HANS-THIES, *Tragedy and Dramatic Theatre* (London: Routledge, 2016)

——'Den Tod sterben: Zu Brechts Dedramatisierung des Todes', in *The Brecht Yearbook 32: Brecht und der Tod*, ed. by Jürgen Hillesheim, Stephen Brockmann and Matthias Mayer (Madison: University of Wisconsin Press, 2007), pp. 176–87

LEWIS, J. LOWELL, *The Anthropology of Cultural Performance* (New York: Palgrave Macmillan, 2013)

LEWIS, WARD B., *The Ironic Dissident: Frank Wedekind in the View of his Critics* (Columbia, SC: Camden House, 1997)

LONDRAVILLE, RICHARD, '*Our Town*: An American Noh of the Ghosts', in *Thornton Wider: New Essays*, ed. by Martin Blank, Dalma Hunyadi and David Garrett Izzo (West Cornwall, CT: Locust Hill Press, 1999), pp. 365–78

LÜBECKER, NIKOLAJ, *The Feel-Bad Film* (Edinburgh: Edinburgh University Press, 2015)

LUCKHURST, MARY, and EMILIE MORIN, 'Introduction: Theatre and Spectrality', in *Theatre and Ghosts: Materiality, Performance and Modernity*, ed. by Luckhurst and Morin (New York: Palgrave Macmillan, 2014), pp. 1–23

LUGNANI, LUCIO, 'In margine ai *Giganti*', in *Pirandello e il teatro, Atti del XXIX Convegno Internazionale*, ed. by Enzo Lauretta (Milan: Mursia, 1993), pp. 117–29

LYONS, JOHN, D., *The Tragedy of Origins: Pierre Corneille and Historical Perspective* (Palo Alto, CA: Stanford University Press, 1996)

LYSAGHT, PATRICIA, '*Convivium Mortis*: Feast and Death in Irish Literature and Oral Tradition', *The Life Cycle: SIEF's Third Congress April 8–12, 1987, Zürich Switzerland* (Stockholm: International Society for Ethnology and Folklore, 1987), pp. 1–10

——*The Banshee: The Irish Supernatural Death-Messenger* (Dublin: O'Brien Press, 1986)

MACCHIA, GIOVANNI, *Pirandello, o La stanza della tortura* (Milan: Mondadori, 1981)

MACINTOSH, FIONA, *Dying Acts: Death in Ancient Greek and Modern Irish Drama* (Cork: Cork University Press, 1994; New York: St Martin's Press, 1995)

MACLEOD, EMMA VINCENT, *A War of Ideas: British Attitudes to the Wars against Revolutionary France, 1792–1802* (Aldershot: Ashgate, 1998)

MALACHY, THÉRÈSE, *La Mort en situation dans le théâtre contemporain* (Paris: Nizet, 1982)

MARCHAND, SOPHIE, *Théâtre et pathétique au XVIIIe siècle: pour une esthétique de l'effet dramatique* (Paris: Champion, 2009)

MARTIN, MATHEW, *Tragedy and Trauma in the Plays of Christopher Marlowe* (Farnham: Ashgate, 2015)

MARTÍNEZ NADAL, RAFAEL, *El público: amor y muerte en la obra de García Lorca* (Madrid: Comunidad de Madrid, 2019), <http://www.madrid.org/bvirtual/BVCM019761.pdf> [accessed 16 April 2021]

MARTINO, ERNESTO DE, *Morte e pianto rituale nel mondo antico* (Turin: Bollati Boringhieri, 2008)

MASLAN, SUSAN, *Revolutionary Acts: Theater, Democracy, and the French Revolution* (Baltimore, MD: Johns Hopkins University Press, 2005)

MAZOUER, CHARLES, 'Chantelouve et la Saint-Barthélemy: *La Tragédie de feu Gaspard de Colligny* (1575)', in *Les Ecrivains et la politique dans le sud-ouest de la France autour des années 1580*, ed. by Claude-Gilbert Dubois and others (Bordeaux: Presses universitaires de Bordeaux, 1982), pp. 129–40

——*Le Théâtre français de la Renaissance* (Paris: Champion, 2002)

MCDONALD, MARIANNE, 'The Irish and Greek Tragedy', in *Amid our Troubles: Irish Versions of Greek Tragedy*, ed. by Marianne McDonald and J. Michael Walton (London: Methuen, 2002), pp. 37–86

MCMANNERS, JOHN, *Death and the Enlightenment: Changing Attitudes to Death among Christians and Unbelievers in Eighteenth-Century France* (New York: Oxford University Press, 1981)

MCPHERSON, HEATHER, 'Masculinity, Femininity, and the Tragic Sublime: Reinventing Lady Macbeth', *Studies in Eighteenth-Century Culture*, 29 (2000), 299–333

MEERE, MICHAEL, *Onstage Violence in Sixteenth-Century French Tragedy: Performance, Ethics, Poetics* (Oxford: Oxford University Press, 2021)

MEEUWIS, MICHAEL, *Property and Finance on the Post-Brexit London Stage: We Want What You Have* (London: Routledge, 2020)

MENKE, CHRISTOPH, 'Die Gegenwart der Tragödie. Eine ästhetische Aufklärung', *Neue Rundschau*, 111 (2000), 85–95

——*Die Gegenwart der Tragödie: Versuch über Urteil und Spiel* (Frankfurt am Main: Suhrkamp, 2005)

MOLIÈRE, *Dom Juan. The Feast of the Stone*, trans. by Daniel Smith <https://www.academia.edu/22112254/Translation_of_Don_Juan_by_Moliere> [accessed 9 November 2020]

MONVEL, BOUTET DE, *Les Victimes cloîtrées*, drames en quatre actes et en prose; new edn (Paris: Barba, 1796)

——*Les Victimes cloîtrées*, ed. by Sophie Marchand (Cambridge: MHRA, 2011)

MOORE, SALLY FALK, and BARBARA G. MYERHOFF (eds), 'Introduction: Secular Ritual: Forms and Meanings', in *Secular Ritual* (Amsterdam: Van Gorcum, 1977), pp. 3–24

Most, Glenn W., and Leyla Ozbek (eds), *Staging Ajax's Suicide* (Pisa: Edizione della Normale, 2015)

Mountford, Fiona, 'Death Stalks Sesame Street', *Evening Standard*, 22 June 2006, <https://www.standard.co.uk/culture/theatre/death-stalks-sesame-street-7387447.html>

Müller, Heiner, *Gesammelte Irrtümer 2: Interviews und Gespräche*, ed. by Gregor Edelmann and Renate Ziemer (Frankfurt am Main: Verlag der Autoren, 1990)

Muratore, M. J., *Cornelian Theater: The Metadramatic Dimension* (Birmingham, AL: Summa, 1990)

Naugrette, Florence, *Le Plaisir du spectateur de théâtre* (Paris: Bréal, 2002)

Navarro, Rosa, 'Dos mujeres de tragedia en el teatro de Lorca', *El Ciervo. Revista Mensual de Pensamiento y Cultura*, 783 (2020), 32–33

Neill, Michael, *Issues of Death: Mortality and Identity in English Renaissance Tragedy* (Oxford: Clarendon Press, 1997)

Nelson, G. E., 'The Birth of Tragedy out of Pedagogy: Brecht's "Learning Play" *Die Maßnahme*', *The German Quarterly*, 46 (Nov. 1973), 566–80

Neruda, Pablo, *Para nacer he nacido* (Barcelona: Seix Barral, 1978)

Nietzsche, Friedrich, *The Birth of Tragedy and Other Writings* (Cambridge: Cambridge University Press, 1999)

Oesmann, Astrid, 'Brecht's Economies of Death and the Gestus of Mourning', in *The Brecht Yearbook 32: Brecht und der Tod*, ed. by Jürgen Hillesheim, Stephen Brockmann and Matthias Mayer (Madison: University of Wisconsin Press, 2007), pp. 188–97

Oulton, W. C., *A History of the Theatres of London*, 2 vols (London: Martin & Bain, 1818)

Owens, Margaret E., *Stages of Dismemberment: The Fragmented Body in Late Medieval and Early Modern Drama* (Newark: University of Delaware Press, 2005)

Parker, Robert, *Miasma: Pollution and Purification in Early Greek Religion* (Oxford: Oxford University Press)

Pascoe, Judith, *Romantic Theatricality: Gender, Poetry and Spectatorship* (Ithaca, NY: Cornell University Press, 1997)

Patterson, Michael, *The Revolution in German Theatre* (Abingdon: Routledge, 2016 [1981])

Pavis, Patrice, *Dictionary of the Theatre: Terms, Concepts, and Analysis*, trans. by Christine Shantz (Toronto: University of Toronto Press, 1999)

Perovic, Sanja, *The Calendar in Revolutionary France: Perceptions of Time in Literature, Culture, Politics* (Cambridge: Cambridge University Press, 2012)

Petre, Zoe, 'La Représentation de la mort dans la tragédie grecque', *Studii clasice*, 23 (1985), 21–35

Pettitt, Thomas, 'Formulaic Dramaturgy in *Doctor Faustus*', in *A Poet and a Filthy Play-Maker: New Essays on Christopher Marlowe*, ed. by Kenneth Friedenreich, Roma Gill, and Constance Kuriyama (New York: AMS Press, 1988), pp. 167–91

Phelan, Peggy, 'Introduction', in *The Ends of Performance*, ed. by Peggy Phelan and Jill Lane (New York: New York University Press, 1998), pp. 1–19

Pincombe, Mike, 'English Renaissance Tragedy: Theories and Antecedents', in *The Cambridge Companion to English Renaissance Tragedy*, ed. by Emma Smith and Garrett A. Sullivan (Cambridge: Cambridge University Press, 2010), pp. 3–16

Pirandello, Luigi, 'I pensionati della memoria', in *Novelle per un anno*, ed. by Mario Costanzo, 6 vols (Milan: Mondadori, 1987), II, 734–39

——*Diana e la Tuda: Libero Andreotti e Pirandello* (Florence: Giunti, 1994)

——*La nuova colonia, Lazzaro, I giganti della montagna*, ed. by Marziano Guglielminetti (Milan: Garzanti, 1995)

——*Lettere a Marta Abba*, ed. by Benito Ortolani (Milan: Mondadori, 1994)

——*One, No One and One Hundred Thousand*, trans. by Samuel Putnam (New York: Dutton, 1933)

——*Pirandello's Love Letters to Marta Abba*, ed. and trans. by Benito Ortolani (Princeton, NJ: Princeton University Press, 1994)

——*Questa sera si recita a soggetto. Trovarsi. Bellavita*, ed. by Roberto Alonge (Milan: Mondadori, 1993)

——*Shoot! The Notebook of Serafino Gubbio, Cinematograph Operator*, trans. by C. K. Scott Moncrieff (New York: Dutton, 1926)

——*Three Plays*, trans. by Anthony Mortimer (Oxford: Oxford University Press, 2014)

——*Tonight We Improvise and 'Leonora, Addio!'*, ed. and trans. by J. Douglas Campbell and Leonard Sbrocchi (Ottawa: Biblioteca di Quaderni d'italianistica, 1987)

——*Trovarsi*, ed. by Marta Abba (Milan: Mursia, 1971)

——*Tutti i romanzi*, ed. by Giovanni Macchia (Milan: Mondadori, 2010)

POLLARD, TANYA, 'Tragedy and Revenge', in *The Cambridge Companion to English Renaissance Tragedy*, ed. by Emma Smith and Garrett A. Sullivan (Cambridge: Cambridge University Press, 2010), pp. 58–72

POOLE, KRISTEN, 'Garbled Martyrdom in Christopher Marlowe's *The Massacre at Paris*', *Comparative Drama*, 32.1 (1998), 1–25

POSADA, MIGUEL GARCÍA, 'Las tragedias lorquianas', in Federico García Lorca, *Teatro completo*, 4 vols (Madrid: Debolsillo, 2004), III, 9–16

PRIESTLEY, JOSEPH, *Letters to the Right Honourable Edmund Burke* (Dublin: J. Shepherd, 1791)

Programme of 'Blood Wedding', dir. by Yaël Farber (London: Young Vic, 2019)

PRYNNE, WILLIAM, *Histriomatix* <https://quod.lib.umich.edu/e/eebo/A10187.0001.001?view=toc> [accessed 20 November]

PUPPA, PAOLO, 'La scena e i suoi fantasmi: dai *Sei personaggi* ai *Giganti della montagna*', *Rivista italiana di drammaturgia*, 6 (1977), 71–102

RADWAY, JANICE, 'Foreword', in Avery F. Gordon, *Ghostly Matters: Haunting and the Sociological Imagination* (Minneapolis: University of Minnesota Press, 2008)

RAYNER, ALICE, *Ghosts: Death's Double and the Phenomena of Theatre* (Minneapolis: University of Minnesota Press, 2006)

REISS, TIMOTHY, 'Renaissance Theatre and the Theory of Tragedy', in *The Cambridge History of Literary Criticism*, III: *The Renaissance*, ed. by Glyn Norton (Cambridge: Cambridge University Press, 1999), pp. 229–47

RENO, ROBERT P., 'James Boaden's *Fontainville Forest* and Matthew G. Lewis's *The Castle Spectre*: Challenges of the Supernatural Ghost on the Late Eighteenth-Century Stage', *Eighteenth-Century Life*, 9 (1984), 95–103

REYNOLDS, FREDERICK, *The Life and Times of Frederick Reynolds*, 2 vols (London: Henry Colburn, 1826)

RIST, THOMAS C. K., 'Miraculous Organ: Shakespeare and "Catharsis"', *SKENÈ Journal of Theatre and Drama Studies*, 2.1 (2016), 133–50

RITCHIE, FIONA, *Women and Shakespeare in the Eighteenth Century* (New York: Cambridge University Press, 2014)

ROACH, JOSEPH, 'Deep Play, Dark Play: Framing the Limit(less)', in *The Rise of Performance Studies: Rethinking Richard Schechner's Broad Spectrum*, ed. by James Harding and Cindy Rosenthal (Basingstoke: Palgrave Macmillan, 2011), pp. 275–83

——'History, Memory, Necrophilia', in *The Ends of Performance*, ed. by Peggy Phelan and Jill Lane (New York: New York University Press, 1998), pp. 23–30

——*Cities of the Dead: Circum-Atlantic Performance* (New York: Columbia University Press, 1996)

ROBINSON, MARC, 'Realism against Itself', in *The American Play* (New Haven, CT, and London: Yale University Press, 2009), pp. 106–56

ROBINSON, MARY, *Monody to the Memory of the Late Queen of France* (London: T. Spilsbury, 1793)

ROCHE, MARK W., 'The Tragicomic Absence of Tragedy', in *Signaturen der Gegenwartsliteratur: Festschrift für Walter Hinderer*, ed. by Dieter Borchmeyer (Würzburg: Königshausen & Neumann, 1999), pp. 265–76

ROGERS, GAYLE, *Modernism and the New Spain: Britain, Cosmopolitan Europe, and Literary History* (New York: Oxford University Press, 2012)

RÖHLE, JURGEN, *Das gefesselte Theater* (Cologne and Berlin: Kiepenheuer & Witsch, 1957)

ROSENBERG, MARVIN, 'Macbeth and Lady Macbeth in the Eighteenth and Nineteenth Centuries', in *Focus on Macbeth*, ed. by John Russell Brown (London: Routledge and Kegan Paul, 1982)

—— *The Masks of Macbeth* (Berkeley: University of California Press, 1978)

ROSENTHAL, LAURA, 'The Sublime, the Beautiful, the Siddons', in *The Clothes that Wear Us*, ed. by Jessica Munns and Penny Richards (Newark: University of Delaware Press, 2003)

ROSSLYN, FELICITY, 'Lorca and Greek Tragedy', *The Cambridge Quarterly*, 29.3 (2000), 215–36

ROUSSEAU, JEAN-JACQUES, *Lettre à d'Alembert* [1758], ed. by M. Launay (Paris: Garnier-Flammarion, 1967)

RUBIDGE, BRADLEY, 'Catharsis through Admiration: Corneille, Le Moyne, and the Social Uses of Emotion', *Modern Philology*, 95.3 (1998), 316–33

RUHL, SARAH, 'Re-runs and repetition', *Contemporary Theatre Review*, 16.3 (2009), 283–90

—— *100 Essays I Don't Have Time to Write* (New York: Farrar, Straus and Giroux, 2014)

—— *Eurydice* [2003], in *The Clean House and Other Plays* (New York: TCG, 2006), pp. 325–411

RUSSELL, GILLIAN, *The Theatres of War: Performance, Politics and Society, 1793–1815* (Oxford: Clarendon Press, 1995)

RUTTER, CAROL CHILLINGTON (ed.), *Documents of the Rose Playhouse* (Manchester: Manchester University Press, 1984)

SAGLIA, DIEGO, '"A portion of the name": Stage Adaptations of Radcliffe's fiction, 1794–1806', in *Ann Radcliffe, Romanticism and the Gothic*, ed. by Dale Townshend and Angela Wright (Cambridge: Cambridge University Press, 2014), pp. 219–36

SAINTE ALBINE, PIERRE RÉMOND DE, *Le Comédien* (1747), in *Sept traités sur le jeu comédien et autres textes*, ed. by Sabine Chaouche (Paris: Champion, 2001), pp. 515–670

SANTIAGO ROMERO, SANTIAGO, 'Nietzsche en el nacimiento de la tragedia española contemporánea' (unpublished doctoral thesis, Complutense University of Madrid, 2019)

SCHECHNER, RICHARD, 'Ritual and Performance', in *Companion Encyclopedia of Anthropology*, ed. by Tim Ingold (London: Routledge, 2002)

—— *Performance Theory* (London: Routledge, 2003)

—— *The Future of Ritual: Writings on Culture and Performance* (London: Routledge, 1993)

SCHÜRER, ERNST, 'Provocation and Proclamation, Vision and Imagery: Expressionist Drama between German Idealism and Modernity', in *A Companion to the Literature of Expressionism*, ed. by Neil H. Donahue (Rochester, NY: Camden House, 2005), pp. 231–54

SEGAL, CHARLES, 'Euripides' *Alcestis*: How to Die a Normal Death in Greek Tragedy', in *Death and Representation*, ed. by Sarah Webster Goodwin and Elisabeth Bronfen (Baltimore, MD, and London: Johns Hopkins University Press 1993), pp. 213–41

SHAKESPEARE, WILLIAM, *Hamlet, Prince of Denmark. A Tragedy. Taken from the manager's book, at the Theatre Royal, Drury Lane* (London: Rachael Randall, 1787)

—— *The Arden Shakespeare Complete Works*, ed. by Richard Proudfoot, Ann Thompson and David Scott Kastan, 3rd series (Walton-on-Thames: Nelson, 1998)

—— *Hamlet*, MIT Shakespeare <http://shakespeare.mit.edu/hamlet/full.html> [accessed 9 November 2020]

SHAW, PHILIP, *Romantic Wars: Studies in Culture and Conflict, 1793–1822* (Aldershot: Ashgate, 2000)

SHERIDAN KNOWLES, JAMES, *Lectures on Dramatic Literature: Macbeth* (London: Francis Harvey, 1875)

SIDDONS, HENRY, *The Sicilian Romance: Or, the Apparition of the Cliffs* (London: J. Barker, 1794),

SIDDONS, SARAH, 'Remarks on the Character of Lady Macbeth', in Thomas Campbell, *Life of Mrs. Siddons*, 2 vols (London: Effingham Wilson, 1834), II, 10–39

SIMMEL, GEORG, 'Der Begriff und die Tragödie der Kultur', in *Philosophische Kultur: Gesammelte Essays* (Berlin: Wagenbach, 1983 [1911]), pp. 183–207

SIMON, RALF, 'Theorie der Komödie', in *Theorie der Komödie — Poetik der Komödie*, ed. by Ralf Simon (Bielefeld: Aisthesis, 2001), pp. 47–65

SKRINE, PETER, *Hauptmann, Wedekind and Schnitzler* (Basingstoke: Macmillan, 1987)

SMITH, JULIAN, *The Theatre of García Lorca* (Cambridge: Cambridge University Press, 1998)

SOBEJANO, GONZALO, *Nietzsche en España* (Madrid: Gredos, 2004)

SOKEL, WALTER H., 'Brecht's Split Characters and His Sense of the Tragic', in *Brecht*, ed. by Peter Demetz (Englewood Cliffs: Prentice-Hall, 1962), pp. 127–38

SPERRY, EILEEN M., 'Decay, Intimacy, and the Lyric Metaphor in John Donne', *Studies in English Literature, 1500–1900*, 59.1 (2019), 45–66 <https://doi.org/10.1353/sel.2019.0002>

STEINER, GEORGE, *Antigones: How the Antigone Legend Has Endured in Western Literature, Art, and Thought* (New Haven, CT, and London: Yale University Press, 1996 [1984])

——— *The Death of Tragedy* (London: Faber and Faber, 1961; New York: Alfred A. Knopf, 1961)

STEINWEG, REINER, 'Brechts *Die Maßnahme* Übungstext, nicht Tragödie', *Alternative*, 14 (1971), 133–43

STEINWEG, REINER, *Das Lehrstück: Brechts Theorie einer politisch-ästhetischen Erziehung* (Stuttgart: Metzler, 1976)

STONE, SIMON, *Yerma* (London: Oberon, 2017)

STOPPARD, TOM, *Rosencrantz & Guildenstern Are Dead* (New York: Grove Press, 1968)

——— *Rosencrantz and Guildenstern Are Dead* (London: Faber and Faber, 1967)

STRASBERG, LEE, *A Dream of Passion: The Development of the Method* (New York: Plume, 1988)

SYNGE, JOHN MILLINGTON, *Collected Works*, vol. II: *Prose I*, ed. by A. Price (Oxford: Oxford University Press, 1966; repr. Gerrards Cross: Colin Smythe Ltd, 1982)

——— *Collected Works*, vol. III: *Plays Book I*, ed. by A. Saddlemyer (Oxford: Oxford University Press, 1968; repr. Gerrards Cross: Colin Smythe Ltd., 1982)

——— *Riders to the Sea* (Boston, MA: John W. Luce and Company, 2011)

SZONDI, PETER, 'Theory of the Modern Drama, Parts I–II', trans. by Michael Hays, *boundary 2*, 11.3 (1983), 191–230

——— 'Versuch über das Tragische', in *Peter Szondi: Schriftten I*, ed. by Jean Bollack and Henrietta Beese (Frankfurt am Main: Suhrkamp, 1978), pp. 149–260

——— *Theorie des modernen Dramas, 1880–1950* (Frankfurt am Main: Suhrkamp, 2004 [1956])

——— *Versuch über das Tragische* (Frankfurt am Main: Suhrkamp, 1961)

TAYLOR, DAVID, *The Politics of Parody: A Literary History of Caricature, 1760–1830* (New Haven, CT: Yale University Press, 2018)

TAYLOR, GEORGE, *The French Revolution on the London Stage, 1789–1805* (Cambridge: Cambridge University Press, 2000)

TELLINI, GIULIA, 'Pirandello e i Giganti: persone e personaggi', *Antologia Vieusseux* XXII, 64 (2016), 5–23

TERRY-FRITSCH, ALLIE, 'Execution by Image: Visual Spectacularism and Icononclasm in Late Medieval and Early Modern Europe', in *Death, Torture and the Broken Body in European Art, 1300–1650*, ed. by John Decker and Mitzi Kirkland-Ives (Farnham: Ashgate, 2015), pp. 191–206

The Revenger's Tragedy (1744) <https://www.gutenberg.org/files/46412/46412.txt> [accessed 9 November 2020]

TISSERON, SERGE, 'La Catharsis: purge ou thérapie?', *Les Cahiers de médiologie*, 1 (1996), 181–91

TORRENTE BALLESTER, GONZALO, *Teatro español contemporáneo* (Madrid: Guadarrama, 1968)

TOWNSHEND, DALE, 'Gothic and the Ghost of Hamlet', in *Gothic Shakespeares*, ed. by John Drakakis and Dale Townshend (Abingdon: Routledge, 2008), pp. 60–97

——'Gothic Shakespeare', in *A New Companion to the Gothic*, ed. by David Punter (Malden, NJ: Wiley-Blackwell, 2012), pp. 43–49

TURNER, VICTOR WITTER, *The Anthropology of Performance* (New York: PAJ Publications, 1988)

VALERO, ENCARNA ALONSO, *La tragedia del nacimiento: el teatro de Federico García Lorca* (Granada: Atrio, 2008)

VALLADARES, SUSAN, *Staging the Peninsular War: English Theatres, 1807–1815* (London: Routledge, 2015)

VARAMUND, ERNEST [ALIAS HOTMAN], *A True and Plaine Report of the Furious Outrages of Fraunce* (London: H. Bynneman, 1573)

VICARIO, MIGUEL MEDINA, 'La tragedia en Lorca', *Acotaciones*, 1 (1998), 42–53

VILETTE, CHARLES, *Lettres choisies de Charles Villette sur les principaux événemens de la Révolution* (Paris: Clousier, 1792)

VINTER, MAGGIE, *Last Acts: The Act of Dying on the Early Modern Stage* (New York: Fordham University Press, 2019)

VOGEL, PAULA, and SARAH RUHL, 'Sarah Ruhl by Paula Vogel', *BOMB*, 99 (2007), 54–59

VORK, ROBERT, 'Witnessing the Trauma of *Our Town*', *Comparative Drama*, 51.3 (2017), 338–63, <https://muse.jhu.edu/article/677376> [accessed 29 April 2020]

WALLACE, JENNIFER, *The Cambridge Introduction to Tragedy* (Cambridge: Cambridge University Press, 2007)

WEBSTER, JOHN, *The White Devil* <https://www.gutenberg.org/files/12915/12915-8.txt> [accessed 9 November 2020]

WEDEKIND, FRANK, *Frühlings Erwachen (1891)*, in F. W., *Werke. Kritische Studienausgabe*, ed. by Elke Austermühl, Rolf Kieser and Hartmut Vinçon, 15 vols (Darmstadt: Häusser, 2000), II, ed. by Mathias Baum and Rolf Kieser, pp. 259–322

——*Spring Awakening*, trans. by Tom Osborne (London: John Calder, 1981)

WHEELER, DUNCAN, 'Pain, Passion, Poetry and Politics: A Reworking of Federico García Lorca's Rural Tragedy', *TLS*, 4 October 2019, < https://www.the-tls.co.uk/articles/pain-passion-poetry-and-politics/> [accessed 16 April 2021]

WIESE, BENNO VON, *Zwischen Utopie und Wirklichkeit: Studien zur deutschen Literatur* (Dusseldorf: Bagel, 1963)

WILDER, THORNTON, 'Preface to three plays' [1957], in *Collected Plays*, ed. by J. D. McClatchy, pp. 682–88

——*Our Town* [1938], in *Collected Plays & Writings on Theater*, ed. by J. D. McClatchy (New York: Library of America, 2007), pp. 145–209

——*Pullman Car Hiawatha* [1931], in *Collected Plays*, ed. by J. D. McClatchy, pp. 93–108

WILKE, SABINE, 'Ökonomie und Sexualität in Georg Kaisers *Von morgens bis mitternachts* und seiner Verfilmung durch Karl-Heinz Martin', *Orbis Litterarum*, 54 (1999), 203–19

WILSON, EMILY R., *Mocked with Death: Tragic Overliving from Sophocles to Milton* (Baltimore, MD: Johns Hopkins University Press, 2004)

WITOSZEK, NINA and PATRICK F. SHEERAN, *Talking to the Dead: A Study of Irish Funerary Traditions* (Amsterdam-Atlanta, GA: Rodopi, 1998)

WOLFRAM, NATHALIE, 'Gothic Adaptation and the Stage Ghost', in *Theatre and Ghosts:*

Materiality, Performance and Modernity, ed. by Mary Luckhurst and Emilie Morin (New York: Palgrave Macmillan, 2014), pp. 46–61

WOLLFE, LISA, *La Tragédie à l'époque d'Henri III*, vol. 1 (1574–1579), ed. by Enea Balmas et al., (Florence: Olschki, 1999)

WOLLSTONECRAFT, MARY, *An Historical and Moral View of the Origin and Progress of the French Revolution* (London: J. Johnson, 1794)

YEARLING, REBECCA, 'Emotion, Cognition and Spectator Response to the Plays of Shakespeare', *Cultural History*, 7.2 (2018), 129–44

YOUNG JEAN LEE and FUTURE WIFE, *We're Gonna Die*, <https://youngjeanlee.org/work/were-gonna-die/> [accessed 5 June 2020]

ZAIXI, TAN, 'Censorship in Translation: The Dynamics of Non-, Partial or Full Translations in the Chinese Context, *Meta*, 62.1 (2017), 45–68

ZAMIR, TZACHI, 'Theatrical Repetition and Inspired Performance', *Journal of Aesthetics and Art Criticism* (2009), 365–73

Periodicals and Newspapers

Evening Mail
Evening Standard
L'Esprit des journaux français et étrangers
Moniteur universel
Morning Chronicle
Mercure de France
Monthly Museum
New York Times
Nuova antologia
The Examiner
The Gentleman's Magazine
The Guardian
The Hampshire Syren: or Songster's Miscellany
The Scots Magazine
The Weekly Entertainer
Times
Walker's Hibernian Magazine

Multimedia

Live interview with Anne Bogart. Park Avenue Armory. Artist Talk, '*Yerma*', <https://www.youtube.com/watch?v=QficpneoITo> [accessed 16 April 2021]

GILBERT, RHOD, *Stand up for Infertility* (BBC 2, 2021)

INDEX

❖

Italicized page numbers refer to the artist or subject of an illustration

www.ingramcontent.com/pod-product-compliance
Lightning Source LLC
Chambersburg PA
CBHW080542090426
42734CB00016B/3181